Transforming Psyche

Barbara Weir Huber explores the myth of Psyche, interweaving research from such diverse disciplines as current feminist and educational theories, mythology, literature, psychology, and cultural anthropology. She offers an original, critical reinterpretation of the myth, highlighting the way it overtly portrays female experience in a patriarchal context while covertly affirming all aspects of female life.

In *Transforming Psyche* Huber shows that the myth of Psyche and Eros can be interpreted to illuminate the experiences of twentieth-century women. In contrast to the portrayal of Psyche as indecisive and amorphous, Huber emphasizes those aspects of the tale that describe Psyche's connectedness – to her sisters, her own sexuality, her earthbound experience, and, ultimately, to the birthing of her child.

Using the works of such writers as Emily Carr, Margaret Laurence, Gertrude Stein, and Virginia Woolf, Huber demonstrates that feminist theory and women's autobiography mirror the insights uncovered in her retelling of the Psyche story.

BARBARA WEIR HUBER is a sessional lecturer in the English department, University of Manitoba.

Transforming Psyche

BARBARA WEIR HUBER

McGill-Queen's University Press
Montreal & Kingston · London · Ithaca

© McGill-Queen's University Press 1999
ISBN 0-7735-1844-4 (cloth)
ISBN 0-7735-1857-6 (paper)

Legal deposit second quarter 1999
Bibliothèque nationale du Québec

Printed in Canada on acid-free paper

This book has been published with the help of a grant
from the Humanities and Social Sciences Federation of
Canada, using funds provided by the Social Sciences
and Humanities Research Council of Canada.

McGill-Queen's University Press acknowledges the
financial support of the Government of Canada
through the Book Publishing Industry Development
Program for its activities. We also acknowledge the
support of the Canada Council for the Arts for our
publishing program.

Canadian Cataloguing in Publication Data

Huber, Barbara Weir, 1943–
Transforming Psyche
Includes bibliographical references and index.
ISBN 0-7735-1844-4 (bound)
ISBN 0-7735-1857-6 (pbk.)
1. Women. 2. Psyche (Greek deity).
1. Title.
HQ1206.H787 1999   305.4   C99-900355-0

Typeset in ITC Sabon 10/12 with Monotype Centaur
display by Caractéra inc., Quebec City

To Henry

and
in memory of

Lila B. Weir

Contents

Acknowledgments

Because this project began as a doctoral dissertation for an interdisciplinary degree at the University of Manitoba, I am especially indebted to my advisor, Dr Evelyn J. Hinz, and to Drs Joan Walters and Keith L. Fulton for their guidance and encouragement. I would also like to express my appreciation to the anonymous readers for their constructive suggestions and recommendations, and to Judith Turnbull, Joan McGilvray, and Aurèle Parisien at McGill-Queen's for shepherding the manuscript to its final form. Any faults or errors that remain are my own.

To my friends and extended families, my gratitude for the warmth and consideration which enrich my life. To my mother, Audrey W. Weir, who taught me many lessons, not the least of which is the importance of "lots of love" and laughter, my gratitude for the daily example of an upright and courageous spirit. To Henry, a special thank you for your reliable strength, love, and unselfish support. To our sons, Heinrich and Andreas, my thanks for your unfailing enthusiasm and affection and the pleasure that you and your friends contribute to our home.

Transforming Psyche

Even the best attempts at explanation are only more or less successful translations into another metaphor. (Indeed, language itself is only a metaphor.) The most we can do is to *dream the myth onwards* and give it a modern dress. And whatever explanation or interpretation does to it, we do to our own souls as well, with corresponding results for our own well-being.

> C.G. Jung (1951)

> We are, I am, you are
> by cowardice or courage
> the one who find our way
> back to this scene
> carrying a knife, a camera
> a book of myths
> in which
> our names do not appear.
>
> Adrienne Rich (1973)

> I too am a rare
> Pattern. As I wander down
> The garden paths.
>
> Amy Lowell (1928)

Introduction

Ours is a culture that is frequently defined in shorthand as patriarchal, revolving around and servant to the (metaphorical) Fathers. Feminist analyses critique patriarchal society by investigating the concomitant suppression and absence of a woman-centred view of reality, and much of feminist criticism is directed towards the foundations of the Western intellectual tradition itself.[1] In Western, Eurocentric and scientifically oriented thinking, human society and the natural world are seen as mutually exclusive units that are defined in terms of opposition, conflict, and aggression. Many feminists see society as especially impoverished by the intellectual construction of polarities, dichotomies, and gender.[2]

Character traits have been linked directly to gender in ways that compound what has been excluded from the material of that intellectual tradition. The definition of male in terms of certain psychological traits leaves men with logic, reason, and aggressiveness. The masculine nature of commerce, law and justice, science and technology signifies prestige and tradition. Definitions of female are criticized for their association with the feminine; such qualities are deemed undesirable in men. The conflation of the feminine with female biology has meant that women are regarded as emotional, passive, and intuitive. Furthermore, femaleness is associated with nature, the flesh, procreation, and physical pleasure.[3] From the conjunction of feminine qualities with reproductive responsibility in childbirth comes the view that women are by nature maternal, compassionate, empathetic, (over)loving, and hence morally weak.

Because our Western and Eurocentric tradition privileges men's ideas, these are the ones that have, until recently, been given precedence within the public domain. As women, we learn about ourselves through what men have thought and written about us.[4] Thus, formal education is expressly problematic because it takes place within a system set up to reflect male experience. Because women live a differently gendered social and cultural experience, it may readily be argued that women face particular and specific problems within a male-designed education system.[5] Obviously, in a system that is based on male experience, on exclusivity, and on the attendant hierarchy of values, women's place is doubly difficult.

In addition, the arrangement given these different values is teleological and translates readily into a power structure that is equally gender based. Those values associated with the female and feminine are seen as existing to service the higher values of the male and masculine. Reflected throughout Western culture, this adversarial system continues to define the self primarily in male terms and human experience for the most part in male experience. Through its pervasiveness, this equation influences all aspects of social life and culture, and men as well as women. Identity and selfhood, the self as human, as singular changeless Subject, is regarded as male, masculine, Man. The Other, in such a system, of necessity and automatically becomes object, female, feminine, Woman.

Because education was historically and traditionally the exclusive right of men, its structures and methodologies were designed to fit and reflect male experience. In an examination of curriculum and its social context entitled *Transforming Knowledge*, Elizabeth Kamarck Minnich challenges the conceptual errors that underlie this dominant intellectual tradition. These errors she defines as a faulty universalization that conflates human into man and as a circular argument that justifies and defines what is appropriate for intellectual consideration. She sees two more errors issuing from these. First, the curriculum emphasizes the products of thought rather than process and consequence. Second, this partial knowledge excludes all that can be defined as other or different. As she observes about this knowledge, "It makes the part the whole, and that whole is partial to the interests of those thus defined at the defining, controlling center" (148). These faults are so deeply embedded within the meaning system that they have become nearly invisible.

Unquestionably, much has been left out in the constructions of a male-defined universe. In the research into human development, Carol Gilligan's *In a Different Voice* introduces an ethic of care and responsibility – regarded as female – to balance Lawrence Kohlberg's work about (male) ethical development, a development seen as based in a paradigm of competing rights. In discussing the work of William Perry and his examination of intellectual and ethical development, she comments on the absence of any recognition of the problems and failures that arise out of either excessive detachment or unsatisfactory and inadequate attachment. Gilligan describes these as difficulties that ensue from an overemphasis on separation and a specifically male anxiety about connection. As she sees it, both men and women move towards contextual complexity in their development, but they do so out of differing ethics.

About formal learning itself, the authors (Belenky et al.) of *Women's Ways of Knowing* note that the women whom they interviewed regarded learning as gleaned through the lessons inherent "in relationships with friends and teachers, life crises, and community involvements" (4). Further, the authors recognize that "little attention has been given to modes of learning, knowing, and valuing that may be specific to, or at least common in, women" (6). Whether this is because of the general cultural perception of the nature of the female mind/psyche as emotional, intuitive, and irrational or the more universal male dominance in a culture that privileges male experience and masculine values, the effects are the same – the absence of a female presence in the tradition of what is termed intellectual development and a devaluation of what is defined as the feminine. "'Thinking'" is concerned with "the abstract and the impersonal" and is "attributed primarily to men," whereas "the personal and interpersonal" are categorized by "the rubric of 'emotions' and are largely relegated to women" (7). This description couples either/or dichotomous thinking and its corresponding teleological valuation to the detriment of women's pursuit of the intellectual and men's understanding of the emotional.

Just as *Ways of Knowing* provides a pattern for the process of women's learning that evolves from silence and passivity to an integrated and self-constructed knowledge, Sara Ruddick's "Maternal Thinking" evolves intellectual theory out of maternal practice and Adrienne Rich's *Of Woman Born* distinguishes between social or cultural attitudes and the experience of motherhood. Similarly, in *Representations of Motherhood* (Bassin et al.), literary analysts, psychologists, anthropologists, artists and activists continue the revaluation of motherhood to reclaim what has previously been obscured.[6] Winnie Tomm, in *Bodied Mindfulness,* articulates her own need and subsequent search to find a way to *"feel rationally* and *think passionately"* (1), thus combining two perceived opposites. Her study claims the need for a reconnection with the spiritual and natural worlds, for women's self-determination, and for a "spiritual creative power that is imaged predominantly in female symbols" (3).

These texts encouraged my own search for a female figure who carries with her the potential for imagining women's personal empowerment. In a study of the learning experience of practising women artists in the Mentor Program of Manitoba Artists for Women's Art (now Mentoring Artists for Women's Art, Inc.), I noted how women artists searched for ways to integrate creative life, affective connection, and community and family responsibilities. By sharing in the concerns and individual struggles of these women artists, I came to understand the need for female symbols and for a figure, a model, or even, in Jungian terms, an archetype whose story might express female experience in an androcentric social context and yet provide a model of affirmation for all aspects of female life – biological, emotional, intellectual, and spiritual. At the same time, I became aware that the ancient image of the spiral could supply an important pattern, that its significance might be found through a direct – even unflinching – examination of the constellation of devalued ideas named feminine and of the physicality of female life. Again, I could see that such an examination would be given an important larger dimension if it could be discussed in conjunction with an ancient, already existing figure or story.

In the figure of Psyche in the story of Psyche and Eros, I, as have many others, find one that resonates with interpretive potential.[7] As James Gollnick observes in his overview of the psychological analyses of the myth, the story has received a "striking variety" of interpretations. Gollnick adds that most of its many interpretations are guided by theory rather than by the text itself (3). Inasmuch as others are more open to those aspects of the story that reflect their own interests, I also admit to responding to various components of the story, to elements that resonate for my own investigations into women's lived experience. As I see it, the story itself may be read as metaphor, as a way to reveal masculinist and male-centred ideologies; yet it is also rich and complex enough for a revisioned view, a more woman-centred interpretation of experience, and for a more gender-neutral and holistic approach to theorizing knowledge.

In this myth, Psyche is a princess whose beauty, it is said, brings her in conflict with the goddess Aphrodite. Psyche is sacrificed on a mountain top, and then she is carried off by Eros, the god of love, son to Aphrodite. Because he visits Psyche only in the dark of night, she is curious about his appearance and contrives, with the aid of her jealous sisters, to see him by lamplight. When she succeeds, he leaves her. Her four tasks, set by Aphrodite, are central to the myth and portray Psyche's struggles for reconciliation with her husband. Her success brings a reunion with Eros and her ascendance to Olympus.

To read this ancient representation of female desire for affective (re)connection in conjunction with twentieth-century research on ways of knowing – cognitively based connection – is to discover new ways of considering the complexities and nuances that are inherent in any philosophy about female life experience in the emotional and intellectual realms. That Psyche is pregnant throughout her tasks adds an undeniably female biological basis to complete the experiential orientation of this myth.

Along with the myth of Psyche, which occupies the central place in my exploration, two other myths contribute metaphors of female being and knowing, and worthwhile perspectives on ontology and epistemology. One is the Narcissus and Echo myth, which not only focuses on the dangers accompanying self love but also foregrounds the roles of sight and hearing as each relates to the overall narrative about vision. The figures of Narcissus and Echo constitute both a cautionary tale and an introduction to what I see as central issues of subjectivity, relationship, and the intellectual or theoretical implications of a gendered value system.

The second myth is that of Persephone and Demeter, which may be interpreted as addressing the connections between mother and daughter and between human and the natural or agricultural environment. The seasonal changes that underlie this mythic mother-daughter story, the changes in the relationships between the two goddesses, and my emphasis on the presence of Hecate as a companion figure are all intended not only to illustrate an expanded reading of female relationships but also to support the meanings of "transforming" that I intend in the title of this text.

Transforming, as the action of the verb *transform*, affirms the present, the active and ongoing; as adjective, it implies the power to bring about change. Both make explicit my desire to bring about a change in the interpretations of Psyche as a female figure, to portray her as a representation of the search for the spiritual or "soul" and as an attitude of the mind, an approach to learning. My title rests on the supposition that transforming is a useful descriptor for the process of knowing. Thus, the title illustrates my concern with the idea of making sense of life as change, change as it occurs in all the relationships of Psyche/psyche – to nature, to culture, to learning, to work, to love, and to the spiritual. That Psyche's symbol, a soul symbol, is the fragile and beautiful butterfly foregrounds change, transformation and hope as an earthly possibility.

The verb *transform* is defined as "To change the form of" and "To change in character or condition" (*The Oxford English Dictionary*).[8] *Webster's New World Dictionary* further clarifies the meaning of *transform* by introducing its synonyms with their different nuances. Whereas *transform* "implies a change either in external form or in inner nature, in function," *metamorphosis* "suggests a startling change produced as if by magic," *transfigure* "implies a change in outward appearance" only, and *transmute* "suggests a change in basic nature that seems almost miraculous." My use of "transform," then, emphasizes the continuous, incremental, and integrated nature of knowledge rather than either a magical change or a superficial alteration of appearance.

A transformed, revalued, and re-examined female life experience presupposes a willingness to entertain a number of premises: (1) that biological life, in the body and on the earth, is a central fact of human existence, one that – literally – grounds metaphor; (2) that female behaviour in body, mind and spirit has its own and an inherent "philosophical truth" and that its free expression will change the definition of what it is to be human; (3) that the full range of human attributes (those characteristics labelled masculine or feminine) is available to all individuals regardless of gender; (4) that the characteristics labelled "feminine" are fundamental to human life but have been inadequately and negatively defined and valued; (5) that in a reconsideration of female biological experience and in a revaluation of the socially constructed values applied to the feminine lie the potential for a model of life-long learning and a way to bridge essentialist and cultural theories; and (6) that a willingness to revisualize the full range of human experience is not simply a reversal of dominance and therefore does not place men in a subordinate, dominated position.

If the Western intellectual tradition is, indeed, only a construct that expresses a bias towards male life experience and masculine vision, one based on opposites, conflict, and dichotomies, then to walk out from male-defined experience and into the named Other, the female/feminine, the wilderness, is to walk towards a view of life that restores context and continuity, interconnection and interrelationship. By taking these steps, it is possible to draw towards a concept of community in which an acceptance of difference in face to face encounters replaces (face to face) confrontation, polar opposites are linked in a (side by side) recognition of the continuum between, and all are contained in context.

My undertaking is necessarily interdisciplinary. Although for the most part the range involves literary criticism, women's studies, and education theory, the multiple questions that arise in the process of my investigation also require far-reaching excursions into other fields such as biology, psychology, sociology, cultural anthropology, and mythology. My methodology is as inductive as it appears to be eclectic, but such strategies are necessary, as I propose not only a critical interpretation but also a creative component. My intent is both to uproot old intellectual constructions and to revision new ones. This creative component appears in both my presentation of a new theoretical paradigm in chapter 7 and a revisioning of the story of Psyche in chapter 9.

Whereas I do make use of classical myths, it must be clear from the outset that I in no way intend a traditional or classical interpretation or use of them. I am neither mythographer nor one engaged in purely myth scholarship. My intent is to use ancient myths to illuminate the experiences of present-day women and ultimately to provide positive and affirmative ways for understanding women's "examined" lives. I believe that there is a clearly discernable pattern to Psyche's tale, and by using an interdisciplinary and feminist approach in my interpretations of it, I mean to suggest how the tale can be seen as speaking to contemporary Western women. My approaches to the other two myths, of Narcissus and Echo and Demeter and Persephone, are likewise interdisciplinary and woman centred.

By way of structuring my exploration into female life experience and the theorizing that defines it, I turn in chapter 1 to a consideration of methodology to survey the context and background from which the issues in this study arise. Expanding the scope of this investigation into adult and non-traditional learning experiences allows me to reorient the discussion into the issues of life-long learning, learning that takes place outside present educational systems and in the larger cultural context.

Chapter 2 contains an analysis of the metaphors of vision and hearing. As a way of highlighting the gender-specific implications of these metaphors, I examine them within the context of the story of Narcissus and Echo and use discussions of the myth to shed light on prevailing attitudes towards identity and subjectivity. This not only prepares for my analysis of Psyche's situation and behaviour but also sets the ground for the relationship pattern I introduce in chapter 7.

Chapter 3 introduces Psyche and the goddess Aphrodite, who also figures prominently in the tale. To re-examine the import of the tasks that the goddess sets Psyche, I consider what Aphrodite as goddess represents by exploring her genesis as goddess, the roots and routes of her powers. Chapter 4 interprets Apuleius's story of Psyche and Eros as a story of transformation within this expanded demarcation of the goddess's purview. Chapter 5 returns to epistemological matters by way of a close scrutiny of the implications of Psyche's tasks in the context of what we presently know about women's learning. Here my analysis also includes a consideration of the more ancient shamanic associations of learning and emphasizes the ages-old patterns in the life experiences of women.

Chapter 6 re-examines the tasks once more, here for what they reveal about gendered preferences for narrative form, and considers how Psyche's journey may be interpreted in terms of female life and spirituality. In chapter 7, female reproductive consciousness provides an avenue out of the subject-object dichotomy that so influences our present Western and Eurocentric outlook. This "other" consciousness brings a way of justifying continuum and context within relationship and a way of recognizing their importance as integral factors in any model for problem solving.

If any hypothesis about female experience is convincing, then its main elements must exist embedded in the real experiences of many different women with different life experiences. I choose to examine women's own life writings, specifically those in published autobiographies. Choosing women who are also writers allows me to assume a consciousness, a thoughtful awareness, about writing style, motif, and image choice. Therefore, chapter 8 is devoted to testing hypotheses and surveying some of the ways whereby twentieth-century women articulate the central themes and issues disclosed in the Psyche story; I also explore how variations of the theoretical patterns are present within the lifeprints of contemporary women's lives.

Finally, in chapter 9, instead of a formal conclusion, I offer a retelling of Psyche's story.

Contexts and Circumstances

An interdisciplinary methodology brings with it strengths and weaknesses that, for me, are best illustrated by the metaphor of the quilt. Because issues of gender permeate the different traditional disciplines, feminist research has relied upon an approach that brings together information from different knowledge fields to make new connections or to highlight what has previously been overlooked. The finished product requires an external design and a process akin to hand or machine sewing to make it whole. Along with the image of the artist, artisan, or agent who makes the patchwork patterns, sewing is an appropriately woman-centred image for the methodology necessary in redirecting inquiry and rearticulating theoretical issues.[1] This kind of quilt suggests the age-old female necessity of constructing the practical (and beautiful) out of the already outworn, of transforming the thread-bare and no longer useful into the creative and useful. In addition, the weaving needle moves, but the needlewoman has a place centredness; she is stationary. The quilt does not carry but is carried. Clearly, whereas sewing, like its sister craft of weaving, is a portable skill, it does not move the self out from the private sphere.

Because an interdisciplinary methodology takes "separate pieces" out from the discrete discourses and disciplines of the Western intellectual tradition, those who are familiar with the original "fabrics" may find it difficult to suspend judgment. Removed from their individual frameworks of investigation, considered primarily for the contribution they make to new knowledge, for what is revealed in a juxtaposition with other information from other disciplines, these displaced rearranged pieces are more vulnerable to critique from many directions. Deviation from the traditional frameworks is not taken lightly.

Standing against the possibilities inherent in a rearranged knowledge (even though the image of the needle weaving through three layers of whole cloth might suggest an integration of past history and of separate intellectual discourses) is the reality that the quilt does not represent the quilter's personal growth. It remains inorganic. It represents a separate learning, one moment in time, one image of the self; it is no more representative of the ongoing process of being than are the separate pieces from which it is constructed.

For me, therefore, the inadequacy of the quilting metaphor resides in the very action of its construction. A quilt remains an artifact, an article that does not put the individual into the experience or represent any transformation of the quilter's psyche. The image is of recontextualized objects/pieces. While the quilt represents much of my experience of combining approaches out of many disciplines as a way of making a theory about women's experience, I look beyond this act of construction for an image to represent a more self-referential learning, a more organic and holistic theoretical perspective.

The Dynamics of Metaphor

The way that the metaphor of the quilt suggests difficulties in interdisciplinary scholarship discloses some reasons for an examination of metaphor itself. Metaphors have consequences; they expand our understanding even as they impose limits to the significance of the comparisons made. In their theoretical examination of the uses of metaphor in everyday life, George Lakoff and Mark Johnson remind us that metaphors are not merely the vehicles of "poetic imagination"; they are fundamental to the ways we think and act in our daily lives (3). Metaphors are central to perception because they make up much of our conceptual structure: we use the forms and patterns from one kind of experience to give order and framework to another experience that may be new.

Our ability to transpose experience intellectually from one form to another gives metaphor importance as a way of deriving meaning from sense experience, perception, language, and action. Again, according to Lakoff and Johnson, metaphor is basic to our way of structuring *"imaginative rationality"* and permits us to understand "one kind of experience in terms of another." They go on to state: "New metaphors are capable of creating new understandings and, therefore, new realities" (235). Furthermore, the information conveyed through metaphoric depictions is selective because metaphor allows us to focus on one aspect of a comparison while excluding others that may be equally pertinent to understanding. Lakoff and Johnson note the value of paying particular attention to the "entailments," the necessary consequences, of metaphoric comparisons in order to heighten the features that direct and contain understanding. The entailments in comparisons can convey information about experience that brings significant new meanings to the metaphor.

In addition, Lakoff and Johnson describe two polarized systems of metaphoric understanding, the subjective and the objective, and indicate their inadequacies: "What the myths of objectivism and subjectivism both miss is the way we *understand* the world through our *interactions* with it" (194). Suggesting a third or experientialist myth, they synthesize objectivist interest in truthful, factual knowledge of the external world, fairness, and impartiality with an internal and personally meaningful subjective concern for individual experience, feeling, and intuitive insight. To this synthesis they then add context, the "perspective of man [*sic*] as part of his environment, not separate from it": "From the experientialist perspective, truth depends on understanding, which emerges from functioning in the world" (229–30). Experientialist myth accepts that "meaning is always meaning *to* a person" (228).

Metaphors of Voice and Sight

Women's Ways of Knowing identifies the metaphor of voice as an especially powerful one for women and applicable to many aspects of women's experience – even as it is used to distinguish that experience from men's. The authors note how speaking and listening are "at odds with the visual metaphors" that equate "knowledge with illumination, knowing with seeing, and truth with light," those metaphors that "scientists and philosophers most often use to express their sense of mind." They emphasize that the metaphors of vision and voice may also encourage different types of social behaviour. Metaphors of vision, as in "'the mind's eye,'" imply "a camera passively recording a static reality" and advance "the illusion that disengagement and objectification are central to the construction of knowledge." These metaphors "encourage standing at a distance" as a way of detaching "subject and object from a sphere of possible intercourse" (18).

In contrast, in *Women's Ways of Knowing*, Belenky et al. note that "the ear operates by registering nearby subtle change" and "requires closeness between subject and object. Unlike seeing, speaking and listening suggest dialogue and interaction." The authors also note the way that our cultural preference for the visual leads to a paradoxical approval of its loss: "philosophers and scientists who use visual metaphors to connote 'mind' value the impairment of that sense" (18). *Ways* illuminates what has been obscured even from the mind's imaginings:

how *intentional* blindness limits very obviously "what one can 'see' with the mind's eye" (19). Behind the privileging of sight lies a distrust of all sensory perception, *including* vision, the *preferred* metaphor.

In this context, one of the most interesting observations in my own earlier study of women artists was that even women with an *obvious* visual orientation – that is, who were practising visual artists – were as inclined to use a metaphor of voice and hearing to describe their experience of self and mind as the women in the study by Belenky et al., who were presumably not as specifically or vocationally oriented to sight. Indeed, that these artists relied on the hearing metaphor even as they described their love of a creativity expressed through visual artifacts seems now to suggest that women tend to affirm all sense experience rather than to foreclose one while advancing another. Moreover, these women's written responses indicated not only a concern with the creativity of a visually available expression of self and a joy in the visual objects themselves but also a concern with maintaining affective connections to family and community (both the wider social and the more specific art communities) and keeping open the lines of communication, connection, and relationship within and to those constituencies.

Experiential Learning

The relationship between visual metaphors and the functioning of the mind has also influenced our understanding of the learning process. In her investigation of experiential, body-centred learning and the "two-sided mind," Linda Verlee Williams relates how the focus has been on visual thinking, whereas learning might be better based on all the senses and, in fact, in an expanded definition of all the senses. After listing the five senses of sight, hearing, touch, smell, and taste, she continues by reminding us of "the proprioceptive senses – the kinaesthetic, vestibular, and visceral systems which monitor internal sensations" (144). This inventory of what has been left out in the construction of visually based metaphors of learning and education suggests that we have an intellectual system that might readily be called impoverished and that it would be enriched by a more inclusive use of sense experience.

Not only with respect to sense experience, it has been argued, has the current attitude towards learning been less than generous or expansive. Research psychologist Howard Gardiner developed a theory of multiple intelligences to suggest other possible definitions of human intelligence. Stressing that his is an "opening list," he adds musical, spacial, bodily kinaesthetic, interpersonal, and intrapersonal intelligences to the already accepted linguistic and logical-mathematical aptitudes that are measured in standardized tests. Explaining how people evidence these separate gifts, Gardiner tells us that musicians, architects, and dancers demonstrate the first three, that actors, teachers and therapists show interpersonal intelligence, and that diarists – and, I would add, autobiographers – show a special intrapersonal ability. Furthermore, Gardiner suggests that all these faculties may be avenues to the creative: "intelligences singularly or in combination may be put to artistic uses" (20). Presenting his two assumptions, that "not all people have the same minds" and that "life is short," he argues for an individual-centred school, one that would allow for these personal differences and accept a wider range of learning styles (22). Gardiner warns, too, that "intelligence and creativity are not always used benignly. They are value neutral." He goes on to illustrate the essential factor of context: "One can compose for Hitler or paint for Stalin" (27).

Both Gardiner's and Williams's differing assessments of an impoverished learning experience underscore Lakoff and Johnson's description of an experientialist myth of understanding. Both grant an increased significance to aptitudes and contexts; both accept that we are part of an environment, know it, and interact with it. In a similar vein, in his exposition of, and support for, a sensory-based and experiential learning process, Edward Cell describes how experience is necessary to, and must be acknowledged in, learning: "All learning is from experience. The experience may be our own or it may be that of others" (61). He continues by arguing that we respond emotionally to experience, that this emotion brings a mutuality of meaning and strength to learning, and that it grows from self-knowledge (91, 110). This personalized knowledge, in turn, contributes to interpersonal relationship: "Personal knowledge of another is based on our knowledge of ourselves" (118).

In his search for a new understanding about learning, Cell correlates empathy with sight and employs a spacial metaphor to expand its meaning: "we take up residence in two countries, seeing the other and his world from both his point of view and from our own simultaneously, although it is his view that is dominant, our own functioning only as the means by which we understand his" (119). Leaving aside the difficulty of being, even imaginatively, in two places at once, the introduction of the dominance of the other's point of view makes the metaphor problematic for women. (As Gilligan notes, women have tended to put others first to the detriment of their own development.) Cell continues by linking sight to touch. He believes that touch is basic to knowledge, that it is "an act of recognition." By his definition, "'respect' means 'to look at'" (125). Although he recognizes the importance of love to empathy and knowing, his philosophy is conventionally gendered, and he switches to the female pronoun to discuss the object in the knowledge exchange: "Genuine empathy, then, in which we enter into the viewpoint of the other and see her on her own terms requires love as does knowledge of ourselves" (128).

William G. Perry's work discusses the positive valuation our cultural context gives to the ideas of progress and achievement; he links growth and creativity to separation and transcendence. The problems raised by such a definition of growth are in turn addressed by Robert Kegan in his study of the structure of development entitled *The Evolving Self*. Although Betty Bardige has argued that Kegan's approach implies a self-centredness that may not exist, he does acknowledge and represent our cultural bias for understanding knowledge and meaning in the familiar metaphors of mind and vision. He also includes an affective dimension: "what the eye sees better the heart feels more deeply" and "[m]eaning depends on someone who recognizes you. Not meaning[,] by definition, is utterly lonely" (16, 19).

Introducing a metaphor of the spiral or helix to illustrate his concept of interindividuality and developmental growth, Kegan images growth as an evolutionary and twofold process of differentiating self from, and integrating self with, others. Distinguishing between these two human yearnings for inclusivity (connection) and integrity (independence), he suggests that their relation in tension is what accounts for creativity in life experience (107). Rather than seeing growth as separation and repudiation, he believes that it is "a matter of transition," a spiral that involves reconciliation and recovery (140). The spiral represents an evolution of meaning that sees the self moving between poles of integration and independence. He suggests that there will be a development "beyond psychological autonomy" that will have as a central feature "a new orientation to contradiction and paradox," one that "seems to shift to the relationship between the poles in a paradox rather than a choice between the poles" (228, 229).

Continuous Learning

Other educators have looked for ways to make learning more meaningful and inclusive by studying adults who continue to learn throughout their life span. Cyril O. Houle not only suggests the variety of continuing learners by distinguishing three types – goal, activity, and learning oriented – but also studies the "whys" and the "cataract of consequences" that make for continuous learning. To Houle, the role of the teacher is not of ultimate significance, but the presence of a public library and a strong relationship with parents – either positive or negative – are profoundly influential factors (72–3, 75, 69). In this way, he sees continuous, lifelong learning as linked to strong emotional connections in the family and to an accessible and nourishing cultural environment.

That the teacher is not perceived by Houle as having a long-term influence is at first glance surprising in view of the importance of the emotional response to parent figures, but his findings do confirm the sense that something is missing in present educational practice. This failure of influence may simply be one of form: the traditional teacher (Houle's book was published in 1963) functions in a hierarchical arrangement, and such an organization works against connection. Thus, teachers in hierarchical situations may make for the efficient transmission of that package of knowledge required by a democratic society, but hierarchy itself may work against the development of what Houle terms the "inquiring mind."[2]

An "inquiring mind" implies a learning that grows from experience and is of a piece with the person's life and life journey; the development is transformative because of the interactive nature of self with environment and life with experience. This change in educational goals from the transmission of a set package of what is known to a transmission of the skills of inquiry is a central concern for Malcolm S. Knowles. His interest in learning as a lifelong process encompasses connection and continuity. His accent on self-directed learning "assumes that learners are motivated by internal incentives, such as the need for esteem (especially self-esteem), the desire to achieve, the urge to grow, the satisfaction of accomplishment, the need to know something specific, and curiosity" (21).

Calling this adult and self-directed learning "andragogy," Knowles distinguishes it from traditional pedagogy, the transmission of already parcelled knowledge to children. Whereas the shift from child (*paido*) to man (*andro*) has a male accent, the change in name does nonetheless clearly signal a modification in the role of the teacher from an authority figure to facilitator and cooperative co-learner. Changing the environment in this way shifts the emphasis to the student and to a process of designing for individual learning. The emphasis is on acquisition – getting for oneself – rather than on transmission – being given – and the switch compels learners and teachers into active sharing of available resources (71). The teacher becomes an associate, a mentor, rather than an organizer of a pre-established curriculum content.

Mentoring

Learning and development theory places special emphasis on mentoring. In writing about male development, Daniel J. Levinson describes male mentors, their importance for individual learning and success, and a little understood connection with the negative and potentially destructive emotions of envy and resentment. He lists the mentor's functions as those of teacher, sponsor, guide, and exemplar but states that the most developmentally crucial role of the mentor is "to support and facilitate the realization of the dream" (98). He calls mentors "transitional figures" but notes that the "good enough" mentoring relationships that he studied often ended unhappily. Even when the young men felt "admiration, respect, appreciation, gratitude and love for the mentor," these feelings could not "entirely prevent" feelings of resentment, inferiority, envy, or intimidation. Only after the separation was it possible for the young men to take in more fully "the admired qualities of the mentor" (101). For men, Levinson states, "the mentor relationship in its developed form is rare. It is sundered, with other things, as part of *Becoming One's Own Man*" (149).

Other metaphors for the multiple dimensions of the mentoring relationship have emphasized the spiritual nature of the role. Laurent A. Daloz expands the guiding and friendship aspects of the mentoring relationship to evoke their presence in a transformational life journey. In addition, he suggests that one has a personal responsibility for choosing a mentor and notes that "mentors are creations of our imaginations, designed to fill a psychic space somewhere between lover and parent. Not surprisingly, they are suffused with magic and play a key part in our transformation" (17). He emphasizes teaching as a transaction, as a relationship and development, as both change and new direction, and his description of learning as knowing more and thinking differently also evokes the spiral image.

Daloz uses Dante's epic poem and the myth of Odysseus to illustrate the links between mentor relationships and the idea of the journey as a metaphor for learning. He notes that "[a]t some point, mentors always depart, generally before the journey is over. The trip belongs, after all to the traveller, not the guide – and the mentor has his own promises to keep" (33). Applying the theories of Gilligan, Kegan, Levinson, and Perry to the mentoring relationship and learning, Daloz describes mentors as "gatekeepers as well as guides" who are able to accept chaos as necessary for attaining enlightenment, who balance polarities and introduce new ways of seeing. They are powerful liminal figures who "stand at the boundary of the old and new worlds and, as such, hold the keys for successful passage. That they are in the position to make judgements and select or reject us gives them considerable power" (96).

Furthermore, Daloz stresses hearing and "sees" teaching as listening. His description of good teaching echoes the emphasis given by Belenky et al. and by Gilligan to the metaphor of voice. Downplaying the accumulation of "a shelfful of knowledge" or "a repertoire of skills," Daloz observes: "In the end, good teaching lies in a willingness to attend and care for what happens in our students, ourselves, and the space between us. Good teaching is a certain kind of stance ... of receptivity, of attunement, of listening" (244).

Learning as Journey

The journey, as path and quest, occurs frequently as a metaphor of learning because it implies change – usually growth – and putting ourselves into the centre of the learning experience. John A.B. McLeish, writing of age and creativity, uses the myth of Ulysses and the Ulyssean path to explore new possibilities in middle age. As he describes it, the Ulyssean path is the path of the warrior-adventurer, a journey of detachment, separation, and confrontation, with a final return home to reconnection; it is circular. This view of the journey represents an experience gendered as male, adventure that chafes at the confines of home and seeks enterprise for its own sake.

If men's learning and the hero's journey are linked in an emphasis on adversarial conflict and detachment, by way of contrast, Carol P. Christ uses the journey metaphor and ties it to both silence and women's spiritual quests. Women's quests begin "in an _experience of nothingness_ (self-hatred, self-negation, being victim)," continue "on to _awakening_ (powers of being revealed) through _mystical insight_ (in nature or with other women) to a _new naming_" (13). Her analysis of "nothingness" evokes the "silence" of the learning pattern set forth in *Women's Ways of Knowing*. Christ's "experience of nothingness" is explicitly tied to women's cultural otherness, but even if this experience is profoundly negative, Edward Cell's study of learning experience reminds us that "more often than not our most significant growth processes take place subconsciously precisely at those times when it seems to us on the surface that nothing is happening at all" (230–1).

In addition, Christ suggests that women's narratives share a spiral pattern: "The moments of women's quest are part of a process in which experiences of nothingness, awakenings, insights, and namings form a spiral of ever-deepening but never final understanding" (14). The spiral, which Kegan has also offered as a metaphor to suggest a balance between autonomy and interrelationship, could have especial value as a metaphor of the stages of knowing described in *Ways* and as an image integral to women's own experience of life and spiritual values. Perhaps any circumstance that requires a new perspective, a new way of dealing with a changing world, causes women to move to silence. Perhaps, too, silence might indicate the beginning of another cycle, a germination of new ways of dealing with and making sense of the world.

In her examination of mind, gender, and the paradox of developmental theories, Gisela Labouvie-Vief uses the dual structure implicit in the myth of Psyche and Eros to argue for a revaluation of the feminine mythos and a union of logos and mythos to represent the values of the cognitive and affective/imaginative in the aging process. She likewise suggests that these two modes are indicated by quite different patterns: one narrative and dialogue, one reason and rule. To her, the core metaphor becomes one of playful dialogue between equals that is well represented by Psyche's joining the divine Eros on Olympus. Arguing for a new language, Labouvie-Vief sees these individual patterns thus resolved in cooperation and integration.

Myths and Fairy Tales

The differences that distinguish male and female journeys are analogous to the distinctions Bruno Bettelheim draws between the structures of myth and fairy tale. In fairy tales, the lack of polarization, of good and evil, is an assurance that even the meek may succeed and that even the most unpleasant of feelings is acceptable; "the difference between myth and fairy tale is highlighted by the myth telling us directly ... The fairy tale never confronts us so directly, or tells us outright how to choose" (34). Myths and fairy tales are likened to shamanic journeys, as all "were derived from, or give symbolic expression to, initiation rites or other *rites de passage* – such as a metaphoric death of an old, inadequate self in order to be born on a higher plane of existence" (35).

Bettelheim's description of the relationship between children and the everyday objects around them suggests that, in their eyes, the "magical" simply represents an enhanced perception, an ability to discern and respond to an inherent beingness within nature. "To the child," he comments, "there is no clear line separating objects from living things; and whatever has life has life very much like our own. If we do not understand what rocks and trees and animals have to tell us, the reason is that we are not sufficiently attuned to them" (46). Because this kind of interaction with the natural world is not acknowledged in our technological culture, it remains visible primarily within myth and fairy tale.

In spite of this, the simple fact that myths and fairy tales endure, have been handed down to us, indicates a level of social sanction. The act of recording signifies that the myths reflect the views of those who record them – those who have the power to record. In the Introduction to *Whence the Goddesses*, Miriam Robbins Dexter cautions us to "remember that myth is political" and that it may be perceived as giving "divine sanction to the social patterns of a culture" (x, xi). According to Dexter, what is sanctioned in the Western tradition is patriarchal because myth is a male construct expressing masculine values. This does not, however, mean that myth is necessarily myth in the conventional sense, though its doubled definition as "fictitious" indicates a desire to downplay its less acceptable meanings. To Ken Dowden, myth does not reveal history or even event. At most it relays a tradition that may be both fiction and ideology: "Myth addresses, explores, expresses the complexity of [cultural] data, but is not claimed itself to be the source of that data" ("Women," 46). Writing specifically about Apuleius and how he imposes his own viewpoint, his own symbolic order, Judith K. Krabbe states that "every writer is a transformer, shaping new reality out of his experiences, personal and literary" (42).

Leslie A. Fiedler makes another useful distinction. Using the term "Archetype" instead of "myth," he refers to it as an immemorial pattern that illustrates our response to death, love, the biological family, and spiritual relationship. Because of this patterning, the Archetype carries what he describes as an unspoken awareness or consciousness of the universality of human experience. For Fiedler, the "Signature" is the sum of the individuating characteristics of a work of art, and as such, it carries overt information about the social collectivity. This is where cultural bias may be inscribed. "The difference in the communal element in the Signature and that in the Archetype," he states, "is that the former is *conscious*" (319). What he also contends is that an understanding of Archetype requires an interdisciplinary analysis, specifically anthropology and psychology, to reveal the underlying and transhistorical truths about human life that lie hidden there.

Acknowledging the influence of the psychoanalytic and universalist perspectives, Marina Warner nonetheless argues that stories like Psyche and Cupid have much to offer to historical interpretation. Such tales reveal "how human behaviour is embedded in material circumstance, in the laws of dowry, land tenure, feudal obedience, domestic hierarchies and marital dispositions" (xviii–xix). Comparing fairy tales to archeological sites, she sees them as presenting clear evidence of past social conditions. The narrative strategy, too, suggests both history and gendered value. Noting that Apuleius uses the term "an old wives' tale," Warner makes the connection between "old women's speech and the consolatory, erotic, often fanciful fable" (14). That the Latin root of the word "fairy" refers to a goddess of destiny and incorporates the suggestion of oral speech leads her to suggest that the power of these tales rests in a knowledge of the past, in an association with foretelling the future and with forewarning.

If myth and fairy tale endure, in their longevity, then, they reveal not only this personal (usually male) perspective and cultural or historical (patriarchal) reality or Signature but also the underlying and more universal experience or Archetype. Even in explicitly patriarchal narratives, women may respond to extant though obscure truths lying in and energizing their centres. Sarah B. Pomeroy suggests that a doubled reality may also have existed in the practice of ancient patriarchal religions. She differentiates myth from cultic practice by the way each represents the goddesses in their relationship to women. Myths, she contends, show goddesses hostile to women, but cults, in the actual ceremonies and rituals of worship, pay attention to women's roles and answer women's needs. Since the myths, usually transmitted through male-authored stories, are what have survived, the anti-woman, anti-feminine biases in the goddesses have also been handed to us through the centuries. Myth is dualistic, binary in its female/male, feminine/masculine divisions and emphasis on conflict; its biases are ancient and have acquired many levels of meaning, and yet, this in no way denies their contemporary relevance. Within these prejudices, however, women have been able to reclaim and revision female experience.[3]

Learning Roles

The cultural construction of social roles that both mask and constrict women's lived experience is a central concern of sociologists such as Lillian B. Rubin and Caryl Rivers et al. who have examined women's life patterns in modern society and discussed the ways that these role assumptions for women are changing. In spite of perceived advances, however, Rubin's examination of mid-life women reveals an underlying and pervasive culturally embedded fear of women – particularly of aging women. Though women have great emotional power privately within the family, they still lack equality in society. For men, Rubin contends, "adult means to do something in the world out there" and "there is no *being* without *doing*." Women are "expected to be – *be* good, *be* pretty, *be* patient, *be* kind, *be* loving. *To be* – the quintessence of woman" (57). As a creature of *being*, woman is by implication "done to," and underlying these definitions are implications and expectations for female behaviour in relationships.

The repression and fear of women's sexuality and emotional power in relationships are subsumed into cultural values. The behaviours expected of women all stress the well-being and comfort of the others in the relationship; female selfhood and desire are consumed in care for others. The usual implication is that the others are husband and children. Relationship, however, also implies a mutuality of give and take. This is nowhere more significant than in sexual expression. Here, Rubin observes that "this very quality of giving ... is necessary to turn the sex act into a relationship. Only when two people wish to give at least as much as they wish to take does sex become a nourishing and enriching experience" (79). The ascription of gender-based behaviours often results in relationship failures and in crushing the needs or feelings that are deemed inappropriate (in either gender).

This scheme, even if or especially if unspoken, renders intellectual life or public life that is not exclusively for the service of others' needs particularly difficult for women to undertake. Any non-traditional and self-expressive activity will be regarded as un/non-feminine or un/non-womanly, and in addition, any traditional female activity will be denigrated or ignored. Cultural anthropologist Emily Martin documents how these views continue to influence even present-day North American culture and specifically medical practice. Christine Battersby shows how ingrained and historically slippery attitudes to gender and to creative and intellectual abilities in men and women continue to prejudice attitudes towards "genius" and women's creative work.

Because there is an equal penalty for women in the idealization of the mother-child relationship, to counter this idealization, Rivers et al. have argued that what they term "hostile mothering" has real benefits: a "reasonable amount of conflict and tension is inevitable and appears to help children grow into 'separate people.'" They go on to declare that a measure of maternal antagonism in an otherwise loving and supportive relationship may be especially beneficial to girls: "Encouraging independence – and being careful not to reward dependent behaviour – is the first key step in helping girls become self-reliant and free to develop their full potential" (137).

Rivers et al. emphasize the fact that girls are educated in incompetence and do not learn to recognize their own success: "Girls have to learn to take credit for their own accomplishments. Too many girls and women do something good and then write it off to luck" (137). The authors also link the failure to become one's own woman with "chronic, unexpressed anger" (202). This loss of voice and unexpressed anger has obvious detrimental effects for the woman herself, but learning to express the needs that result in anger, conflict, and tension has real benefit for all of a woman's relationships. In this way, the struggle to express unhappiness with inhospitable circumstances can, in fact, result in changes that improve interpersonal relationships.

Women and Science

Nowhere is women's struggle to change roles and find a place in an inhospitable community – while at the same time working to change the contours of that community – more evident than in the field of science. The examination of the lives and careers of women scientists is paralleled by an intense scrutiny of the very forms of the scientific process. Evelyn Fox Keller has provided both in her exploration of the work of scientist Barbara McClintock. Keller recounts McClintock's career to show the ways in which she does scientific observation *differently*. McClintock's struggles to reconcile objective and scientific observation with empathic understanding serve to test concepts about "the limits of verbally explicit reasoning." Keller tells us that McClintock's stress on the importance of a "feeling for the organism" in phrases that "sound like those of mysticism" has made her suspect among her peers (xiii–xiv). Her work was unrecognized throughout most of her career, and McClintock lived her life at the boundaries of the scientific community.

In describing McClintock's attempt to reconcile scientific observation and intuitive understanding, Keller portrays her work on corn genetics as taking on a life of its own and as being focused on the individual details and the unique characteristics of individual plants (86, 101). Understanding and insight combined with "respect for the unfathomable workings of the mind" and "regard for the complex workings of the plant" all illustrate a concept of research based on connection and relationship, on interrelationship between known and knower, object and subject (104–5). An image of attunement and sympathy pictures an observational approach that is profoundly different from the strategy of the objective scientist who is outside of, and removed from, the area of inquiry. Keller's description of "artists and poets, lovers and mystics," who wrote "about the 'knowing' that comes from the loss of self – from the state of subjective fusion with the object of knowledge," provides a clear contrast to scientists who "pride themselves on their capacities to distance subject from object." She goes on to note that scientists' "richest lore" is a result of "a joining of one to the other, from a turning of object into subject." Keller asserts that often the best results come from this desire to lose the sense of a distanced self in the interaction implicit in intellectual experience (*Feeling*, 118).

Keller further observes that McClintock's ability to "see" is central to her methodology: "For all of us, our concepts of the world build on what we see, as what we see builds on what we think. Where we know more, we see more" (148). This interrelationship between visual and the cognitive – reading "simultaneously by the eyes of the body and those of the mind" – exists within a relationship of "shared subjectivity"; it involves "a way of looking that is necessarily in part determined by some private perspective" and "a capacity for union with that which is to be known" (148, 149, 150, 201). Keller links mysticism and spiritual experience to this "commitment to the unity of experience, the oneness of nature, the fundamental mystery underlying the laws of nature" (201).

Sex as Metaphor

In a series of essays exploring the relationship between gender and science, Keller moves from her study of the experience of one scientist to explore the general sexualization of knowledge. She indicates that the way in which the gap between object and subject, known and knower, is traditionally closed is in the compelling and powerful metaphor of "sexual relation." Knowledge is described as "a form of consummation, just as sex is a form of knowledge. Both are propelled by desire." Emphasizing that even without metaphor "the experience of knowing is rooted in the carnal," her study is arresting for the paradox this metaphor is used to reveal. The classical distinction in knowledge is "its essential thrust away from the body: its ambition is to transcend the carnal. Mind is not simply immanent in matter; it is transcendent over it." Keller stresses that "all visions of knowledge must accordingly struggle with the dialectic between immanence and transcendence" (18). The sexual metaphor also shows the differing valuations applied to body and mind and to immanence and transcendence. The suspicion of embodied sense experience results in a paradigm of knowing that separates the mind from the *only* means through which we collect information, embodied sensory perceptions.

Maintaining that objectivity has become the cult of objectivism to the detriment of true understanding and knowledge, Keller first traces the development of these ideas through history, from Plato to the present, and contends that modern science carries a "projection" and a "reflected self-image" which is specifically male and which undercuts any claims of objectivity. She then moves through a discussion of object-relations theory and the tensions among power, dominance, autonomy, and love to explore the failures in a concept of science based on the "laws of nature"; in turn she suggests shifting "to an interest in the multiple and varied kinds of order actually experienced in nature" and "more global and interactive models of complex dynamic systems" (134).

According to Keller, the scientific belief in the blindness of the "laws of nature" contrasts markedly with McClintock's extraordinary emphasis on, and definition of, seeing and response: "'Laws' of nature name nature as blind, obedient, and simple; simultaneously, they name their maker as authoritative, generative, resourceful, and complex. Historically, the maker is God; but as discoverer and maker converge, the scientist inherits the mantle of creativity along with that of authority" (134). Keller, describing nature "as orderly, and not law bound," argues that this "allows nature itself to be generative and resourceful – more complex and abundant than we can either describe or prescribe." Nature is regarded as "an active partner in a more reciprocal relation to an observer, equally active, but neither omniscient nor omnipotent" (134).

Keller especially recognizes what such a shift entails for the ways in which we conduct investigation. This "different style of inquiry" would be "no less rigorous," yet "modesty and open attentiveness" would "allow one to 'listen to the material' rather than assum[e] that scientific data self-evidently speak for themselves" (134). Suggesting an integrative, responsive, and passionate learning that exists outside of, or at the very least on the edges of, present learning theory, Keller confronts the importance that is traditionally accorded the idea of transcendence, of the mind as having a power which (sexually) penetrates and subdues (rapes) nature. As it relates to learning, transcendence presupposes a subject matter that is passive, outside and apart from the learner. Not surprisingly, this construction of a passive subject matter accords fully with patriarchal constructions of female roles and feminine behaviours.

Paradox

Keller's analysis of the sexual metaphor in scientific approaches to research recalls the gendered valuations with which my discussion began: of body/female/feminine/immanent spirituality as defined and seen to exist in opposition to mind/male/masculine/transcendent spirit. These are well understood binaries or dichotomies, and I recall to the reader those comments made early in the chapter about their hierarchical and teleological valuations.[4] The gendered associations of these binaries make self-evident the rationale for the metaphor of sexual union as a way of combining opposites. Here, however, this particular metaphor becomes blurred with paradox. The term "paradox" contains and unites the dichotomies that do not ordinarily exist in proximity. Unlike metaphor, paradox does not rely on process.

In his *Glossary of Literary Terms*, M.H. Abrams notes that a paradox "seems on its face to be self-contradictory or absurd, yet turns out to make good sense" (126). He goes on to state that "it was a central device in seventeenth century *metaphysical* poetry." Paradoxes that conjoin two contrary terms are oxymorons and often are found "in Elizabethan love poetry" and "in devotional prose and religious poetry as a way of expressing the Christian mysteries, which transcend human sense and logic" (127). In both these ways, paradox not only links sexual intercourse and transcendent spirituality but also conjoins other oppositions that seem to exist "outside" our definitions of "sense and logic." If they exist outside, then they cannot be seen to be subject to process. The elision of continuum creates paradox.

Subjectivity and Experience

A concern with the construction of female subjectivity and authenticity and with the search for a way to articulate female experience requires a philosophical definition of experience. Teresa de Lauretis declares that "the notion of experience" is "very much in need of clarification and elaboration," yet it "bears directly on the major issues that have emerged from the women's movement – subjectivity, sexuality, the body, and feminist political practice" (159). According to her, experience results from a process of continuous transformation, in a "process" where "one places oneself or is placed in social reality, and so perceives and comprehends as subjective (referring to, even originating in, oneself) those relations – material, economic, and interpersonal – which are in fact social and in a larger perspective, historical." She asserts that this "process is continuous, its achievement unending or daily renewed. For each person, therefore, subjectivity is an ongoing construction, not a fixed point of departure or arrival from which one interacts with the world" (159).

After surveying the dualities inherent in various theories of subjectivity and the difficulties for women within current discourses, de Lauretis moves to a discussion of semiotics and the split subject. From that vantage point, she defines experience as "a complex of habits resulting from the semiotic interaction of 'outer world' and 'inner world,' the continuous engagement of a self or subject in social reality" (182). De Lauretis warns against "becoming woman" and, in the self-consciousness present in feminist theory, articulates a future direction for feminist theory as "political, theoretical and self-analyzing practice." Her warnings are against seeing "in femininity" a "privileged nearness to nature, the body, or the unconscious" or "an essence which inheres in women." She warns about seeing "a female tradition simply understood as private, marginal and yet intact, outside of history but fully there to be discovered or recovered." For her, a direction for theory lies not "in the chinks and cracks of masculinity, the fissures of male identity or the repressed of phallic discourse" (186).

I emphasize these warnings because in all these areas, in spite of all clear and present dangers in the list, I intend to take on what de Lauretis describes as "the subtle, shifting, duplicitous terms" of contradiction. I do believe that facing into these very real perils is one way through the labyrinth of phallocentric discourse. I add them to her injunction to create a "political, theoretical, self-analyzing practice" whereby "the subject in social reality can be rearticulated from the historical experience of women" (186).

Narcissus and Echo

The myth of Narcissus is characterized by its haunting images of vision, beauty, and passionate love. In complex and subtle ways, it intertwines inequalities of power with gendered social roles, perception, aesthetics, identity, and love. This narrative, in which the protagonist is male, the spectator-owner and object-projection of his own reflection/obsession, and in which the female figure of Echo makes a brief appearance, dramatizes how issues of vision and voice reveal both women's social position and the status of those qualities named "feminine" in Western tradition. In addition, this tradition has made use of both the positive and negative aspects of the myth to illustrate specifically male anxieties about identity, sexuality, and power, and twentieth-century psychoanalysis from its Freudian beginnings has codified the myth in such a way as to re-enforce masculinist attitudes in modern culture.[1]

Ovid's *Metamorphoses* is the source for the story of Narcissus.[2] The narrative begins with violence in the ravishing of Liriope by Cephisos, the river-god: he "caught hold" of Liriope, "confined her," and "took her violently." It also begins in blindness, with the blind see-er, who is consulted by Liriope about whether her son, Narcissus, will have long life. Tiresias's response, "If he does not get to know himself," introduces the complicating factors of identity and self-knowledge. Because of his beauty, Narcissus is loved by many but "(there was in his delicate beauty so stiff a pride) / no men, no girls affected him." Echo, "still a body, not a voice," falls in love with Narcissus, but he rejects her and will not allow himself to be touched by her: "Hands off, do not embrace me. / I would die before I would offer myself to you." As a result, she grows thin, wastes, shrivels until "only ... her voice remained; her bones they say, took on the appearance of stone."

Narcissus also rebuffs young men: "disdained," one youth "raised his hands up towards the ether / and said, 'so may he too love, and so may he not gain / what he has loved.'" The young man's prayer is granted by Rhamnusia [Nemesis]. Narcissus sees himself in a pool, "a beautiful reflection," and "loved a hope without a body"; "He did not know what he was seeing, but he was on fire for what he saw." Authorially the poem warns: "What you are looking at is a shadow, a reflected image. / It has nothing of its own." Understanding the image as his own reflection, as himself, Narcissus wishes "that I were able to withdraw from my body." He longs for escape from embodied life because he knows that only in transcending the physical (into the imagination) will he be able to achieve his desire to join with his reflection. He, like Echo, pines and wastes, but his body metamorphoses magically – is totally changed – into a flower, the narcissus.

Image and Voice

Narcissus vividly enacts the kind of scientific observational stance that Keller critiques. Narcissus falls in love with the projection of himself, his own and the male/masculine dichotomized version of culture (history, philosophy, religion, etc.).[3] Narcissus sees a projection of himself on the surface of a pool – his image *on* nature – a nature that he does not see and in which he does not therefore include himself. Thus, the image that he adores excludes context and is *partial*. His projected "reality" is selective, exclusive, and prohibitive: he selects his own youthful male image, excludes nature and the world as context, and prohibits any relationship that could interfere with self-love.

If Narcissus can be read as a representation of Man-as-male/masculine and sight, then Echo can equally represent Woman-as-female/feminine and hearing. Echo can express herself only through a partial repetition of what is said to her: in this case, the last part of Narcissus's speech. Echo's plight is a punishment by Juno/Hera. Echo distracted the goddess from seeing her husband Jove/Zeus's marital infidelities with the nymphs. The female figures are presented as divided and set against one another over issues of sight and sexuality, and female authority is portrayed as demanding and vindictive. Further, marriage is depicted as the province and protection of a spiteful goddess who directs her anger at Echo (instead of at the profligate Jove/Zeus) and punishes her by depriving her of the means for the direct expression of her own will: "the nymph began only to reiterate words at the ends of speeches, and repeat what she had heard."

As embodied female and as part of the named feminine, Echo is already unable to speak her own reality or her Self; she is forbidden to "touch" Narcissus. He cannot "hear" her. Significantly, the definition of touch allies it with hearing: touch is derived from "*toccare*, to strike," as in "[t]o strike the strings, keys, etc. (of a musical instrument) so as to make it sound." The term has a specifically sexual meaning as well: "[t]o have sexual contact with." These multiple meanings of "touch" suggest that Echo's presence in Narcissus's tale accounts for some crucial absences, even if her story is but a minor theme. Echo is as (sexually) unfulfilled as is Narcissus; she pines to a stone-like bone. An early, if sad, by-product of Narcissus's self-obsession is that Echo's fate, like her being, is of no concern to him. As Amy Lawrence explains, "even when he is alone (watched by Echo) speech is the one thing that could break his absorption in the image, language the medium that could explain the image's status as reflection" (1).

Not only is Narcissus lost in image reflection but Echo is lost in "accoustic reflection" (2). Lawrence describes Echo as a representation of "woman's voice": she represents a woman's physical ability to make a sound, a woman's relationship to sound or verbal discourse, and a female point of view. The separation of voice-as-echo from the embodied female comes about because Echo cannot "touch" or affect Narcissus; female life and feminine values – as biologically, culturally, and socially reproductive and generative – are disregarded, unheard.

Disembodied, disconnected sound, the Word is all that remains of Echo, and even that is not her own. She may respond only with part of what Narcissus says: "the one thing not forbidden / Is to make answers," but these answers are mere and partial repetitions of what she has last heard. She does not even have access to the history, the words, that have come before what she repeats. As an image of the plight of woman's place in the Western intellectual tradition, Echo reverberates with truth. Like the surface image that Narcissus sees in the pool, she speaks an incomplete and superficial reality, unable to create her own self-expressive language. Ignored by Narcissus, left as intellectually and creatively infertile as her love leaves her unfulfilled, Echo may only "bear witness." She is destroyed, almost accidentally, by ignorance, by being ignored.

The Mirroring Pool

In this saddest of tales, both Echo and Narcissus are lost in a dichotomized world of oppositions, but like a stone dropped in that pool, the story has rippled forward through time to present a provocative image, warning us of what is lost in this construction of disconnection and this failure in expression of identity. Poolside, Narcissus is rooted in the contemplation of his own beauty; he is locked into the visual and into visual imagery as the means of expressing self-identity. Narcissus discounts, does not see, the pool that mirrors and reflects his image; he does not register the pool as context, a very real element in the natural world.

As symbol, water represents generative nature, the life source, the mother, and gives "birth to 'spirit,' supposedly a male principle" (Walker, *Encyclopedia*, 1066). The mother of Narcissus is Liriope, a name that refers to a water grass that grows around shallow pools, a "grass-leaved" herb (described further as having "a superior ovary" in *Webster's Third New International Dictionary*). In the notes to his translation of Ovid's *Metamorphoses*, D.E. Hill states that "liriope" means "lily-like" and that the lily is botanically related to the narcissus; Barbara G. Walker discloses that the lily represented Astarte, Hera/Juno, Venus/Aphrodite, and the Virgin aspect of the triple goddess (*Encyclopedia*, 542–3). By the myth's representation, however, the pool is specifically named as Narcissus's paternal source: Cephisos is a river god. In this way, the pool is a symbol representing his parents (especially his father) and implies his own personal past, his social, cultural, and family history.

His conception in rape and its effects on his perception are understood as influential by David C. McClelland, who uses this aspect of the Narcissus myth to illustrate the issues of power and violence in what he refers to as the Icarus complex. Drawing on the writing of Octavio Paz, McClelland describes the alienation and isolation experienced by the sons born of the rape of Mexican women by Spanish conquerors. The violence inherent in rape results in a profound, painful, and traumatic estrangement for the son: from identification with the father and from a mature and affective sexual identity. Both are doubly difficult because of an understandable emotional identification with the mother's trauma. A third consequence of rape is illustrated by cultural anthropologist Wenda R. Trevathan. In *Human Birth*, she writes of how important the father's loving support is to the mother's optimum bonding with her infant. Because Narcissus is conceived in rape, the primary – primal – bond of affective connection is made more difficult.

The Nature of Reflection

The pool, then, is an element of nature that contains Narcissus's own familial history, yet is a surface that functions as a mirror. By definition, a mirror is both "a polished surface which reflects images of objects" and a process: "to reflect in the manner of a mirror." The word "mirror" comes from the Latin *mirari,* meaning "to wonder at." On the one hand, Narcissus's beautiful image in the pool is a mirror reflection, a product of the mirroring process, the object of his sight and love, "a hope without a body." On the other hand, mirroring is a "wonderful" process, a by-product of the pool's character, a process also called reflection.

Reflection, which encompasses process and product, is both means and ends: "[t]he action of a mirror or other polished surface in exhibiting or reproducing the image of an object; the fact or phenomenon" and "[a]n image or counterpart thus produced." At the same time, however, reflection is also defined as a process and product of thinking: "[t]he action of turning (back) or fixing the thoughts on some subject" and a "meditation, deep or serious consideration." Philosophically, it is the "mode, operation or faculty by which the mind has knowledge of itself and its operations, or by which it deals with the ideas received from sensation or perception." What is left out of Narcissus's perception is the pool as nature, parent, personal history, and the process of reflection. His thought, a reproductive procedure, reflects the world only through his own being and guarantees a partial understanding of reality.

His is an overdeveloped and self-absorbed emphasis on the end product, the image. Narcissus cannot see through his image to the process of his own desiring or to the means, the pool behind it. This ensures that he is unable to embrace – to love – or to understand either his image-as-repetition or the process in context, the pool he does not see. His blindness to the pool (the mirror, the continuum, the middle, the reflective process, his own reflective thought), on which and by which his desire has been created, means that there can be no resolution, no consummation; his mental action is unproductive, ungenerative. This blindness, the need for more sight, carries its own judgment. The last of the dictionary definitions given for "reflection" is of blame, censure, and reproof: "[a]n imputation; a fact or procedure casting an imputation or discredit on one."

Repetition and Aesthetics

In Western tradition, a process that is repetitive, like Echo's repeating of words, has little or no aesthetic value; yet repetition in the form of repeated images like that of Narcissus – an object – does. Thus, repetition has been employed to distinguish art from craft and thereby to establish a hierarchy of aesthetic values. In an essay that explores this double standard in aesthetic criticism, Judith Barry and Sandy Flitterman-Lewis quote Lucy Lippard. Although Lippard is discussing the work of a particular woman artist, the observations she makes about repetition as process have a general validity. According to Lippard, in some women's art, repetition "refers not to form but to process" and to repeated actions like unravelling, binding or nailing (92). Barry and Flitterman-Lewis view the negative attitude towards repetition-as-process as a kind of repression. In this instance, what is repressed, overlooked, and disregarded is complexity and skill. In the realm of women's art production, this negative view results in dismissal; women's art, especially the traditional art forms, is relegated to the lesser domain of craft. Traditional art forms of weaving, quilting, and pottery necessarily rely on repetitive processes, and the discrepancy in assigned aesthetic value epitomizes the devaluation of process.[4]

In contrast to the idea of repetition as process, repetition as form reifies stillness. However tension filled, Narcissus's world remains stationary, solipsistic, and self-referential. There is no breath (no life) to disturb his own reflection as he sees it on the surface of the pool. The primary focus of his reflection is his head – doubly read as intellect and phallus. As image, his head represents a concern for things of the mind, an intellectual knowledge on top of, surmounting, a male body, disconnected both from nature and from the female. This disconnection represents a purification of understanding by removing – disengaging – subject from context. Scientific understanding is represented as "pure" by just such a removal of context; aesthetic value, by a removal of process.

Fire and Passion

The passion for his own image becomes the unquenchable, internal fire that destroys Narcissus: "He did not know what he was seeing, but he was on fire at what he saw." In *Love's Fatal Glance*, Lance K. Donaldson-Evans discusses the role of eye imagery and traces the "aggressive eye topos" back to Ovid and the philosophy of Plato. Not only does the sight of the beloved itself generate love but the beloved's glance engenders and nurtures love: "Briefly, the efflux theory of vision represents the eye not as a mere receiver or reflector of light rays, but as possessing its own internal illumination in the form of fire" (12).

The mix of water, fire, and voice metaphors with eyesight and passionate love is evident in the quotation from Plato that Donaldson-Evans uses to illustrate the effects of this gaze: a "'flood of passion' pours in upon the lover," is partly absorbed, and "as a breath of wind or an echo" returns to its origin and "re-enters the eyes of the fair beloved." In the myth, then, Narcissus's "fiery" eye beam is reflected back from water to consume him in passionate fire whereupon he drowns. Plato might well be writing of Narcissus when he observes: "So he loves, yet knows not what he loves ... not realizing that his lover is as it were a mirror in which he beholds himself" (17). As Donaldson-Evans observes, other ideas associated with these metaphors include the belief that love is "a kind of illness which can be transmitted by the effluences from the eyes" and that "the eyes shoot arrows" and they "project fiery beams which burn the soul and kindle love's flame" (18, 21). Thus, the fire imagery and the "primary role given to the eyes in the experience of falling in love [are] well established in the pre-Christian era of Greek literature" (21).

Narcissus's blindness to process and his failure to include it within his reasoning result in his entrancement by his own beauty. This creates in him a constant tension, a desire that is unattainable, unembraceable. The attainment of an unreal desire – an image – may be realized (made real) only in transcendence, by rising above and out of the physical body into the imagination. Narcissus's body is consumed by a desire that blinds him, a "hidden fire," and he is changed magically into another form, a flower.

Playfully accurate and misleading, Tiresias's augury ("If he does not get to know himself") has been fulfilled. Narcissus is immortal and lives forever as story because he does not understand. As a morality tale of what and how not to love, he endures. In the same vein, he immortalizes transcendence, the escape from the physical body and any sense perception beyond a limited vision of "beauty." As the (male) subject-spectator in a magic and delicious projection,[5] he loves himself as the (male) object-surveyed and suppresses any knowledge labelled the other: nature, affective relationship, or the maternal/parental.

By a magical species change into a flower, he becomes a vision of beauty and gains the illusion of endless life perpetuated in cultural memory. Present as subject and shadow self – thus representing both sides of the gaze – Narcissus manifests repeating sites, a repetition of sights and consequently a perpetual and sexualized tension. His desire is to embrace a projection of himself, to embrace a reproduction as an end that stands for the origin(al). Sanctioned as action, as a kind of methodology, Narcissus is the image of masculinist desire: circular, separate, closed, origin-as-end.

The Death Wish

Not only are Narcissus and his reflected face a vivid example of repetition, but as image and myth they have also been used in psychoanalytic theory as an explanation for masochism. In his discussion of Sigmund Freud's theories, Jeffrey Berman describes how repetition operates in masochism and how the desire to repeat unpleasant experiences functions as a kind of self-punishment. Berman combines Freud's theory of drives in human beings (the pleasure principle and the death drive) to explain the insecurity inherent in narcissism. First, "Freud reasons that depression is caused by the internalization of an object originally loved but now hated because of its association with rejection or disappointment," and in this way the "cause of narcissistic injury then is the incorporation of a poisonous object." Berman goes on: "Behind narcissists' self-love lies self-hate; beneath their grandiosity lies insecurity" (18). As a psychoanalytic term, narcissism is, paradoxically, a result of too little genuine self-love and is linked to a failure of parenting such as maternal loss and cold or disapproving fathers (26, 53). According to Berman's analysis, Narcissus's rejection and disappointment lie with Cephisos, in the rape of Liriope, in a failure of affective connection with the father and perhaps with his mother; Narcissus was conceived in violence.

In an examination of the social construction of visual symbol in film theory, Noel Carroll comments that in the oedipal period, "the male child, putatively fearing castration by the father, leaves the quest for the mother and seeks to emulate the father in a process called introjection" (68). Carroll stresses that this introjection is not just a biological role that is assumed, but is, more importantly, a cultural position: "For Freudians, the introjection process of the oedipal stage is the means by which the culture reproduces itself," and "for Lacanians, the investiture of the child with its social roles, ideals, and values is also the point at which the child is said to enter language" (68).

In both theories, the introjection, the unconscious incorporation of characteristics, is by way of image, an imaginative and mental repetition of pattern. One enters language by copying the form or image of power, by being able to copy that form. Thus the voice, language, the Word, belongs only to Narcissus, a son, and never, by definition, to Echo. While Echo does repeat, she is allowed only "to answer"; she will never access the power of self-expression in this paradigm. The patriarchal tradition repeats the male and masculine image alone; that image *is* Narcissus.

In his analysis of Freud's influence on Lacanian psychoanalytic theory, Richard Boothby ties Freud's writing on narcissism together with the development of the theory on the death wish. Highlighting the backward looking, negative, and pain-filled nature of Narcissus's experience, Boothby illuminates Freud's concern with the way in which unpleasant experiences are repeated to re-enforce the destructive, death-oriented conclusion of Narcissus's desire: "Alongside the homeostatic principle of pleasure there must exist a second basic principle, a destabilizing, disruptive force that tends not toward equilibrium and harmony but toward conflict and disintegration" (3).

About the strange and radical nature of this death-drive theory, Boothby writes: "It amounts to saying that the true goal of living is dying and that the life course of all organisms must be regarded as only a circuitous route to death" (3). He agrees with Freud and describes the problems inherent in repetition as necessarily involving "a tendency to reach into the more and more distant past," but suggests that it is "not repetition as such but only repetition of unpleasurable experiences" that led to the creation of a death-drive theory (80).

The Mother-Child Monad

In *New Essays on Narcissism*, Bela Grunberger, like Berman, Boothby, and Carroll, describes psychosexual development as taking place in a polarized mother-child bond with dualistic phases. The monad consists of the infant and the "envelope" of the responsive mother's touch and gaze. She, the mother, is asexual, removed; she serves only as a landscape that predates object relations. Describing his own approach as "bioanalytic," Grunberger traces "narcissistic phenomena" to prenatal nature and biology, to "an unconscious and archaic lived experience," which he then "extends to the social, the intellectual, the cultural and the mystical" (1, 2). He records the positive, even spiritual feelings that are part of "the matrix" of this state. These he lists as serenity, happiness, sovereignty, completeness, omnipotence, self-worth, exultant expansionism, freedom, independence and autonomy, vulnerability, eternity and immortality (2). In the prenatal narcissistic state as he describes it, the fetus "exists in a state of perfect completeness," and he argues that the prenatal experience has a masculine cast: "the phallus is emblematic of all the attributes of prenatal coenesthesis, and its image – a primal fantasy – is present within the psyche from, and probably before birth" (16). In his interpretation, then, this matrix of feelings before birth is irrevocably and psychically gendered male. Following birth, the infant must cope psychologically with the memory of the difficult physical passage as well as with the loss of this wonderful prenatal psychic condition. Grunberger draws in Freud's Oedipal complex and the theory of castration as explanation for this loss: "this prototypical castration provokes an enormously aggressive response" which "might be the *primal source of a future and equally powerful sense of guilt*" (17–18).

Post-birth, the mother/care giver attempts to reproduce the well-being of the prenatal world. The mother-child monad is "a binary unit" where "the infant merges with the surface of the internal envelope" that serves as a transitional subject between narcissistic projection and true object relations. In this post-birth, monadic relationship, "the one thing that the child asks of its mother is that she 'be with' ... it in a certain way" that is "not to be confused with the child's instinctual demands" (4). While the "instinctual demands" are necessarily the demands for bodily care that accompany infant life, the post-birth phase that Grunberger emphasizes is tied to gaze and "pure narcissistic" reflection and incorporates the father as the image of "narcissistic completeness and phallic energy (the penis)" (18, 19).

Grunberger returns to the myth of Narcissus in order to explore further the ideal of purity as a psychological state outside of physical being and especially beyond sexual and physical love: "Narcissus is pure. We know that he rejects both hetero- and homosexual love and contents himself with worshipping the reflection of his face in the water." Grunberger portrays "double unit" as the infant's internal psychological state: "the term monad gives an accurate description of a state surrounding something which, in its view, merges with it. That substance is its universe (cosmic narcissism), even though it does not *physically* merge with it" (92).

In a description of the disembodied nature of the post-birth monad, Grunberger tethers the absence of the maternal body to purity, vision, and the experience of self-identity: "At the moment of birth, the mother does not exist as such, but her gaze (narcissistic confirmation) and her touch may act as a substitute for prenatal bliss and may therefore compensate for the basic existential trauma." From now on, "the child's narcissistic existence will be supported by the monad, which has now been reformed" (92). Purity is attained in a progression away from embodied connection and embodied self: from a disappeared maternal body, through the absence of touch/embrace, to a sense of elevation away from an embodied understanding of reality (93).

This movement signals a sense of agency and mastery. "Dreams of flying or levitation are probably an expression of the same fantasy of disembodied purity and of a fantasy of omnipotence involving the phallic emblem," and, as Grunberger makes clear, "in the unconscious the phallus and penis are represented by the same emblem" (94). Grunberger extends his analysis to emphasize the importance of male descendants. Underscoring the legal concept of marriage as a way of legitimating offspring, he describes the line of descent as "a continuous sequence of male individuals; the founder of the line is therefore the father" (178).

Grunberger's interpretation of incest is equally bound up with this concern for legitimacy and lineage, and as a result, women's affective connections are dismissed as totally as the myth obliterates Liriope and to the same extent that Narcissus ignores Echo. To Grunberger, incest "represents a search for narcissistic fulfilment by returning directly to the mother's womb (incestuous coitus)." To avoid incest, then, and if "the line of descent is to be perpetuated, it must be constantly crossed or cut by the introduction of a mother from the outside (exogamy)." Exogamy constrains women into new family groups; daughters are compelled out of their kinship communities.

For the son, staying in the family (with the mother) has its own difficulties and dangers: "the return to the mother brings an impasse because coitus with the mother means the death and obliteration of the father." Furthermore, Grunberger argues, "[i]n so far as the prohibition of incest takes a socialized form which gives rise to rites and taboos, we can conclude it has more to do with the breaking of the line than with the prohibition of an individual sin" (179–80). Thereby and conveniently, incest is regarded primarily as a mother-son taboo. This interpretation of incest makes an ongoing lifelong affective connection between mother and son culturally problematic, at least theoretically. Grunberger reiterates the view that psychosexual maturation demands the oedipal transition, the break from the mother. What Grunberger also notes is the pain inherent in this (perceived) transition: "Even within psychoanalysis itself, man is striving to lay down the burden of his conflicts and his primal narcissistic wound" (181).

Romantic Love

In discussing Freud's theories of development, Elizabeth Young-Bruel explains that this burden, this "narcissistic wound," is transferred and the transferral is used to explain heterosexual attraction: "The boy's overvaluation of the penis is narcissistic: to give up his certainty that all people have penises – to experience 'castration threat' – is to experience the limits of self-love" (29). Freudian theory, to explain the transfer of the adolescent male's affection to "the girls they love," at the same time encodes narcissism, an overvaluation of self, as a cultural norm.

Linking this traumatic discovery occasioned in the male child to an examination of vision and difference in her book of the same name, Griselda Pollock explains how disavowal and fetishism are linked to anxiety and are acknowledged by the male child, but only by displacement to another object. As she sees it, this "form of fetishism, which involves not just displacement but fetishistic conversion, also takes the form of reshaping the whole of the female form into a fetish, a substitute for what appears to be lacking on the maternal body, the phallus" (139). She lists these fetishes, these displaced lost parts, as they appear in the male depictions of woman: in fragmented bodies, schematized faces, blank looks (140).[6] These fetishes and fragmentations are a constant reminder of what is obviated, hidden, but not forgotten (140).

There is a connection between the origin of the fetish and the role of beauty in women's lives. John Berger clearly articulates the equation between the mirror and the cultural perception of women's vanity.[7] He describes the mirror in art as a symbol of women's vanity and recognizes the importance of the pleasure that is involved in the (male) painter's gaze: "You painted a naked woman because you enjoyed looking at her, you put a mirror in her hand and you called the painting vanity, thus morally condemning the woman whose nakedness you had depicted for your own pleasure" (51). Female nakedness masked as woman's narcissism and vanity is revealed as a way to disguise and transfer anxiety about the phallus and masculinity, the male wound.

Sensitive to the particular burden this culturally entrenched male gaze represents for women, Teresa de Lauretis explores the way this matrix of ideas surrounding woman as a specular, visual image and fetish relates to the prohibition of incest, and she includes the theories of Levi-Strauss: "[T]he "historical" event instituting culture and found in all human societies, requires that woman be possessed and exchanged among men to ensure the social order." She concludes: "One then understands that women are not simply objects exchanged by and among men but also messages which circulate among *individuals* and groups, ensuring social communications" (18–19). In this way, woman becomes a sign system as well as a displaced narrative object (fetish); woman exists in the realm of symbols, a sign that means something more, however extrapolated from the real (23).

In his classic essay *On Narcissism,* Sigmund Freud inscribes self-centred narcissism as a neurosis specific to "normal" women who, "especially if they grow up with good looks, develop a certain self-contentment which compensates them for the social restrictions that are imposed upon them in their choice of love object." He continues by noting that "it is only themselves that such women can love with an intensity comparable to that of a man's love for them" (Young-Bruel, 192). This he directly ties to his theory of penis envy in women, to what he calls women's "narcissistic wound," and to what he sees as their inability to overcome this wound and obtain "object-love." One way to gain this ability involves seeing the child that they bear as "a part of their own body [that] confronts them like an extraneous object, to which, starting from their narcissism, they can then give complete object-love." Another way exists for those women "who do not have to wait for a child in order to take the step in development from (secondary) narcissism to object-love": "Before puberty they feel masculine and develop some way along masculine lines." When they reach "female maturity, they still retain the capacity of longing for a masculine ideal – an ideal which is in fact a survival of the boyish nature that they themselves once possessed" (193–4).

In her discussion of this essay, Elizabeth Young-Bruel not only notes the way that Freud endorses the masculine as human ideal, but recognizes how Freud sees loving as active and thereby masculine, while defining narcissistic desire or being loved as passive and thereby feminine. Young-Bruel relates this attitude specifically to Freud's own nineteenth-century cultural context: "Given this interplay of anatomical and social factors, boys and girls end up complementing each other in the manner of the Beauty and the self-sacrificing Beast characters so common in nineteenth-century novels" (30).

The creation of gender stereotypes re-enforces the roles that were so important then and that continue to linger into the twenty-first century, roles which imply that the only relationship possible is heterosexual and wherein the girl/wife replaces the mother in the son's life. Young-Bruel goes on to record that even Freud knew that such stereotypes were limited and that sons can "not only love their mothers but identify with them" (31). That the flower, narcissus, is "grass-leaved" and shares with the grass, liriope, "small whitish or blue or violet flowers" vividly suggests that possibility.

The Mirror Stage

Jacques Lacan uses the metaphor of the mirror to describe the stage of human development that precedes the oedipal and is marked by the child's identification with the visual representation of his own body. The recognition of the self in a mirror causes in the child the beginning of two identities. These two identities are constituted in a consciousness of a self that perceives and in an awareness of the sense perceptions themselves. A corollary to this "narcissistic structure" is the "notion of aggressivity" (22). Lacan draws on Freud's oedipal theory to explain how the child is able to transcend these aggressive feelings by identifying with a symbolic authority.

Lacan also suggests that the genital libido operates to suppress the individual's immediate desires or interests in favour of the species through an act of sublimation, an "aggressive" conversion "upon the subject's own self" (25). This is defined as a "castration," is viewed as occurring in the subconscious, and represents not only a sexual identification but also the child's movement into culture and language. Consciousness is accompanied by the sense of loss, of lack; Lacan signifies "lack" with the term phallus, "a signifier" that represents "as a whole the effects of the signified" and "conditions them by its presence as a signifier" (285).

Elizabeth Grosz makes special note of Lacan's "ocularocentrism," his vision-centredness, which like Freudian theory "privileges the male body as a phallic, virile body and regards the female body as castrated" (39). Furthermore, according to Grosz, Lacan describes love as "always structured with reference to the phallus, which, in a sense is the third term coming between two lovers" (137). In contrast, Jane Gallop views Lacan's approach as a gain for women, since the loss applies to both genders. Taking heart from Gallop's comment that Lacan's writings are "impossible to understand fully," I pick up on his observation that "the unconscious castration complex has the function of a knot" (281). Here, his metaphor of function seems to be at odds with his naming the phallus as symbol. Although Lacan insists that the phallus is not the penis but may symbolize either penis or clitoris, anatomical differences make interpretation "especially difficult in the case of women" (282). Contrasting the Real, where there is no lack, with the Imaginary (as in narcissistic reflection), where there is, the phallus, for Lacan, becomes both a sign of difference and a way to reconciliation. This phallus likewise distinguishes male and female entry into language. It marks the way the child attempts to identify with the father, with authority, with symbolic language, as a means of overcoming the sense of loss, the condition of lacking.

Echo and Voice

By way of illustrating core issues in attitudes towards identity, sexuality, voice, and vision as I believe they may be employed to interpret both Psyche's initial situation and as a contrast to the paradigm that I set up from her story, I have strayed rather far from the story of Narcissus. Here, I turn to focus more closely on Echo. As noted, Echo is witness to Narcissus's dilemma, a witness who cannot voice her own desire. She does not have a language with which to voice an authentic self and life-experience. In Amy Lawrence's examination of the role played by women's speech in contemporary Hollywood cinema, she elaborates on the crucial significance of speech to meaning in Narcissus's myth. Calling it "a cautionary tale" that warns "against what is conceived of as the unnatural and dangerous separation of sound and image, woman and man, hearing and seeing, she goes on to note that "[b]oth Echo and Narcissus are ravished by perception, subjected to obstacles of expression or comprehension and ultimately to die from the missed connections" (2). This multiple relationship of "woman's voice" to sound, discourse, and authorial point of view is one which prompts Kaja Silverman to suggest the term "acoustic mirror" as a way of indicating a combined image of sound and sight for the female voice.

Echo fades away to exist only as a repeating voice. The first reason Ovid's recounting gives for this decline is that after Narcissus rejects her, Echo retreats to nature: "Spurned, she hid in the woods and, in her shame, covered her face / with foliage and lived henceforth in lonely caves." Echo, a figure representing woman, is hidden by a shame that is not rightfully hers. As the outcome of the tale implies, however, penalty is shared by both. The second reason Ovid provides for Echo's loss of embodiment is that her love for Narcissus grows with his rejection; she values him too much: "and yet her love clung to her and grew with the pain of rejection." What is unsaid but may be inferred is that she loves herself too little. Echo's failure to care for herself parallels Narcissus's over-loving self-regard. Her misplaced caring leads to waste – and to her wasting: "her cares kept her awake and made her body pitiably thin, her skin wasted and shrivelled up and all her body's / moisture went off into the air." Echo cannot speak – may not speak – for herself, and this leaves her a hard, stony "skeleton" of her former self: "only her voice and bones were left: her voice remained; her bones, they say, took on the appearance of stone." The outcome of the story for Echo is underscored by her loneliness out in the natural world where she remains unbodied and disconnected: "Since then she has hidden in the woods and is never seen on the mountains, she is heard by all: but it is only sound that lives in her." And, as I noted earlier, even the language of that sound is not her own.

In her discussion of feminist art criticism theory, Joanna Frueh describes a painting of such an Echo-like female figure in nature. Her description of Gustave Courbet's *The Source* presents an Echo voiceless but still fleshed: "A fleshy woman sits by a stream. One hand holds a branch, seems almost molded to it, as if she herself were part of the tree; and her contours, from the buttocks up are eaten by shadows, so that nature absorbs her flesh, is actually one with it." She goes on to point out: "Woman and nature literally mirror one another for the material of the female body is the material world" (157). The significance of Courbet's painting lies not only in the equation of woman with nature and fecundity but especially in the lack of consciousness signified in the association. The image presents an incomplete female being.

Arguing for a feminist art criticism that is "alive," Frueh calls for a rejection of the "phallic tongue" and for the exercise of an intelligence integral with female physical being. Her argument suggests that the "path to freedom" exists in a body ownership: "Once a woman owns her body she will speak a different language. When the organ in her mouth belongs to her, we will know that all tongues, all words are flesh" (160). Also writing about art criticism, Arlene Raven presents this embodied thinking as a way of transforming thinking "to a model of rhythms and relationships upon which a society can be built" (238).

As myth, Narcissus demonstrates and isolates the two solitudes of gendered life in an intellectual and social patriarchal system, two solitudes that make a vivid backdrop to the story of Psyche and Eros. Since it is not possible to restore to Echo her own embodied experience, to restore to her an independent relationship to language and the authority of her own desire, then in order to break these ancient dichotomies – feminine/masculine, nature/culture, other/self, site/seer, spoken/speaker – into which female and male life experience have been placed, it is necessary to turn away from Narcissus and towards Psyche. In her narrative exist both difference and potential.

Introducing Psyche, Attending Aphrodite

Like the Narcissus tale, the story of Psyche exists within a larger work, entitled *Metamorphoses* but also known as *The Golden Ass*.[1] Written by Lucius Apuleius, a second-century Platonic philosopher from Madauros in North Africa, it recounts the Psyche and Eros story as one told by an old woman to a young bride who has been kidnapped by bandits. Both women are subsequently killed, but because the tale was overheard, it persists as part of the (male) narrator's adventures. The manner in which Psyche's story is overheard and carried onward by this narrator, named Lucius, accentuates the powerlessness of the women. The precarious transmission of their story parallels the role of Echo and likewise underscores women's loss of voice and agency.

In the Introduction to his translation of Apuleius's *Metamorphoses*, J. Arthur Hanson* indicates some of the many conflicting viewpoints of critical opinion about the text: "It can be, and has been, read as Platonic allegory, psychic autobiography, Bildungsroman, and literary parody" (xi,xii).[2] Stressing the complexity of the work, Hanson warns that irony is a central feature. In this regard, the fact that the evocative and memorable tale of Psyche and Eros exists within a series of Milesian or pornographic stories that are told by a man who has been changed into an ass (and later back again) and who then culminates his adventures in an initiation into the rites of the goddess, Isis, serves as a lengthy caution to any reader who might take the events in the tale at face value.[3] The wide variety of interpretations of the story that already exist and the many signatures given to it are ample evidence of its powers of attraction and wealth of resource.

As the Psyche and Eros myth begins, there is a concern with beauty and gendered power relations, with perception and image, that is

---

* Hanson's translation of Apuleius's tale of Cupid and Psyche appears in the Appendix.

comparable to that found in the story about Narcissus. The narrator
tells us that Psyche is beloved in her father's kingdom because of her
"so dazzling and glorious" beauty, because others believe her – see and
judge her – as beautiful. This beauty evokes many responses: "Many
citizens, as well as multitudes of visitors ... were dumbfounded in their
wonderment at her unapproachable loveliness and would ... venerate
her with pious prayers as if she were the very goddess [Aphrodite]
herself" (237).[4] Various reports are offered for the origins of this
vision of beauty, for Psyche's derivation. She is the goddess herself
"mingling amid human gatherings"; she is "a new germination of
skyborn drops, not the ocean but the earth had sprouted another
[Aphrodite]."

Psyche's beauty causes Aphrodite's anger because it has estranged
the goddess's own devotees; Aphrodite is "inflamed" because "[h]er
rites were postponed, her temples fell into disrepair, her cushions were
trodden under foot, her ceremonies neglected, her statues ungarlanded,
and her abandoned altars marred by cold ashes." As Apuleius emphasizes, "It was the girl that people worshipped: they sought to appease
the mighty goddess's power in a human face." Furthermore, while it
is not overtly stated, Apuleius also implies that Aphrodite's son Eros
falls in love at his first sight of Psyche's beauty, and this provides a
rationale for Eros's manipulation of Aphrodite's wishes for Psyche's
destruction (241, 295).

Psyche as Beauty

In *Ways of Seeing*, an explorations of gender, authority, and artistic
expression in the visual arts, John Berger describes what is, in fact, a
crucial part of Psyche's dilemma: "To be born a woman has been to
be born, within an allotted and confined space into the keeping of
men" (46). Berger lists the effects that this power arrangement has in
the beauty equation; three of these are useful to my analysis of Psyche's
role as a beauty. The first is that women conventionally are "seen and
judged as sights" by men; they are beautiful or not, simply according
to the discrimination of the (male) viewer (47). Beauty exists outside
the control of the woman judged as having it. Because it is an arbitrary
designation and changes with fashion and over time, beauty is not a
source of power to those who "have" it. Power lies in the bestowal;
power belongs to those who have labelled Psyche beautiful.

The second is that, as a sight and site, beauty as woman is given
the "prize" of being "owned" by the (male) judge, thence, sexually
available to the judge (52). The label "beauty" magnifies the woman's
physical appearance – over which she has relatively little control – to

mask a real powerlessness. As a daughter to a king, Psyche is under his governance. Later, when Eros singles out her "beauty," he becomes her "owner"; yet Psyche gains no reward: "Psyche, for all her manifest beauty reaped no profit from her charms" (245).

The third effect is that "[w]omen are there to feed an appetite, not to have any of their own" (55). Sexual desire is active for men and therefore assumes a masculine guise. By an extension of the logic of thinking through dichotomy, desire is perceived as passive in the feminine and thus absent for/in women. Psyche "weeping over her forlorn loneliness" is "sick in body and wounded in heart" (245). Subsequently, the prohibition is played out more directly: she is forbidden to look at Eros, her lover/husband who visits her, his bride, only at night (259). Psyche, whom conventional slang would designate a "looker," may not look at Love.

Berger sums up the consequences of this visual exchange and their implications for contemporary women, but such consequences could apply equally to the situation of the storybook Psyche: "This unequal relationship is so deeply embedded in our culture that it still structures the consciousness of many women. They do to themselves what many men do to them. They survey, like men, their own femininity" (63). The price exacted is of "a woman's self being split in two. A woman must continually watch herself. She is almost continually accompanied by her own image of herself" (46). As Psyche might attest, even having beauty does not preclude the exaction of such a price and, in fact, can simply raise it. Unlike Narcissus, "[s]he hated in herself that beauty of hers which the world found so pleasing" (245).

In *The Beauty Myth*, Naomi Wolf not only documents the price that acquiring beauty exacts from modern women but also highlights the major import of the "beauty myth": it "is always actually prescribing behaviour and not appearance" (15). The only role available to Psyche, the prescribed behaviour, is that of marriage, and perversely, this is made impossible by the very declaration of her beauty: "Everyone gazed at her, but no one, neither king nor prince nor even commoner, desired to marry her and came to seek her hand" (245). The response to Psyche's beauty brings with it an ironic emphasis. Her beauty does not bring her a husband.

Beauty's Consequence

Psyche is named beautiful in a kingdom, the quintessential patriarchal community. Her father, the King, "wretched" and "fearing the gods' anger," consults an "ancient oracle" to request a husband for his "hapless" daughter (245). He does not consult Psyche, nor is he under

any obligation to do so. As her father's daughter, Psyche is his responsibility. Like the perception of her beauty, the request for a husband
and marriage is not hers.

The King's request is to Apollo. Through an oracle, the King is told
to prepare a "funereal marriage" wherein Psyche is "abandoned" on
the "summit" of a "steep mountain" (251). First Psyche is singled out
from her community by her beauty, and then she is physically separated from all she has known and loved. The attendant losses of
community, family, and agency are her second birth, her twice-born,
"born again" entrance into culture. Psyche's role as beauty masks a
danger that is literally present in the events of the story. In the absence
of power lies the real fear that any judgment about the beauty of
women obscures. A close analogy to woman as visual object is an
animal as quarry. The hunter requires keen sight; out of fear, the
hunted relies on vigilance, constant wariness, and camouflage.

In *Death and the Maiden*, Ken Dowden uses myth as a way of
examining girls' initiation rituals. As a consequence, he exposes the
intricate equations of beauty, marriage, sacrifice, and death that are
central to them. Beginning with a description of Iphegenia, whose
name he deciphers as meaning "most beautiful," he identifies several
motifs that I see as equally present in Psyche's story. First, the special
nature of the initiand is signalled by a recognition of "beauty." Next,
a goddess is angered – in Iphegenia's situation because Agammemnon,
the king and her father, shot a deer and bragged of outdoing Artemis.
Then, the goddess sends a punishment of stormy winds. Subsequently,
a priest declares that, in propitiation, the daughter must be sacrificed.[5]

As Dowden puts it, in such initiation stories, "the child dies, though
not literally" (37). Explaining what he calls "Bremmer's Principle" –
that ritual symbolizes but myth exaggerates – he reiterates that, in
these initiations, death is a sign of a passage to marriageability (13).
For the initiand, death represents both a status change from unmarried
to married and a transferred authority – from "her father's *kore*" to
"her husband's *gyne*" (2). In this way, women's concern for their
appearance, which may be interpreted as narcissism, mere vanity, may
represent a real and present danger. In a comment that I read as a
re-enforcement of my own comparison of visual object and quarry,
Dowden states that sacrificial substitutions were an accepted part of
the myth; in one version of Iphegenia's story, Artemis saves her by
substituting a deer to be sacrificed in her place.

Whereas neither Iphegenia nor Psyche rebels against her situation,
Psyche does lament it and, more importantly, recognizes its derivation
from her being called "a new [Aphrodite]" (249). Yet, she in no way
avoids her fate or attempts to argue against it: "the maiden fell silent

... abandoned ... frightened, trembling and weeping at the very top of the cliff" (251). Likewise, she is "carried" to a paradise. There, she continues obedient, even "to the suggestions of the disembodied voice"; finally, she "promised to behave as her husband wished" (257, 259).

Even as Psyche's story presents the issues surrounding beauty, it demonstrates the silences of women and the relationship of silence to lack of power. To parallel and emphasize Psyche's silencing, there appears the original silenced woman in the myth, the queen, the mother. As mother, she listens and grieves (247). In their silences, Psyche and her mother represent the sacrifices that patriarchal family continuity requires from women and from the relationships between them. As sign and exchange, daughters and mothers may only grieve their losses.

Silence and Self-Esteem

If such a view of marriage is less a reality in the Western world at the end of the twentieth century, what does remain is a clearly measurable and profound loss of self-esteem in young women. Even though the trappings have changed – in marriage and apart from marriage – the devaluation of female life remains unchanged, and Psyche's situation continues to have a meaningful resonance. In *Meeting at the Cross-roads: Women's Psychology and Girls' Development*, Lyn Mikel Brown and Carol Gilligan emphasize how the forfeiture of feeling "right," of being "okay," is directly related to growing up female. Arguing that "[w]omen's psychological development within patriarchal societies and male-voiced cultures is inherently traumatic," they stress that "[f]or a girl to disconnect herself from women means to dissociate herself not only from her mother but also from herself – to move from being a girl to being a woman, which means 'with men'" (216). The authors continue by linking this trauma to loss of voice (becoming Echo): "For girls at adolescence to say what they are feeling and thinking often means to risk, in the words of many girls, losing their relationships and finding themselves powerless and all alone" (217).

In this way, Psyche may be interpreted as encoding the losses in self-esteem that come with female adolescence; what has been labelled her beauty obscures the sacrifices coincident with growing up female in a male-defined culture. The constriction of female agency into beauty, sacrifice, and abandonment is a twofold betrayal. Loss of personal agency or action (voice) is rewritten into an objectified form of male power (beauty); like Echo's, female desiring is subsumed in male power structures. This is fittingly described by Annis Pratt as a model for "growing down" rather than "growing up," especially as it is so crucially linked to sexual maturity.

Sacrifice and Marriage

In Psyche's story, isolation and loss are encoded as beauty and marriage. In Psyche's circumstances, Erich Neumann sees "the basic mythological situation," the "ancient, primordial motif," in terms of "marriage as the marriage of death." Arguing that "every marriage is a rape of Kore," he goes on to state: "The character of rape that the event assumes for womanhood expresses the projection – typical of the matriarchal phase – of the hostile element on the man." Whereas, for the woman, patriarchal marriage is separation of "the primordial relation of identity between daughter and mother" and "a mystery of death," for the man, it is "primarily an abduction, an acquisition – a rape" (61–3). Neumann remarks that the metaphor used to imply female youth and beauty is the flower and highlights the sexual implications of such a symbolism: "it is extremely significant that for the consummation of marriage, the destruction of virginity, should be known as 'deflowering.'" As he continues, his diction suggests that female loss of self is coincident with femininity, sexual experience, and real life: "For the feminine, the act of defloration represents a truly mysterious bond between end and beginning, between ceasing to be and entering upon real life" (63–4). What Neumann's language reflects is the complex of relationships that are used to justify female loss of agency, will, and desire. Entry into marriage equates "beginning" and "real life" with "ceasing to be."

Significantly, the kind of sacrifice/betrayal that Psyche experiences is recognized in other interpretations of the myth. Robert A. Johnson, for example, writes of this sense of pain and abandonment: "there is a Psyche in every woman, and it is intensely lonely. Every woman is, in part, a king's daughter – too lovely, too perfect, too deep for the ordinary world." Johnson appreciates that this "is terribly painful" and that "[w]omen are often excruciatingly aware of this situation without knowing its origin." This origin, however, Johnson interprets as "the Psyche nature, and there is nothing that can be done about it. That part will remain untouched, unrelated, unmarried most of one's life" (10–11). Complex equations of pain, inevitability, perfection, and identity with a nothing-can-be-done-about-it attitude makes Psyche's story reducible to woman's destiny rather than to a cultural or social construct. Psyche is made responsible for her own alienation and for her own violation because it is her "nature."

Johnson further describes the "Psyche nature" as being solely relational, passive, and dependent on the marriage (love) relationship. Introducing the "sacrificial element" of a wedding, he also brings in the goddess, Aphrodite, to suggest that all is not well in such a dependency: "Aphrodite does not like maidens to die at the hands of men. It is not her nature to be subject to a man" (13). Paradox is inherent in this view of weddings and of the goddess: Aphrodite both "condemns Psyche to death" and "brings about weddings in the first place"; she "weeps and rages at the wedding for the possible loss of the bride's freedom and individuality, for the loss of her virginity."

Johnson's choice of diction reveals the conflict between progress and loss: "The forward push of evolution toward marriage is accompanied by a repressive tug of longing for the autonomy and freedom of things as they were before" (14). For Psyche, the rape is of possibility, of personhood, agency and desire, independence and voice; patriarchal marriage precludes the search for selfhood. In a culture that subsumes female autonomy and personhood, love – of a sort – is readily available; agency and voice are not.

Sacrificing the Goddess

There remains one other sacrifice/betrayal of female experience that is fundamental to Psyche's (and Echo's) loss of voice. That is the betrayal inherent in the way that Aphrodite expresses her wrath. As Apuleius recounts the tale, Aphrodite proclaims her neglect: "My name which is founded in heaven, is being profaned with earthly pollution" (241). Psyche, victimized by an unwanted adoration, is then blamed for this transfer of allegiance and is made the focus of Aphrodite's violent wrath: "But, whosoever she is, she will certainly get no joy out of having usurped my honours: I will soon make her regret that illegitimate beauty of hers!" (241). As an object of beauty, a fetish, Psyche is without power and denied action; nonetheless she is condemned for usurping Aphrodite's honours. Similarly, Psyche's beauty, described as "illegitimate," disguises the "illegitimacy" of the adoration. The faithful in the kingdom transfer adoration from the never-virgin goddess to the girl "with the bloom of virginity" (237, 239).

Psyche appears to concur in this devaluation of the goddess and at the same time to join in the erasure of her own interests, her own plight. Admonishing her parents and referring to Aphrodite, she reminds them that "the blow which destroys *you* is dealt by wicked Envy." She then adds that "it is [Aphrodite's] *name alone* that has destroyed me" (249, emphasis added). Psyche's speech reveals the

absence of power, innate in patriarchal societies, of a fully female –
even fully feminine – divine.[6] At the same time that Psyche appears
to gloss over her own losses, however, she reclaims them, and at the
same time as she appears to blame Aphrodite, she says that Aphrodite's "name," not the goddess herself, has destroyed her. In these
ambiguities and in an analysis of what this transfer of adoration
illustrates, there is an underlying truth: Aphrodite is defamed by "an
earthly pollution."

Apuleius's Goddess

In the larger framework of the *Metamorphoses*, Apuleius combines a
male quest motif with devotion to a female deity. As protagonist,
Lucius autobiographically represents Apuleius's submission to, and initiation into, the Mysteries of Isis. Marie Louise Von Franz, Elizabeth
Hazelton Haight, and Ben Edwin Perry see Lucius's adventures as a
personal, interior, masculine, and male search for union with the feminine as represented by Isis. P.G. Walsh calls the adventures of Psyche
an allegory of Lucius's spiritual quest, an extended metaphor of the
second or frame narrative, and "a Platonist-Isiac myth" (223).

Apuleius not only describes the goddess Isis in terms of the feminine
but calls her a "true reality" and makes her the reigning deity of an
external world. Again according to Walsh: "When Isis reveals and
describes herself to Lucius, she pronounces herself identical with the
[Aphrodite] of Psyche's story" (222). Thus, the two named goddesses
potentially depict one aggregate figure, and with the description of
Isis, Apuleius's figure of Venus-Aphrodite surpasses the patriarchally
defined feminine love goddess. Moreover, the very real possibility and
potential of this figure are often at odds with what Apuleius as author
has Aphrodite do and say. Although he presents the patriarchally
defined "symbolic order" and the one-dimensional love goddess, he
strengthens both with the potential of the much older core figure. In
Lucius's vision, Isis names herself "mother of the universe, mistress of
all the elements ... mightiest of all the deities, queen of the dead," and
called by many names, Minerva [Athena], Venus [Aphrodite], Diana
[Artemis/Selene], Proserpina [Persephone], Ceres [Demeter], Juno
[Hera], and "my real name, which is Queen Isis" (2:299, 301).

By linking Aphrodite with this ancient power, Apuleius encourages
the reading of Aphrodite as a Great Mother figure and life goddess
in Psyche's tale and paves the way for an interpretation of Aphrodite
as a mentor of wholeness, of holiness, and of transformation for
Psyche. Indeed, within Psyche's tale, Aphrodite names herself "the
primal mother of all that exists, the original source of the elements,

the bountiful mother of the whole world" (239, 241). As Psyche is forced beyond patriarchal culture and out into "the whole world," she moves out into the realm of "the all that exists" that is patterned in Aphrodite, the "primal" and "bountiful" mother.

The Goddess's Attributes

Cultural anthropologist and linguist Paul Friedrich uses an interdisciplinary approach to examine the constellation of meanings surrounding both the figure and history of Aphrodite. He begins his exploration by noting her origins and background in the Old European Great Bird goddesses and fertility figures, in the Sumerian Inanna, Semitic Ishtar, and Phoenician Astarte figures, in the Minoan Great Mother and Mistress of Animals or Wild Things, and in the Egyptian goddess, Isis; all substantiate and give credence to her figurative and emotional power. She is the most potent of the goddesses in the Greek world because she is "the most golden, the most beautiful, and the most charged with fertility and the powers of creation" (101). In addition, "Aphrodite was more important in popular cult than any of the other goddesses" (2).

Friedrich gives a list of Aphrodite's associations or dimensions that includes islands and mountains, apples, roses, lilies, poppies, pomegranates, birds that are not predatory, water or aquatic birth (73, 75, 80). Geoffrey Grigson sees Aphrodite "blended" with Isis as "goddess of nature, goddess of earth and waters" (197), and in this way, Aphrodite may be linked to the "green world" and "special world of nature" described by Annis Pratt. Because of Astarte's associations with water, Grigson links her and Aphrodite with the dolphin, calling it "Aphrodite's animal" and emphasizing its associations of "exemplary" parenthood, music, and kindness in distress (136–7). From one story of her birth out of the sea (from the east as Astarte), she is closely allied with the seashell, a female genital symbol. Like Friedrich, Miriam Robbins Dexter and Erich Neumann describe Aphrodite as a goddess of earth and waters, of animals, of birth, life, and death, of regeneration and transformation, of birds and snakes.

Above all, Aphrodite is a golden goddess. While Dexter and Friedrich describe her as encompassing the chthonic, David Kinsley suggests that more emphasis should be placed on her association with light, golden sunshine, and warmth, with fertilizing dew and rain, with flowers, seasonal growth, and fruitfulness. He attributes the chthonic to her close connection to Persephone. For Friedrich, Aphrodite's goldenness is intrinsic and so sets her apart from the other goddesses. He notes that her antecedents are solar and dawn goddesses and that she is the "least lunar" of the goddesses.

In her relationship with the natural world, Aphrodite is also and specifically a sexual goddess of passion and its physical expression. While she regularly attends to marriages and wedding celebrations, hers is not passion that confines itself to patriarchal wedlock or to heterosexuality, for in her earliest manifestation she is able to give birth parthenogenetically: "The autonomy of Aphrodite, the fact that she was not bound by the rules of chastity which were imposed upon other goddesses and mortal women, also bespeaks her power" (Dexter, 115). Her sexuality is so powerful that she was never virgin (Dexter, Friedrich). In a particularly happy association with life, sexuality and love, Grigson quotes Sappho, who names Aphrodite "lover of laughing" (110).

Bias and Ambivalence

Emerging from the descriptions of Aphrodite's attributes are several broader issues that pertain to her role in Apuleius's narrative. The first is the general observation by Friedrich that many scholars avoid Aphrodite or dismiss her powers because "they are made anxious and puzzled by the conjunction of meanings, particularly the religious ones." He contends that, in spite of Aphrodite's "universal human relevance" as a goddess of love, Judeo-Christian cultural biases against Aphrodite arise because she represents "profound values and great ambivalences" (2). Sarah B. Pomeroy, too, notes "inconsistencies and mutually contradicting qualities," yet believes that these are "readily encompassed" by the goddess (218). Jane Ellen Harrison ties Aphrodite's spirituality to her origins, to her triple nature, and to the natural world. Aphrodite is "earth-born," "sea-born," and "more than any other goddess, she becomes Ourania, the Heavenly One ... the only goddess who in passing to the upper air yet kept life and reality" (314). Thus, Aphrodite adds the "upper air" – earth's essential atmosphere – to earth and sea to be truly triple in her origins. Earth goddess and sea-born, Aphrodite is yet "Heavenly" and thus a spiritual being. The Judeo-Christian tradition, however, defines "heavenly" as a polarized opposition to things earthly. In fitting into this kind of dichotomous reasoning, the constellation of meanings ascribed to Aphrodite loses much of its power as well as its complex and original triplicity.

In Kinsley's linking of her overt sexuality, her strong connection to the earth, and her triplicity, Aphrodite represents feeling and sensory perception in spiritual consciousness. In her "green world," the body as sense perception, intellect, and emotion are all integral to spiritual awareness. But in comparing her "complex type of intelligence" to the intellects of other goddesses, Friedrich notes one story of her birth as a daughter of Zeus and describes her "mental powers" as "deceits, wiles, persuasion, and other arts for amorous ends between men and women" (90). Although he also describes Aphrodite's ability to mediate between the dyadic oppositions of nature and culture, it is his perception of Aphrodite's "liminality" that provides another way to envisage her powers. He sees her as a figure who "overrides" or "stands between" opposing categories. Some of these categories he lists as female/male roles (in relation to nudity and sexual activeness, passive vs active sexuality): mortal/immortal, prostitution/marriage, nature/culture. He states clearly that he in no way sees this as a "set of logical rules for getting from one category to another" but rather as an "emotional assertion" (147). He regards this as an aspect of her "potency" that exists within a given structure. Further, the ways in which Aphrodite stands between categories and interacts with them recalls her ancient prehistoric and historic origins, serving to enhance this "synchronic liminality."

Whereas I will return to the significance of this structural positioning of Aphrodite in chapter 7, one more of Friedrich's revaluations of Aphrodite is significant to a discussion of her role in Psyche's narrative. Drawing on the similarities between Demeter and Aphrodite, he contends that there has been a consistent suppression of the mother archetype in the representations of Aphrodite, the love goddess. Seeing this as an outcome of the "larger symbolism of incest and sexual taboos," he hopes that this "split" between "sensuous sexuality and motherliness-maternity" can be healed by religion, a "system of ideas," or a changed world-view (191). However that comes about, these wider observations, added to those attributes directly associated with Aphrodite and combined with her naming of her own powers in Apuleius's rendering, all magnify her role far beyond that of the classical "beauty queen" of Paris's judgment.

Aphrodite and Power

Aphrodite possesses primacy and bounty, but as Pomeroy observes, "in her omnipotence she was not threatening, for she was loving and merciful" (218). While the philosophic tradition has rendered Aphrodite into a goddess of sexuality, in *Psyche's Sisters,* Christine Downing likens one's relationship to Aphrodite with that between siblings, and in *The Goddess,* she describes the impossibility of relating to Aphrodite as a distant goddess addressed only as a third person, a "she," because she is the relationship goddess: "You are to me not only a you but that in me that is you directed, which comes into being as it is shared with another, a you apart from whom I cannot imagine myself" (186).

In her sexuality, sensuality, and multiplicity, Aphrodite represents an interaction of feeling, understanding, and awareness.

Both an expanded view of Aphrodite's powers and this view of relationship to her coexists with a redefinition of power as it is exercised by the goddess. Dexter defines two sorts of goddess power: "power *over*, which is the power exercised by one who dominates, and power *within*, autonomy, connectedness to the life force, which is the power of those engaged in a sharing society." Dexter goes on to note that "[t]his power within belongs to those who connect themselves to the life force and who as nurturers, augment that life force." Paradoxically, this energy is not spent but grows: "the more one gives to life, the more one is filled with that energy" (143).

The view of goddess power as a "power within" is important to Dexter's vision of how the triple energies of the goddess have been appropriated by patriarchal society. To Dexter, these energies are transferred to men by the awarding of sovereignty, by the granting of warrior energy, and by the transferring of nurturance. In the goddess, this energy is imaged in three forms. As kore, she represents stored energy; as wife/mother, she releases that stored energy to men in sexual intercourse and progeny. In patriarchal cultures, the third or grandmother phase is broken into two dichotomous views: as the "wise old woman" honoured for her wisdom or as the witch, "an object of fear or derision" (Dexter, 160). The triple goddess is reinterpreted as four: the mother/daughter binary and the witch/wise-woman dichotomy.

The contradictions in the interpretations of the grandmother phase emphasize the danger to androcentric societies of the old and/or not-virgin, not-married woman. As Dexter indicates, "she became a threat to the patriarchal, patrilineal establishment, because she became autonomous." This autonomy was interpreted as specifically threatening to patrilineal inheritance and sexual mores: "Any woman who took control of her own sexuality ... was both condemned and feared" (164). In this loss of the third phase of the triple goddess, in its breakdown into two dichotomous antithetical figures, we have imaged the loss of the autonomous woman, the self-directed woman of wisdom, experience, and power.

Whereas all three of the phases that Dexter describes have relevance in the myth of Psyche, in the attitudes towards the goddess as virgin there are clues about the reasons for the worship of the virgin Psyche: "And so the virgin, the maiden who stored her powers and held them in abeyance for the men of her society, was a woman who was cherished and revered" (173). Here exist the motivations obscured by, yet underlying, the change of worship from Aphrodite to the maiden, Psyche. Aphrodite's power is circumscribed; the goddess as never-virgin, as model for an active sexuality and sexual/reproductive energy, as old wise-woman of female and feminine wisdom, is replaced by the patriarchal daughter who has yet to attain wisdom, whose "energy" is controlled for dispensation by the father and will be appropriated by the husband.

Aphrodite is deprived of the reverence of the community that has turned to the adoration of a girl princess, a situation which Apuleius describes as an "extravagant transfer of heavenly honours to the cult of a mortal girl" who is worshipped for her "illegitimate beauty" (239, 241). The issue of beauty is used to disguise a very real appropriation of power. The devotion given Psyche relegates Aphrodite to a "vicarious veneration" (241), and the result is not only the loss of the outward authority and inner power of the triple goddess but also the trivialization of Psyche as a representation of human female experience.

This change in the object of worship may function as an allegory, as a mythic "exaggeration" of the processes whereby ancient cultures supported male power structures and were transformed into patriarchal societies. Psyche's story illustrates how the arrogation of Aphrodite's power to a human maiden supports a male social order that is sanctioned by the male-ordained and -defined pantheon of gods. Aphrodite's command to Eros that Psyche "be gripped with a violent flaming passion for the meanest man," one who lacks "rank, wealth, and even health," becomes the priest's insistence that she prepare for "a funereal wedding" to "a cruel and wild and snaky monster, / That flies on wings above the ether and vexes all, / And harries the world with fire and sword" (243, 247).

This interpretation of Aphrodite's request is made by Apollo's Oracle, but Apuleius outlines no direct communication between Aphrodite and the Oracle or the priest. There is communication only between the priest and the King, who feared "the gods' anger," and between the priest and the Oracle of Apollo (245, 247, 283). Ken Dowden discloses a similar gap between event, interpretation, and the role of the priest as he quotes Proclus's summary of *Kypria* by Stasinos: "The goddess was angered and sent storms ... Kalchas declared the anger of the goddess and said that Iphegenia should be sacrificed to Artemis" (*Death*, 10). Only male priests and oracles interpret goddesses' commands.

Aphrodite's directive can imply that a social (patriarchal) hierarchy is intended to be upset by Psyche's falling in love with "the meanest man"; this, however, is translated into a lawful and "funereal marriage" to a "monster" on "wings" who "vexes" all. If Aphrodite's command is read to mean that Psyche as princess and daughter to a king should fall in love with the poorest of men, then patriarchal power alliances are upset. Psyche's falling into love and sexual experience, then choosing to love in the knowledge of that experience, denies father and husband the choice, the ordering, of their coalitions and hers.

Cultural Failure

By their inference/interference, king, priest, and Apollo's Oracle determine that passion (and love) are exiled and what is enshrined is coercive marriage, but the transfer of worship from Aphrodite to the maiden has deeper implications for the entire kingdom and its social order. After telling Eros to make Psyche fall in love, Aphrodite departs: "Then she sought the nearest beach ... stepped out ... over the topmost foam of the quivering waves, and ... sat down over the clear surface of the deep sea" (243). Much later, to recall Aphrodite back to her "duties," the seagull recounts that the goddess's "entire household is getting a bad reputation." Describing what has transpired in the kingdom in the absence of Aphrodite and her son, the seagull says: "[T]here is no joy any more, no grace, no charm. Everything is unkempt and boorish and harsh. Weddings and social intercourse and the love of children are gone, leaving only a monstrous mess and an unpleasant disregard for anything as squalid as the bonds of marriage" (303). This absence of Aphrodite and her son is described in terms that indicate a wide-ranging cultural breakdown.

According to James Baird, cultural failure generally results from "the loss of a regnant and commanding authority in religious symbolism"; it is this loss that brings disorder and cultural failure (16). Whereas Baird is speaking of a nineteenth-century Judeo-Christian religion, cultural climate, and loss of faith, in Psyche's tale, cultural failure may be construed as the loss of the full powers of female sacredness and deity, of female life, and of an authority of the feminine. Reading this transfer in the exaggerations of myth, for women and for the feminine, cultural failure is encoded as a failure to reverence Aphrodite and the values that she represents. It is envisaged as an absence of joy, grace, and charm, a sacrifice and breakdown of affective connection and family responsibility. This turning away from the worship of a goddess representing an empowered and powerful female being, together with the reconstitution and limited reinscription of some powers into new values, enforces a male-defined cultural hegemony. To this is added an unrestrained male erotic power; rather than carrying out Aphrodite's directive, Eros has taken Psyche for his own.

Apuleius's image of Aphrodite's retreat underscores the import of this cultural failure. Aphrodite moves "out toward the Ocean" (245); this most golden of goddesses is "shielded" from the "hostile sun's blaze," accompanied by the music of "a tuneful conch shell" while a Triton holds "a mirror before his mistress's eyes" (243). All this can suggest that, because the kingdom does not provide Aphrodite with a true reflection of herself or reverence for her power, she returns to the place of her birth with her mirror – to the mirror of the natural world, to the place of primal origins.

Psyche as Hero

If Apuleius's text has itself encouraged an expanded reading of Aphrodite, so too does his presentation of Psyche encourage an interpretation beyond that of an anima figure. What the anima interpretation omits and glosses over is that the myth of Psyche introduces a female protagonist, a woman who is fully bound up in a culture and who represents a female apprehension of consciousness. As Lee R. Edwards accurately attests, "Psyche's heroism, like all heroism, involves both doing and knowing. The pattern of the tale parallels the growth of consciousness" (11). While Psyche has been construed as an anima figure in masculine consciousness, she also enacts feminine experience, first within a patriarchal world and then in a world overseen by Aphrodite. Moreover, Psyche grows up, gains sexual experience, conceives, and gives birth as a female being. Even if these experiences have been interpreted metaphorically as creative and spiritual consciousness and as an anima representation, they are fundamentally experiences of female reproductive biology, a biology which, presumably, is fully comprehended by the "mother of the universe."

This female body experience also changes the perception and comprehension of the feminine archetype. Erich Neumann sees the "archetypal feminine as a unity" and notes the way in which the patriarchal world divides this unity into "antithetical goddesses." He explains how Psyche's perception differs from this: "But Psyche's experience of the unity of the archetypal feminine is not the experience of opposites … it is the experience of totality" (129). Thus, Neumann distinguishes Psyche's understanding of the goddess from a patriarchal or male mythopoeic interpretation; he notes the difference between Lucius's desire for "unity with" and Psyche's recognition of the "unity of."

Psyche not only presents a different vision of the female goddess, but she in turn also sees differently in the goddess's green world. When Psyche is betrayed and sent out to the mountain top as a sacrifice, her journey moves her out from her father's kingdom with its attendant devaluation of female experience and into a new place, the realm of a goddess, whose contradictions, ambiguities, and powers intimate a different perception of female being.

The Green World

Psyche is abandoned into the green world, on a mountain top, a place which, as Friedrich tells us, is specifically associated with Aphrodite; she then is carried down into a valley. Here, Psyche discovers what concerns are central in an environment no longer obviously bound, as is the kingdom, in patriarchal social order. Psyche's first experiences in this natural landscape are sensual, and in her encounter with Eros, she achieves sexual and reproductive maturity. Paul Friedrich's claims about Aphrodite's "unique synthesis of sexuality, sensuousness, subjectivity" and "fertility-potency" suggest that this valley too may be marked off as hers (181). In this new context, Psyche's sisters visit her, and in the interactions of the sisters are glimpsed new reasons for the action they inspire in Psyche and for their final fate. Playing out these two kinds of relationships in what might be called the larger world of the goddess, one which no longer constrains action or interpretation within patriarchal confines, Psyche begins to understand her own power, the possibilities of relationship, and most of all, she learns to accept the consequences of her own actions. Aphrodite sets Psyche four tasks, and when Psyche completes them, she knows wisdom.

Psyche's Paradise

After being abandoned on the mountain top, Psyche is "slowly lifted by a gentle breeze" that "carried her down the slopes of the high cliff, and in the valley deep below laid her tenderly on the lap of the flowery turf." There, "her great mental distress was relieved and she fell peacefully asleep" (251, 253). The presence of flowers alone affirms Aphrodite's influence, but David Kinsley also relates that one of Aphrodite's epithets, from her association with the poppy, is "She Who Lulls the Senses and Brings Sweet Sleep" (209); thus, in the sleep of Psyche, we recognize another mark of Aphrodite's power in this new environment. (Friedrich states that the poppy, goldenness, and beauty are all symbols that Aphrodite shares with Demeter [208].) Aphrodite's domain is a paradise of the senses, and she controls all aspects of sensory response, including release into regenerative sleep.

In Aphrodite's valley, where all experience is through the body, there is no separation of nature and culture, of embodied life from cultural expression. This comprehension is fully present in Apuleius's description of Psyche's paradisal interlude and the "royal palace" that she finds there.[1] Psyche awakens to a "resplendent and charming residence" of "citronwood and ivory," with "great art" and "pictures made of precious stones" (253). A bath, "a royal feast," "nectarous wine," and music are all part of Psyche's encounter with paradise (257). This "residence of some god" is "supported on golden columns" and built with "divine hands." Those who tread there are twice blessed "and even more." Psyche "crossed the threshold" and "found it amazing that there was not a single chain or lock or guard protecting this treasure house of all the world." Addressed as "Mistress," she is asked, "Why are you so astounded at all this great wealth? All this belongs to you" (253, 255).[2] Significantly, too, her sisters are the only visitors from her old life to be carried here. This is a palace of female being which Eros visits, and it is here that he conceives their child.

Apuleius's description of the particular aloneness that implies youthful self-discovery and sexual awakening has a modern counterpart. Jessica Benjamin reiterates a parallel theme of isolation in the psychological experience of today's adolescent women, who are also "preoccupied with solitude" (129). Relating this directly to the story of Eros and Psyche, she remarks: "It is only when freed from idealization and objectification that Psyche can experience true sexual awakening, first alone, and later in her desire to see and recognise her lover, Eros." Acknowledging that the idea of sexual desire arising from "a state of aloneness" is paradoxical, she observes that isolation nevertheless "offers the opportunity to discover what is authentic in the self" (129). Idealization and objectification are identified as keeping young women from authentic self-hood. Idealized and objectified because of her "beauty," Psyche can experience genuine desire only when she is separated out from the kingdom.

Certainly, this turning inward might be associated with the self-exploration that accompanies puberty and menarche. Penny W. Caccavo suggests that the awareness of sexual potential begins in the seclusion, the turning inward, that accompanies menarche (140). Apuleius does tell us that Psyche's "bridal veil" is "flame-red" (247). Furthermore, Sarah B. Pomeroy states that in ancient Roman society – in Apuleius's time – marriage and puberty were often coincidental (207).

The Green World Eros

In *Archetypal Patterns in Women's Fiction*, Annis Pratt describes the "special world of nature" wherein women writers create for their female heroes "images of desire for an authentic selfhood." Often, Pratt continues, these images involve Eros, "the green world lover," because this natural world represents what is lost in patriarchy, what is lost by the "rape-trauma" archetype. Certainly, Erich Neumann's description of Psyche's interlude with Eros is characterized by the patriarchal implications of this rape-trauma; he terms it an "unworthy servitude," a "state of blind, though impassioned servitude," a "non-existence, a being in the dark, a rapture of sexual sensuality" (74). Psyche's experiences, however, cannot be circumscribed by these negative terms, and this, paradoxically, is equally apparent in Neumann's suggestion: "What for the masculine is aggression, victory, rape, and the satisfaction of desire ... is for the feminine destiny, transformation, and the profoundest mystery of life" (63).

If the relationship with "green world Eros" can represent an awakening to new experience as well as the trauma of lost desire and coercion into bondage, then plainly, Psyche has reached a paradisal green world, and equally plainly, a central aspect of this green world is an authentic female being that includes sexuality. According to Pratt, "Eros is one of the primal forces leading the personality through growth towards maturity, as necessary to human development as intellectual growth and the opportunity for significant work" (74). However significant his presence may be, he is but one element of the green world. Aphrodite herself reminds Eros of her greater power: "I will adopt one of my young slaves and make over to him those wings of yours and torches, your bow and arrows, and the rest of my equipment, which I did not give you to use that way" (307). Further, as Erich Neumann and Robert Johnson inform us, Eros is the daemon of relationship and attachment to others.

In preclassical myth, Eros is a primordial force but one appropriated by Zeus in classical Greek mythology. His appropriation by Zeus and his designation as Aphrodite's son show that Eros's powers have been subsumed under a particular cultural purpose, yet the emphasis on his wings and serpentine form imply that Eros and the erotic retain a potency beyond patriarchal society and the patriarchally defined gods. In her study of Victorian fiction, Karen Chase observes that "[i]n our age, eros has been narrowed from love to sexuality, from a divinity to an instinct" (1). For her purposes, she returns the meaning of eros to the larger affective meanings of loving, desiring, longing, and a more generalized yearning. The attributes associated with the god Eros confirm these wider associations and, moreover, affirm his associations with the goddess of regeneration (Dexter, 140), and Psyche's description of him – after she sees him – emphasizes his integration of both masculine and feminine characteristics.

That his hair is in "neatly shackled ringlets" suggests that his sexuality is bound, perhaps by affection for Psyche, perhaps to the larger life purposes represented in the great goddess, perhaps by Zeus. Hair is generally a symbol of male virility (Neumann; Johnson; Walker, *Dictionary*), and its absence – the "rest of his body was hairless and resplendent" – may imply that he has female aspects as well or that he is child to, or subservient to, the greater life force represented in Aphrodite. Furthermore, his "weapons" are bow, arrow, and quiver. The arrow and the suggestion of eye beams along with the bow are male attributes (Donaldson-Evans; Walker, *Dictionary*), but the quiver as a container is a female symbol. A figure of sexual energy, Eros is both male and female, masculine and feminine, yet even his effects are bound within the greater imperatives of nature and culture.

Within the world and life experience to one side of "civilization," Eros suggests an energy of emotional connection that is an aspect of reproductive life and an additional way whereby intellectual growth and consciousness are achieved. Isolation is essential to new erotic connection. The "within" world of lovers is warm, intimate, sharing. The close and vivid physical relationship is removed and isolated from the patriarchal structures of power. When two people are lovers, they are never more alive, power-full, and never more "dead to the world" or the concerns of power.

Because the early relationship between Eros and Psyche represents a honeymoon of pleasure and sexual experience, for Psyche, the nighttime experience with Eros is pleasurable and reassuring: "This happened thus for a long time, and, as nature provides, her new condition through constant habituation won her over to its pleasure, and the sound of a mysterious voice gave comfort to her loneliness" (259). To Psyche, the "new condition" is an incremental step in her life journey and represents one that is central to human experience. Through sexual need and feeling, individuals are drawn beyond parental connection and dependence to form new love relationships, new families.

The Patriarchal Taboo

Even here, however, centrally portrayed in the myth is the cultural taboo against female sexuality and female desire. In their sexual encounter, Eros forbids Psyche to see him; he comes to her only at nighttime: "Now her unknown husband had arrived, had mounted the bed, had made Psyche his wife, and had quickly departed before the rising of daylight" (257, 259). When Eros forbids sight of himself, he demonstrates the taboo that inhibits female desire and female agency in sexuality. Penny W. Caccavo discusses such prohibitions as a "forbidden room," a taboo imposed by husband or fiancé that forbids a young woman access to "her femaleness, that which permits her to be her own woman, a young goddess" (147). Sidney M. Rosenblatt posits that comparable paradisal isolations may also imply masturbation and self pleasuring, and thus Eros's interdiction might denote these additional proscriptions.

Annis Pratt raises the issues that clarify the dangers to patriarchal society inherent in Psyche's forbidden desire. She explains that the taboo against female sexuality arises because it is a threat to inheritance (42). This is a threat that extends to all the patrilineal family members. Not only is the woman ruined economically and the man not ensured rightful heirs, but the children themselves are endangered, and this is encoded within the tale. If Psyche disobeys, her child will not be immortal – will be disinherited – and so will forfeit a father's protection in a system of governance where little but legitimate paternity counts. As Pratt again points out, such a tragedy results "from a flaw that would not be fatal in a male hero, namely, the desire for sexual fulfilment" (73).

In Psyche's instance, because the taboo is *only* on seeing Eros, the implication seems to be that vision equals knowledge and that with sight comes Psyche's first cognition of Eros; if she does not see, she will not know (or desire) Eros for herself. That first "sight" of Eros, however, might more appropriately be read as a re-cognition of Love. As bride, she already has very real and other-sensory experience of her husband. In the sound of his "mysterious voice" and in the touch and movement "through constant habituation" of his body, Eros "was sensible both to her hands and ears" (259). To this other-sensory knowledge that she has of Eros, she merely *adds* sight.

What is clear in the totality of the description of this paradisal interlude is the importance to Psyche of *all* sensory experience: hearing, taste, touch, smell, movement, *and* sight. The addition of sight emphasizes the multi-sensory nature of Psyche's desire. By choosing to look, to see, what Psyche does is assert an independence of desire – through the knowledge and ownership of her own body and its erotic empowerment but also in the light of her awareness that she is already "Mistress" of a "royal palace."

Psyche and Her Sisters

Notwithstanding its pleasures, Psyche's interlude is interrupted with new information about her family. Eros tells her of her parents' "tireless mourning and grief" and her sisters' attempts to console them with "searching for some trace of you." Psyche is warned: "[D]o not even look in their direction. Otherwise you will cause me the most bitter pain, and yourself utter destruction" (259). Eros's warning highlights a truth of exogamous marriage alliances. As women are passed between men, their personal ties to sisters and families of origin are severed; their relationships continue through the mediation of men. Psyche, however, prevails: "Then she pleaded with him and threatened to die until she wrenched from her husband his consent to her wishes: to see her sisters, to soothe their grief and to converse with them" (261). Her emotional intensity indicates the strength of her desire for a renewed and personal exchange. The sisters, too, "hastily deserted their own homes" and for the sake of their own complex needs are compelled to reconnect in love and grief with their parents and with Psyche (259).

God or no god, daemon or not, clearly Eros and the erotic are not sufficient to Psyche's entire happiness. Where Psyche's resistance to Eros's "injunction to break off relations with her sisters" leads Neumann to see in Psyche a "puzzling persistence that appears to contradict her softness" (75), her obvious and clearly stated desire to visit with her sisters parallels what current research into women's relationships with siblings and friends reveals about the emotional development of modern women. Nancy J. Chodorow's psychoanalytic theory suggests that such a response is based in a specific cultural behaviour. In *Feminism and Psychoanalytic Theory*, she postulates that because children are universally raised by women, they retain the love for their mothers and the need for female love and friendship.

Chodorow explains that boys and girls resolve the issues surrounding this affection for the mother in the oedipal stage. Boys resolve the connection by repressing the affiliation to the mother. Girls differ because their affective interests contain a duality; rivalry with the mother "is always tempered by love for the mother" (70). The result is that women sustain complex affective needs that are not satisfied in an exclusive romantic attachment. Certainly, Psyche's reunion with her sisters is joyful: "the sisters took their delight in mutual embraces and eager kisses."

In spite of this joy, however, upon returning home the sisters "were consumed with the gall of swelling envy" and planned to "return in greater strength to punish her pride" (265, 267, 271). Thus, in the way that Apuleius has drawn the complexities of the relationship between Psyche and her sisters, there are both positive and negative elements. In *Psyche's Sisters*, Christine Downing describes the sororal relationship as being instrumental to female consciousness specifically because siblings are both alike and different: "Likeness and difference, intimacy and otherness – neither can be overcome. That paradox, that tension, lies at the heart of the relationship." This explains the special role of each same-sex sibling in the other's life: "Same sex siblings seem to be for one another, paradoxically, both ideal self and ... 'shadow.' They are engaged in a uniquely reciprocal mutual process of self-definition" (11).

Eros and the Sisters

Eros displays no such doubled, paradoxical vision. He again warns Psyche against the sisters because their plot "is to persuade you to examine my face." Calling her sisters "those deceitful bitches" and "those horrible harpies," he tells Psyche: "your womb, still a child's, bears another child for us, who will be a god if you guard our secret in silence, but mortal if you profane it" (273). By his injunction, secrecy is sacred, truth profane; new ties and responsibilities override kinship and sisterhood. Introducing the dynamics of power into their intimacy, he describes the barriers that Psyche must erect between herself and her sisters, barriers necessary for his primacy and continued authority: "By resolute self-restraint free your home, your husband, yourself, and our little one from the catastrophe of ruin which threatens." He calls the sisters "vile women" who are "trampling on the ties of blood" and "make the rocks resound with their fatal songs" (275). This suggests that the conflict between Psyche and her sisters can be construed as another outcome of a society in the midst of what James Baird terms cultural failure. Psyche's ties of blood to her sisters are trampled; Eros certainly wants to ignore them. The antagonisms between sisters recall the seagull's plea for the goddess's return to restore joy to a "monstrous mess." To underline their losses, the sisters in Apuleius's tale are nameless. They are doubly de-emphasized – in their affective importance to Psyche and in their lacking of any individual nature. Their differences are circumstantial, in the minor differences between their husbands.

The sisters' relationships reveal the breakdown of intimate and personal ties and illustrate the transference of kinship and affective connections that are necessary for the maintenance of patrilineal families. Sisters' ties to their original families are subsumed in economic and social liaisons as a way of providing cultural stability. There are also significant personal issues that the sisters individually represent as women who have been given into patriarchal marriage and who are estranged from their original family connections. About Psyche's situation, Marina Warner observes: "The question of exogamy, or marrying out, and its accompanying dangers lies at the heart of romance" (278).

Understanding this second kinship betrayal requires an understanding of how a male-centred socio-political view is authorized by patriarchal society to interpret female experience in wedlock. "According to Classical Greek and Roman mythopoets," Miriam Robbins Dexter declares, "mother-in-law is to be pitted against daughter-in-law, and sister is in competition with sister. The warrior concept of 'divide and conquer' pertains to the domestic sphere and to the battlefield" (140). This mythopoeic view of female relations describes them as antagonistic; they are made to fall into a pattern of dichotomy and thus replay a view of power as domination. The wider cultural view of the relationships between women influences both the male mythopoeic visions and their interpretations. Because male concepts of maturity have focused on aggression and confrontation, disputes in the family among women are understood in terms of male power structures and male warfare. Such interpretations also foster patriarchal hierarchies because they ensure that relationships between women do not threaten individual male power or the social structure.

Regardless of the subsequent punishments for Psyche and her sisters, what is obscured by a focus on the sisters' envy is the profound importance that all three women attach to the "nature" of the men whom they marry. To outward appearances at least, the two older sisters had made "fine marriages," but they feel differently. One says that her husband is "older than my father ... balder than a pumpkin ... punier than any child, and keeps the whole house locked up with bolts and chains." Of her husband, the other says that he is "doubled over and bent with arthritis, and hardly ever pays homage to my Venus" (209). In the sisters, what is named an envy of Psyche is a very real and justified anger against a (presumed) coercion into, and failure of, their own marriages.

Anger and Envy

In *The Politics of Reality*, feminist philosopher Marilyn Frye makes several comments on the nature of anger that explain much of the sisters' circumstances. Observing with some irony that women's anger "is generally not well received," although it "is in fact sane and sound," she notes that men often misread it and ignore its causes. The sisters' response to the failures and unhappiness in their own marriages is read as envy, and the cause of the anger – the very real failure and inadequacy in the husbands – is ignored. Patrilineal power arrangements evidence little concern for emotional or erotic failures in the daughters' marriage arrangements. The ordained power structures require little more than legitimate male heirs, and marriage does not preclude male desire directed elsewhere.

In a comment that could apply directly to the sisters, Frye goes on to say: "Anger seems to be a reaction to being thwarted, frustrated or harmed." The frustration that generates anger comes out of a sense of being offended and of seeing the offence "as due to someone's malice or inexcusable incompetence" (85). The sisters' anger renamed envy can be seen as arising out of being thwarted in personal fulfilment specifically because of their husbands' physical infirmities, parsimony, and sexual inadequacy. Frye's view that anger also has about it a sense of righteousness resounds in the sisters' plight. If women are allowed only marriage in a patriarchal social structure, then rage is an appropriate response to any perception of failure or injustice. The sisters have been truly wronged because someone else – the king/father – chose their husbands poorly, either maliciously or incompetently or though sheer self-interest.

Psyche is visited twice more by her sisters, and on the third and last occasion, they tell her to take "a very sharp razor" and "a lamp, trimmed and filled with oil and burning with a clear light." Hiding these, she is to wait until her husband is asleep; "then, with as strong a stroke as you can, sever the knot that joins the poisonous serpent's neck and head" (287). Left alone, Psyche experiences a gamut of emotions: "She felt haste and procrastination, daring and fear, despair and anger; and worst of all, in the same body she loathed the beast but loved the husband" (289). In spite of her emotional turmoil, she does carry out the plan; armed with the razor and by the light of her lamp, she sees Eros asleep.

For married women in traditional societies, well-being is almost entirely bound up in the whims and fortunes of the husband. The importance for Psyche of knowing her husband is clearly gauged by her emotional state and is intensified by her pregnancy; while still adhering to the prohibition, she says to Eros that she "will know [his] looks at least in my unborn babe's" (277). Knowledge of her husband is undeniably part of her responsibility to her child. With her first sight of him, however, Psyche is "terrified at this marvellous sight ... overcome ... faint and trembling." She tries to hide the razor "in her own heart," but it slips away. Psyche at first "[i]nsatiably, and with *some* curiosity ... scrutinized and handled and marvelled at her husband's arms." After pricking her thumb on one of the arrows from Eros's quiver, Psyche bleeds "tiny drops of rose-red blood" and "fell in love with Love." She rests *overcome by the sense of being safe* (291; emphasis added).

In spite of this complexity of affection and intent, Apuleius provides for all three sisters a retribution that recalls Pratt's explanation of disinheritance. First, Psyche is cut off from her paradisal life, and her child will be born mortal – disinherited from the father's power and support. Then, when the sisters are told by Psyche that Eros really loves them, each rushes back to Psyche's paradise by throwing herself from the mountain as she had done before, and in this way both the sisters fall "to the self-same deadly doom" (301, 303).

The Sisters' Doom

The sisters' doom is doubly problematic for a woman-centred interpretation of Psyche's adventures. Their deaths provide endings that are both appropriate and inappropriate. That the sisters should die is a fitting ending in terms of the isolation that exists and is compelled between women in exogamous marriage systems. In the "normal" course of these systems, Psyche would lose social contact with her sisters; wives join their husbands' family groups. The deaths are also psychologically fitting, but for more complex reasons. The sisters have not confronted the true source of their envy – that very real and justifiable anger within their own marriage relationships.

In her examination of anger, Carol Tavris reminds us of its importance and especially of honestly confronting its true source: "Ultimately, the purpose of anger is to make a grievance known, and if the grievance is not confronted, it will not matter if the anger is kept in, let out or wrapped up in red ribbons and dropped in the Erie Canal" (160). Making the source of anger and grievance known is the way by which we keep it centred in our own lives, where, presumably, we may make some difference.

Transferring the anger to envy of another moves the emotional action out of our own lives and prevents any appropriate changes. Not expressing their anger prevents the sisters from taking action to change their own circumstances; the sisters die to their own lives at a profound psychological level. And lastly, naming the "grievance" – expressing anger – reveals the purpose of the voicing: to grieve. Hidden in the sisters' welter of angry emotions is the pain and sorrow at the betrayals that they have endured. That each is married to an old and impotent husband supplies reason enough for the erotic longing expressed as a fall from that "steep mountain."

The Sister Goddesses

I would argue against the appropriateness of the sisters' deaths, however, for equally complex reasons. The first is that they are in the mountains, in Aphrodite's realm, where there are strong psychological forces that argue for the continued existence of Psyche's sisters. Reclaiming Aphrodite's multidimensional origins and powers brings the opportunity to change how the relationships among the women in the tale may be viewed. Aphrodite is a goddess who can be interpreted as encompassing many of the creative and destructive variables of life, of the natural world, of passionate relationship, and who is, to a degree, maternal (Friedrich, 182). The myths about her are rich and complex, fully embracing discord and difference, and yet she is the least martial or warlike goddess (Friedrich, 95). Difference and discord are as much a part of her history, especially with Ares and Hephaestes, as are love and generation, but hers is a "relatively peaceful and amatory nature" (Friedrich, 97).

Apuleius's tale provides a second model of sisterhood. There is a second set of three sisters who endure within his tale: Aphrodite and the sister goddesses Hera and Demeter. According to Dexter, Downing (*Goddess*), Kinsley, and Spretnak, the three goddesses are aspects of the Great Goddess. Hera dominates as queen, Demeter rules over agriculture and the seasons, and according to Friedrich, Aphrodite is the most powerful of the three, the most "golden" in her function as goddess of nature, life, procreation, and sexuality. In the tale, Apuleius describes Hera and Demeter as representing a full range of "natural" annoyance and "sisterly" support when they meet Aphrodite soon after the seagull has told her of the chaos in the world brought about by her "abdication" and Eros's dalliance with Psyche. Noting the irony in their appearance at just this moment, Aphrodite calls the meeting "opportune," but nonetheless seeks their assistance to find Psyche, "my elusive runaway" (309). They attempt to soothe her, remind her of her own and her son's respective responsibilities, and reprimand her "for finding fault with your own talents and your own delights in the case of your handsome son." While the tale interprets this as flattering deference to Eros, they give sound criticism and advice; they tell the truth, but since it is not what Aphrodite wants to hear, she "swept past them on the other side" (311).

Juxtaposing the two sets of female figures allows for some comparisons that resolve the unsatisfactory denouement to the relationship of Psyche and her sisters. What is acknowledged in the goddesses is their individual spheres of power: they are named and their names carry the association with their powers. Whether seen as a carry-over of earlier matrilocal lore or as existing in a patriarchal power structure, these goddesses have their individual spheres of influence within overlapping boundaries. In their similarity of powers over the natural world, in their relationships with men, there is also acknowledged a difference of sphere – Aphrodite's flowers and birds, Artemis's wild animals, Demeter's agriculture, Hera's wifehood, Aphrodite's sexuality, Artemis's virginity. What is missing in the mortal sisters is this sense of name, of individual similarity and difference, of individual power. In Aphrodite's sphere, sister goddesses may be wrong, irritating, or too often right, but they are an essential part of her community. Denying Psyche her sisters denies her what Downing has described as mirror and shadow-self reflections.

This loss of the friendship of similars is a profound loss. Linda A. Bell makes the important observation that, in Western culture's traditional views, differences and similarities have not been adequately appreciated. Because difference has been reduced only to gender and heterosexuality, "it has resulted in an enormous and uncritical assumption of the similarity of all women with each other" (226). Unlike the goddesses, the sisters are undifferentiated and nameless, and what they bring to Psyche is also unnamed. This unnamed mirroring therefore is unrecognized and lost to Psyche with their deaths. Acknowledging their similarities and differences – their griefs, anger, and joy – by keeping them alive would add a dimension missing from the final stages of Psyche's journey.

The Wounds

In the tale, however, Eros is the one visibly, undeniably angry, burned – awakened – by "a drop of boiling oil" from the lamp Psyche holds (293). In an article on Greek attitudes towards sexuality, Anne Carson reveals the ways in which women were believed to "pollute" men and describes the imagery surrounding sexual relationship and touch. Early Greek society regarded men as "dry," but women and the emotions were "wet," especially those emotions associated with eros that were liquid and could drip, heat, melt, or boil. Women were regarded as fearsome because they were believed to be more emotional and sexually insatiable. In a way that allows the placement of Eros's response within this paradigm, Carson recounts the perception that a "voracious woman, by her unending sexual demands," not only "'roasts her man' in the unquenchable fire of her appetite," but also "drains his manly strength and delivers him to the 'raw old age' of premature impotence" (141). Carson includes a description that links sight, fire, and danger in the "blazing eye" of the sexually experienced woman, one who has "tasted man" (138).

Neumann views Psyche's intention to cut off Eros's head in less directly sexual terms. To him, this "ancient symbol of castration sublimated to the spiritual sphere" suggests how "the opposition between a psyche that hates the beast and a psyche that loves the husband, is projected outward and leads to psyche's act" (72, 77). Castration as a spiritual sacrifice makes the loss of potency in masculine sexuality the loss of the connection to, or of the way to make connection with, the divine. Even though Psyche's sisters supply her with a razor, she does not use it on Eros. He is burned; he is not "sacrificed." By way of contrast, Psyche's abandonment on the mountain constitutes more of a sacrifice, yet even hers is in the manner of myth, exaggerated, psychological as much as physical.

The dictionary gives the origins of sacrifice as the Latin *sacre*, holy (whole), and *facere*, to make. Thus, another way of being made holy and whole is to be spent, used up, to live in service to life, to generation, and to love. In this way Eros is a "dying god" enlisted in the service of life and regeneration. He is merely wounded, burned, and requires time to heal. Such an image is entirely consistent with the male role in physical reproduction. Eros is "spent" and "dies" in the service of life and rests to recuperate, to "rise" renewed. Page DuBois states that "the theme of male death or sleep after intercourse may refer to the male loss of semen and of force, which is sacrificed to the earth in order to ensure its continued productivity" (54).

Such a definition of sacrifice can also transform our interpretation of Psyche's pricking of her own thumb and bleeding. For her, too, this blood may portray an aspect of entrance into female reproductive life and sexual experience. In M. Esther Harding's description of menstrual blood, we come closer to an evocation of blood spent in the service of life. Likewise, Penelope Shuttle and Peter Redgrove refer to menstruation as a "wise wound" that brings healing and self-knowledge. Bruno Bettelheim interprets such drops of blood in fairy tales as a symbol of sexual maturity (136) and as the "sexual bleeding" of menstruation or of the breaking of the hymen in first sexual intercourse (202). All these interpretations, the "wise wounds" that women bleed without dying and the release of semen with which men die without dying, seem perfectly appropriate to Aphrodite's auspices.

Eros does leave Psyche in anger, however, citing her ingratitude in a temper of sanctimonious indignation: "Illustrious archer that I am, I shot myself with my own weapon and made you my wife, for the pleasure it seems of having you think me a wild beast and cut off my head with a sword, the head that holds these eyes that are your lovers" (295). When Marilyn Frye says that anger implies "a claim to domain," she could be referring directly to Eros, since he clearly claims – a patriarchally warranted "trust" – sole right to sight and to "ownership" of the beloved: Eros, "seeing the ruin of betrayed trust, straightway flew up from the kisses of his poor unhappy wife" (293). Conflating Psyche's justifiable concern about his nature with her wish to see him denies the mutuality and respect that is necessary between equals. He will not grant Psyche this seeing and respect, and he flies away. He intends to be revenged on the sisters but punishes Psyche "merely by leaving." Still, Psyche responds not with anger but, in an action of despair and depression, by throwing "herself over the edge of a nearby river."

Pan's Advice

The river deposits her unharmed on the bank. There, Psyche is addressed by Pan, who is seated nearby with Echo. Pan's significance to the tale is seen by Neumann as that of a wise old man, loving and natural, of nature. Barbara Walker states that Pan represents "the sacred king who died in fertilizing the earth," that his attributes were "goat-hoofs, horns, and unremitting lust," and that he "coupled with all the Dionysian Maenads" (*Encyclopedia* 765). Thus, his wisdom, that of a lusty though undiscriminating male fertility god, would be of little use to a Psyche who is already pregnant and wishes for a more durable reconnection with Eros.

As a fertility god, however, Pan is observant and his first comments direct an immediate attention to Psyche's appearance: "your weak and oft tottering footsteps, your extremely pale complexion, your constant sighing" (297). In a discussion of pregnancy, Robbie E. Davis-Floyd calls the birth process a transformational rite of passage and illuminates Pan's depiction of Psyche's behaviour: "What Victor Turner calls liminality, pregnant women experience as a sense of change, of growth, of detachment, fear, wonder, awe, curiosity, hope, specialness, simultaneous alienation from and closeness to themselves and their families, irritation, frustration, exhaustion, resentment, joy – and a trembling sense of unknown, unknowable potentiality" (24). Davis-Floyd also notes that pregnant women sense that they share a "secret sisterhood" (35) and want to reclaim the sister-mother connections.

Within the tale as Apuleius relates it, Psyche does indeed seek out her sisters, but she does so because of Pan's advice: "Stop your mourning and put away your grief. Instead pray to [Eros], the greatest of the gods, and worship him and earn his favour with flattering deference, since he is a pleasure loving and soft hearted youth" (297). Notwithstanding Pan's suggestion that her behaviour should be of "flattering deference" to Eros, we may assume that she heeds Pan's advice and pleases Eros, as she next confronts her sisters and tells them of Eros's love for them, thereby setting their destruction in motion.

But there, seated on Pan's lap is Echo. Neumann associates Echo's presence with "the unattainable beloved," transforming herself "into music for him" and with whom he holds an "eternal loving dialogue" (97–8). In keeping with my earlier interpretation of the Narcissus myth, I would question the association of Echo with unattainability and argue instead that her presence is cautionary, suggesting that Pan's advice may be differently interpreted. Echo's presence implies a limited repetition or ironic parody of Pan's advice. That Pan is accompanied by Echo emphasizes Psyche's depression and passivity.

As one who – like Echo – only "makes answers," Psyche remains outside the action, and as voice, she repeats to her sisters the information that ensures their destruction. She speaks Eros's intent from the passivity of her own depression. Again the situation emphasizes grief, mourning, and an absence of choice; Psyche is carried along by events even as she was carried by the river. In Marilyn Frye's distinction between the frustrations that cause anger and those that cause depression, there lies a means for assessing what underlies Psyche's passivity. Her acceptance of Pan's advice suggests that Psyche is depressed: her anger is inward. She cannot save herself that way.

Apuleius has already indicated that Psyche is quite capable of feeling anger and of expressing it. When she was to be sacrificed and was confronted with the lamentations of her family, she displayed a justifiable irritation: "When countries and peoples were giving me divine honours, when with a single voice they were all calling me a new [Aphrodite], that is when you should have wept, that is when you should have mourned me as if I were already dead." She recognizes their sorrow as "dealt by wicked Envy," but even this does not detract from a real and rightfully placed anger at her situation, nor does it help her to save herself (249). Since she does not display that ability to be angry when Eros flees, I conclude that she does not see herself as wronged, at least not in her acceptance or love of her husband.

Similarly, she does not seem to regard her loss of Eros as unjust or unfair or the result of someone's malice, and this certainly absolves her sisters. She reacts to this loss with a passivity that suggests depression. According to Frye, "By determining where, with whom, about what and in what circumstances one can get angry and get uptake, one can map others' concepts of who and what one is" (*Politics*, 94). The sisters may take their anger out on Psyche, and she may revenge Eros on them, but none of the sisters may themselves find justice; Psyche behaves as if she does not think she has the power to affect Eros, to effect a reconnection.

Choosing Aphrodite

The deference to Pan's advice and the subsequent retribution delivered to her sisters do not bring peace to Psyche; consequently, in her search for reconnection with Eros, she seeks help from the goddesses Demeter and Hera. They, however, refuse to intervene, citing Aphrodite's goodness and the kinship ties of love and friendship that they owe her, and especially they stress her rightfulness as Psyche's owner. These goddesses in their guises of daughter-lost seasonal agriculture or as lawful queen and patriarchal "wife of" are not Psyche's enablers in this situation. They are, however, goddesses who, like Aphrodite, often subvert patriarchal dictates. Demeter compels the summer return of her daughter from Hades, and Hera continually prevents or makes exceedingly difficult the philandering of Zeus. In this very intransigence, they are appropriate models for Psyche, but as mentor, Apuleius stresses, Psyche herself ultimately chooses Aphrodite.

Unable to find anyone to save her or to restore Eros magically to her, Psyche "took counsel with her own thoughts" and reached a decision: "Hand yourself voluntarily to your mistress and soften her furious attacks by submission, late though it be." She speculates: "Besides who knows but what you will find what you are searching for, there in his mother's house" (321). Certainly, Eros is there in his mother's house, and as the goddess of fertility and creativity, Aphrodite does represent possibility, even that of a reconnection that promises a greater equality. More immediately, however, Psyche is pregnant and must prepare herself for motherhood and its responsibilities.

Psyche's desire for reconnection with Eros and her pregnant condition require a re-examination of mothering relationships as they specifically affect the behaviour of Eros, Aphrodite, and Psyche. By showing how the intensity and exclusivity of the mother-child relationship affects men and women, Nancy J. Chodorow's research into the mothering relationship can be used to reframe the connection between

Aphrodite and Eros, as well as that between Psyche and Eros. Chodorow sees exclusive mothering as having several results. First, women are more emotionally important to men than men are to women. Second, this lopsided importance is exacerbated by men's attempts to repress their own relational needs. Third, a man's first adult experience of loss precipitates depression and an incapacity for forming new relationships (75). All of these features are clearly present in Eros's experience, in the experience of the once primordial god "downsized" to a son of Zeus and Aphrodite.

Eros moves from a dependence upon his mother to a passionate dependence on Psyche. When he forbids Psyche to look upon him, he is denying reciprocity and instead substitutes control for the exchange implicit in relationship needs. Denying what losing Psyche means to him, Eros retreats into depression as a result of losing/rejecting her. He withdraws from the world, away from responsibility and back to Aphrodite. He finds himself unable and unwilling to form another relationship or to reconnect with the old. The strength of his attachment to Psyche, however, is undeniable. As James Hillman notes, there are no myths that tell of Eros's infidelity; he is faithful.

Psyche must find her own way to reconnection. Her seclusion in paradise is paralleled by her solitude as she submits to Aphrodite and takes up the tasks which she is assigned. Aphrodite both sets the tasks and aids Psyche in the guise of her familiars: the chthonic ants, the reeds in the borders between pool and land, and the eagle. She is the reproductive goddess, mother figure and mother-in-nature who directs Psyche to an understanding of the strength of female being and feminine values.

The Tasks

Psyche's tasks are tasks of female achievement and feminine development. She must sort seeds, gather golden fleece, collect water in a flask, and bring a jar of beauty back from Persephone in the underworld. All the tasks symbolize various aspects of goddess power, and most of the associations are already familiar. Seeds are associated both with Aphrodite as a life goddess and with Demeter as an agricultural goddess. Both Erich Neumann and Robert Johnson conflate seed and semen to describe Psyche as learning to differentiate and sort the promiscuous masculine. Yet since seeds are whole and therefore more like a zygote/fetus, it is biologically and genetically inaccurate to link seed with semen in this way. Semen accounts for only one-half of the "seed," whatever the symbol (falsely) implies; the ova supplies the other half. Rachel Blau DuPlessis sees the seeds as Psyche's own fruitfulness, the child(ren) within and the importance of conscious choice in that fecundity. Although Psyche's pregnancy makes the case for such an interpretation, to restrict the symbolism of the seeds to female fertility is also problematic, for seeds do not represent either semen or ova in the literal, grounded, and biological sense.

Literally, the seeds are wheat, barley, chick peas, millet, lentils, poppy seeds, and beans. As Mary Anne Ferguson observes, they are most appropriately read as the manifestations of concrete reality. Indeed, because the list includes wheat, beans, peas, and lentils and so provides complete proteins, its significance to food preparation is obvious. Psyche learns what is required to sustain physical well-being. Charlene Spretnak links the poppy specifically to Aphrodite and "herbal magic" (69), but Apuleius acknowledges Isis/Aphrodite's capacity as a fertility goddess and places all seeds in her realm. In his address to the goddess at his initiation, he states that "seeds sprout" at her "nod" (2:345). This makes Psyche's task represent the goddess's power at the same time as it is symbolic of the traditional female responsibilities for the provision of food and herbal medicine. Johnson adds that sorting is directly related to the tasks of housekeeping (49) and further suggests the psychological aspect involved in keeping orderly track of "the influx of emotions, moods, and archetypes for the family" (52).

The jars of the third and fourth tasks may also imply the uterus as container, and the water in the third task recalls Aphrodite's birth as well as sacred and goddess-associated life-giving powers (Gimbutus, 22). The significance of the golden fleece of the second task is less obvious, although certainly Aphrodite is golden. Jane Ellen Harrison provides a more complete explanation. In preclassical Greece, the fleece was divine, associated with purification and revelation; unwashed, it was left as an offering at the opening of Demeter's cave (159). At Delphi, it was woven into a "net-work of wool-fillets" to cover the omphalos (61). In *Lady of the Beasts*, Buffie Johnson reveals that, in ancient Greek depictions, on coins and medallions, Aphrodite has been shown on the back of a sheep (205). She also notes that the sheepskin or fleece was associated with purification and cleansing during an initiation into the Mysteries, just as the poppy induced the sleep that preceded "rebirth."

The tasks thus depict women's historic and traditional spheres of labour and are also a link to Aphrodite. Women were responsible for agriculture, weaving, medicine, and child care. Sorting seeds implies a knowledge of the uses of plants for food and medicines, gathering fleece is a prelude to carding, spinning, and weaving, and collecting water is the link to birth, life, and the life source.[3] Even in today's society, women remain almost exclusively responsible for food and clothing purchases, general health care, nurturing in the family, and children's religious and cultural education. Thus, the tasks have practical and historic relevance as well as mythic and psychological implications.

The Descent

What gives particular resonance to these tasks is that Psyche is pregnant throughout her entire ordeal, and her pregnancy makes the fourth task specifically and physically female. In this task, Psyche makes a descent journey, a journey inward represented through a journey to the heart of the earth and to the centre of life's last mystery. At this centre, Psyche comes face to face with death. Her last task requires her to replenish "beauty" for Aphrodite, "who used up and exhausted all she had while caring for her sick son." Specifically, Aphrodite gives her the following command: "Take this jar and go straight down from the daylight to the underworld and Orcus' own dismal abode. Hand the jar to [Persephone] and say: [Aphrodite] requests that you send her a little of your beauty, just enough to last her one brief day." Initially, Psyche "headed towards a high tower, with the intention of jumping off it, since she thought this was the most direct and decorous route by which she could descend to the underworld" (341).

The tower is described by Johnson as "a construct, a convention, a set of rules, a tradition, a system" (65), and according to Harding, the moon deity is symbolized by a conic or stone pillar (42). Even though Aphrodite is the "most solar and least lunar" of the goddesses (Friedrich), there remains an oblique association between her sea birth, tides, the moon, and female menstrual cycles. Marija Gimbutus gives information, however, that seems most in keeping with the tower's warning. Gimbutus notes that ancient Old European "life columns" are "the link between non-being and being" and are "inherent in the body of the goddess" (221). In this definition, then, the tower's role is fully centred in the task and in the goddess's powers. Its warning to Psyche, that she should not jump, must be heeded: "this most direct and decorous route," provides no return; "in no way will you be able to return from there" (341). Instead, the tower commands her to go to "Dis's breathing-vent," which is "a dead end road" and "a direct track to Orcus' palace" (343), and warns her "not [to] go forward into that shadowy region empty-handed" (343). In preparation for her descent, Psyche is given other warnings by the tower. In these warnings, Neumann distinguishes between the traditional or more universal motifs of "coin" and "sops" and Psyche's being forbidden to help others

(112). The former pertain to what is regarded as universal (male) payment, while the latter refers to what is regarded as "unlawful" or taboo for female journeys.

The tower tells Psyche what tasks and requests are to be ignored: "you will meet a lame ass carrying wood, with a lame driver as well, who will ask you to hand him some twigs that have fallen off his load. But you must not utter a single word and must pass by him in silence" (343). She is told, in effect, where silence is appropriate. She should not divert her energies to assist those who do not need it or who misconstrue charity. "Some twigs" do not constitute a worthwhile request even from the lame. The tower then provides another injunction: "Likewise, while you are crossing ... a dead old man, floating on the surface, will lift up his rotting hands and beg you pull him into the boat. But be not swayed by unlawful pity" (345). The two directives are linked in their application to the misuses of pity. For Neumann, the injunction against pity "confronts every feminine Psyche on its way to individuation: it must suspend the claim of what is close at hand for the sake of a distant abstract goal." To him, the injunction stresses the importance of ego stability and the need to avoid distraction (113). For Johnson, the prohibition is required because "the fourth task requires all of a person's energy and resources" (68).

Carol Gilligan, however, provides the basis for another interpretation, one that focuses on women's moral and ethical development and stresses the importance for women of integrating the care of self into the desire to care for others. An ethic of recognizing and valuing the independent self within the community, and of being responsible for one's own needs and desires within the social context, is expressed by Gilligan in terms of the seeming paradoxes of separation and attachment: "we know ourselves as separate only in so far as we live in connection with others, and ... we experience relationship only in so far as we differentiate other from self" (63). Rather than taking the form of conflict, what Neumann sees as a "struggle against the feminine nature" (112), Psyche's evolution can be read as a movement towards the inclusion of self into an ethic of care for others. She must grant the same importance to her own journey as she would give to others'.

Next, Psyche is warned not to interfere in the weaving of life and death that is the responsibility of the Fates: "After you have crossed the river and gone on a little farther, some old women weaving at a loom will ask you to lend a hand for a moment. But you must not touch this either" (345). These "old women weaving," suggest the Fates, those old women who dictate life's continuum: its beginning, middle, and end; birth, life, and death. Seeing them, Psyche learns the limits of her personal responsibility for others' lives. This is an essential lesson on the limits of responsibility for someone about to be a mother, and it recalls the silence and absence of her own mother from all but the beginning of the story.[4]

The tower tells Psyche about the proper behaviour in the underworld. Psyche is warned that Persephone "will receive you kindly and courteously" but will "try to persuade you to sit down comfortably beside her and eat a sumptuous supper. But you must sit on the floor and ask for common bread and eat that" (345). While Psyche is encouraged to meet the goddess of death, to know her "shadow" as a part of life, and to "break bread" with Persephone, she must not dwell on death or make of death "a sumptuous supper." In a text co-authored with Jung, C. Kerenyi ties the sowing of corn specifically to the underworld journey and to the decay that heralds "fruitful death" (166). "In most cultures," adds Neumann, "to eat a meal some place is to forge permanent ties with that place, or family, or situation. Where one eats, one is somehow committed" (69). What is forbidden is to overindulge, to give death excessive and hence unfruitful value in life. Thus, the atypical prohibitions concern pity, responsibility, and excessive indulgence in, or fear of, death.

The final warning is "not to open or look into the jar that you will be carrying, and in fact do not even think too inquisitively about the hidden treasure of divine beauty" (347). Psyche pays heed and successfully completes her journey, but on her return to "bright daylight," she decides to "take out a tiny drop of [beauty] for myself" (347, 349). Persephone's jar is supposed to contain "beauty," but it contains a "deathlike and truly Stygian sleep" which attacks Psyche "instantly, enveloping her entire body in a dense cloud of slumber ... She lay there motionless, no better than a sleeping corpse" (349).

Whereas Neumann describes this "beauty" as a personal feminine desire and associates "a woman's preoccupation with beauty or attractiveness, with physical desirability" (71), Marie-Louise von Franz sees women's concern with beauty more appropriately as "part of their persona and their conscious personality" (106). That Psyche's journey is downward and passes through the vent of Dis, a yonic or genital symbol, highlights the essentially female nature of this quest. All these details are in accord with the acquisition of wisdom (beauty) in the realm of Aphrodite-and-Persephone, particularly if we understand wisdom and knowledge of the world as acquired in the experience of the body and through the senses.

Writing of the Sumerian descent myth of Inanna, Sylvia Brinton Perera connects this kind of female descent journey with Jungian theory: Inanna's descent "may be viewed as" a way of incarnating "cosmic uncontained powers into time-bound corrupting flesh," of "retrieving lost values long repressed and of uniting above and below into a new pattern" (143). Such an interpretation is consistent with establishing Psyche's female physicality and feminine values. A direct female experience of the positive or spiritual nature of embodied female life is what women have lost. Regaining this spirituality requires a transformation that takes place in the mind, one that involves the integration of embodied life in the natural world with spiritual values appropriate to an intellectual framework that gives a full and integrated expression of all three – the body, mind, and spirit; this is what Winnie Tomm calls an embodied mindfulness.

Persephone, the goddess of the underworld, is the shadow self of Aphrodite. She represents the realm of unconscious experience. For analysts like Neumann, Johnson, Ulanov, and von Franz, to bring "contents" up from the underworld as Psyche does is to bring them to consciousness. Like Hillman, Annis Pratt links the process directly to Eros energy: "Eros springs from the inner realm of the unconscious experience. Indeed, fully experienced Eros demands the capacity for moving down into and returning from the deepest realms of the libido" (74). If, as she states, one element of romance is the search for "one's heart's desire," then Psyche must look into the "jar of beauty," must see for herself, know her own desire, and experience its power. This opening of the jar indicates that the last of Aphrodite's tasks is successfully completed.

The Choice

Psyche's choosing to open the jar containing "beauty" is for Neumann a failure: "Psyche fails, she must fail, because she is a feminine psyche. But she does not know it is precisely this failure that brings her victory" (121). While I do agree that this symbol is profoundly important, I differ with Neumann in various ways. Foremost, I believe that Psyche succeeds – she is "meant" to open the jar in the sense that she is provided with the opportunity to do so. In moving between Aphrodite and Persephone, she weaves together the mortal, the human, a living continuity, and the goddesses. In her pregnant condition, she reflects the capacity for personal fulfilment, for generation, and for female community itself, even as she is the connecting tie.

Opening the jar to take "beauty" for herself, she chooses to be responsible for her own needs. While Psyche is pregnant with a child, that child, in a very real sense and paradoxically, is herself. Another paradox lies in the way that she dies to be reborn. One of the secrets of the jar – the opening up of the underworld and the opening of the virgin's body – is a liminal event associated with ritual precaution (Carson 1990, DuBois). Unlike her disobedience of Eros, this choice was not instigated by the sisters or dependent on the urging of others. Psyche has undertaken the four tasks of purification, has rightfully chosen for herself, and is an agent willing to accept the consequences of an action that might reconnect her to Eros.

And lastly, Psyche's act does bring what she desires; Eros does take pity on her. As Gilligan explains, men must integrate a care for others into their system of competing rights. For them, to pity is to accept the other as of equal importance to the self; for men, after separation comes reconnection. In their second chances, and representing human lovers, Psyche has emerged with knowledge of a separate strength; Eros, with an understanding of attachment and responsibility. Both recognize the point where they cannot control outside circumstances; they must rely on opportunity, even luck. Coming to terms with life implies an acceptance of things that cannot be controlled and a willingness to trust in one's own perceiving.

Learning Transformation

At the end of the twentieth century, in Western, Eurocentric culture, learning is most often viewed as an enlargement of an intangible intellectual spirit. Analyses of women's learning, for example, have been marked by the desire to present women as intellectually capable, even as there is real effort to remake learning into an exercise more in keeping with women's values. In *Women's Ways of Knowing*, the authors describe different perspectives "from which women view reality and draw conclusions about truth, knowledge, and authority" (3). Their research also marks the transformational encounters, the transitional events, that cause women to change their self-concepts and opinions of their own mental capacities.

Examining the events in Psyche's progress together with the structures provided by the analysis of the stages of women's learning gives Psyche's story a new dimension of particular relevance for twentieth-century women. The tasks that Aphrodite assigns, with their metaphoric associations and entailments, divulge the potential for a different reading of the learning that takes place within Psyche. An expanded reading of Aphrodite's more ancient affiliations and powers gives Psyche a mentor who is fully connected to female gender and feminine values. Laurent A. Daloz defines mentors as guides and explains their significance: "They lead us along the journey of our lives. We trust them because they have been there before. They embody our hopes, cast light on the way ahead, interpret arcane signs, warn us of lurking dangers, and point out unexpected delights along the way. There is a certain luminosity about them, and they often pose as magicians in tales of transformation" (17). In a reclamation of her more ancient and now lost capacities, in the contradictions of her representations, and in her devaluation into love goddess, Aphrodite allows for a reading of Psyche's learning that encompasses the most basic and fundamental aspects of her travails as well as the most profound and evanescent values and philosophy.

Silence

In the beginning, Psyche – like Echo – is paralysed in silence. Her beauty, the sacrifice, and her ensuing marriage to Eros are not of her doing or choosing; she submits. She is both acquiescent and alone, unable to connect with, or exert influence on, those around her. She exhibits an extreme denial of self, a dependence on external authority, and an inability to learn from or connect through language to her own experience. Like the women described in *Ways*, she is locked into the immediate present and into specific and enacted behaviour. The self descriptions of such women appear to hinge wholly on "their own movements in and around the geographic space that surrounds them" (31). Just so is Psyche concretely aware of her surroundings as she crosses the threshold of her palace, "attracted by the allurement of this beautiful place" (255).

In *Ways*, this demeanour is characterized by the authors as passive and dependent; yet, whereas passive is usually construed to mean the opposite of active (that is, without agency, without the will or desire to do or exert influence), here passivity is also perceived as a way of resisting when the outcomes of all alternatives for action are deemed to be, or are perceived as, unpleasant. This latter response could be more accurate as an explanation of Psyche's attitude. She expresses irritation with those around her, but she is not able to influence them; nor does she expect to. Like Psyche, the women described in *Ways* rely entirely on external authority, pure and absolute polarities, and "blind obedience." They are closed in upon themselves, having no vantage point from which to imagine a complete self or even to bring an external physical picture of self into view (26–32).

Belenky et al. suggest that movement out of silence is encouraged by "face to face" conversation and a "sign-rich environment" (33). Certainly, Psyche experiences a sensual and sign-rich environment in the paradise with Eros beyond her father's kingdom, and the face to face encounters are provided by Eros and by her sisters. While her paradisal encounters with Eros are certainly physically close and mutually pleasurable, and his conversations with her are influential, she is forbidden to "see" him in the way that she is able to see her sisters. Her relationships with them provide for a mutuality of equals.

Silence exposes other problems of communication. In Carol Gilligan's view, women's sense of moral values is directly related to hearing the other person's point of view, linking together attention and perception. The failure to listen to another and to respond to another indicates detachment; girls perceive those who do not listen as not caring, and the experience is described in terms of the loss of voice: "When others did not listen and seemed not to care, they spoke of 'coming up against a brick wall.' The image of a wall had as its counterpart the search for the opening through which one could speak" (150). Part of that search was for a way to maintain connection even through the silences of isolation and separation. Belenky et al. also state, however, that the "act of creation ushers in a whole new view of one's creative capacities" (35). Indeed, it is after Psyche becomes pregnant that she listens to – hears – the voices of her sisters, and this listening/hearing precipitates the confrontation with Eros (289).

Significant, too, is the fact that the conflict with Eros and the instigation of the sisters centre not only on Psyche's relationship with her sisters but also on Psyche's curiosity and that of her sisters. Psyche is, in effect, forbidden to be curious about the identity of her husband; she is allowed only a "blind" carnal knowledge. The sisters tell her to use a lamp to uncover his identity, to satisfy her own as well as their curiosity, and to use a razor to ensure her own safety if necessary. When Psyche does equip herself in this way after Eros has fallen asleep, the lamp and razor respond in ways that confirm Psyche's safety with this husband: "At the sight of him even the light of the lamp quickened in joy and the razor repented of its sacrilegious sharpness" (291).

The lamp in its "goldenness" and the razor less directly in its "double edged" nature (like the Old European goddess's double-sided axe) may be credited as representations of Aphrodite's power, but these implements also signify the specifically cognitive abilities of perception and judgment. The experiential, intellectual, and body-centred nature of Psyche's awareness or comprehension of Eros is made clear by the symbolism Barbara Walker attributes to these tools. She refers to the lamp as "an almost universal symbol of enlightenment," and she identifies "light in darkness" as meaning creation or birth and as symbolizing mystical enlightenment through sexual experience – through carnal/body knowledge. The razor she defines as "the cutting edge," a "universal standard of sharpness," and "the keenness of female judgment" (*Dictionary*, 143, 151). This "razor" judgment implies the mental actions of careful separation – dissecting, analysing, scrutinizing, inspecting, observing – and close, "scientific" attention to detail.[1]

Even though designated by the sisters as a useful weapon, the razor is not used on Eros. The lamp enables judgment, and safety renders

the knife-as-weapon unnecessary. Whether his fear of beheading –
castration – is real or not, she does not attack him. Together these
tools may be said to represent her intellectual potential for perception
– her in-sight, reasoning, and understanding; they represent an embodied learning that relies on sense experience and intellectual judgment.
Marina Warner remarks on this central narrative concern in the variants in the Beauty and the Beast fairy tale: "women ... contest fear;
they turn their eye on the phantasm of the male Other and recognize
it, either rendering it transparent and safe, the self reflected as good,
or ridding themselves of it (him) by destruction or transformation"
(276).

Psyche Pricks Her Thumb

As Psyche is satisfying her curiosity about the nature of her husband
and his weapons, she pricks her thumb on one of his arrows. While
others have suggested that this represents a "second defloration" (Neumann, 64; Ulanov, 221), I submit that it enacts the moment when
Psyche actively chooses to love. Although the arrow's prick implies the
male role in heterosexual intercourse as well as love's eye beam, in this
instance it represents an aspect of Psyche's own more cognitively based
experience. What is marked by her action is the element of choice, the
moment when choice enters into love relationships. After Psyche sees
Eros for the first time, she tests the acuteness of her vision by touching
her thumb to the arrow point. At this moment, when love becomes
reasoned choice as well as paradisal erotic enjoyment, judgment is
added to love. This is, likewise, the moment when the lover recognizes
the profound and even irreconcilable differences between self and other
that exist outside of gender difference.

The thumb is defined as an "opposable digit," one that can move
next to or together with the fingers to grasp or hold on to objects. This
ability is also metaphoric: it signals a specific human capacity to hold
on, to hold hands and be together side by side. That Psyche pricks "the
tip of her thumb" reinforces her personal apprehension of care and
responsibility. Symbolically, according to Walker's *Encyclopedia*, the
thumb represents the soul, and as "the innermost Self, dwells forever
in the heart of all things" (997). Such symbolic connotations confirm
a self-directed, experiential, and embodied knowing and highlight the
agency suggested by Apuleius's diction: "She drew one of the arrows
from the quiver and tested the point against the tip of her thumb."
That Psyche "drew out" and "tested" accentuates the contradiction in
the narrator's next observation: "Thus *without knowing it* Psyche *of
her own accord* fell in love with Love" (293; emphasis added).

Walker's designation of the symbolic meaning of the four fingers, conversely, helps to clarify what Psyche does not choose (*Dictionary*, 310, 315). Psyche does not prick the index finger of spells and pointing, which might indicate that she is a witch of either patriarchal or matrilineal defining. She does not prick the phallic middle finger of derision, which might imply that she was taking over from Eros his role or responsibilities and, in effect, illustrating the wish to castrate him. Nor does she prick the ring finger of unions and love, which would emphasize the marriage and the union with Eros as more important than her own life journey. Certainly she does not prick the "pinky" of ineffectuality and thus denigrate her own decision to look at love.

The pricking causes the eruption of tiny drops of blood, a metaphor of life itself, of kinship bonding, and especially of female physicality. Walker also relates blood to female wisdom (*Dictionary*, 299–300). Here, Psyche's pricking her thumb is particularly appropriate. That she draws her own blood from the thumb reaffirms that Psyche has moved through sexual maturity, sexual experience and gratification, towards personal choice. Her experience of love has grown from passion's embrace of body and emotion to include reason's choice, a preference governed by an adult awareness of difference and responsibility. Love becomes agency and is self-chosen; no longer is it compelled by a patriarchal transfer of her body from father to husband. Psyche's choosing to love is a willed, reasoned, sexual, emotional, and passionate choice.

The Taboo

The question of what else is being forbidden remains. Even patriarchal kingdoms want women to be loving, and women who love voluntarily would be more amenable than those coerced. Hence, in the interdiction, there remains something beyond the obvious. Psyche must not look at or see Eros, male love; she may experience him/it only in darkness. When she does see him, Eros is sleeping, defenceless, vulnerable; he is not active, in control, erect. What Psyche is forbidden is to place Eros as object in a passive or feminine position.

A taboo against the explicit depiction of the male (or male genitalia) as love object persists to the present.[2] Rosemary Betterton has identified the power issues that coexist with the eroticization of sight: men have not been eroticized as objects for women's benefit, and women have not been encouraged in the subjectivity of their own experience. This is part of the androcentric taboo that Psyche's look has broken, the "mystery" of the phallus that exists to obscure the actual genitalia, the actual male being. Such a look is dangerous (to male hegemony) because women tend to see the individuality of their male models.

In her examination of the issues affecting women's art practice and criticism, Cassandra Langer describes the censorship applied to women who paint male nudes. Writing of Sylvia Sleigh's male nudes, Langer notes the change from the depiction of "beautiful blanks" when male painters eroticize women to depictions of individualized "self-possessed and sexy male[s]" when women eroticize men. The response is revealing: "The irate male audience is particularly sensitive to the change in position from vertical to horizontal, from superior to object." Contrasting the response of "this same moral male hierarchy" to "the objectification of wombs, vaginas, and breasts by men as perfectly acceptable works of art," Langer continues by noting a paradox: "these same art lovers are capable of censoring the work of women artists who have the unmitigated audacity to use male anatomy in a similar fashion" (120). When we are made aware of the frailties, individual characteristics, and weaknesses of the de-idealized male, men are no longer Man and universally powerful. The act of the female looking at the male body challenges the authority in who has the right to look and reveals the (culturally veiled and suppressed) human frailty of individual men. Either way, men are not valorized, and they lose the right to an unquestioned authority – that only their experiences, knowledge, and vision is truth. This upending of an author-ized and male-defined social structure is what Psyche's action portends. She loves an equal as an equal and now experiences her own desire for him: "Then more and more enflamed with desire for [Eros] she leaned over him, panting desperately for him" (293).

This satisfaction of curiosity has led to new desire. Describing this growth, James Hillman interprets the "awakening of the sleeping soul" as psychic development and sees the entire Psyche myth as offering a pattern of creativity, a "mystery text of transformation" (56). Hillman also tells us that present in the awakening of sleeping Eros through soul, in the "interplay of eros and psyche," is a ritual "between people and within each person" (59). This he describes as a doubled form: within the psyche and "between the human and the divine" (60). Rather than conflating one of the "people" with the divine, I prefer to see the metaphors of psychological growth take a triple form: one in the form of relationship between, between human and divine (Aphrodite); and the other two taking the form of relationships within, within the human couple represented in Eros and Psyche.

Hillman further links the creative spirit to genetic and masculine sexuality: "Eros has particular mythical connections with Phanes, the light-bringer; with Hermes, the male communicator; with Priapus, the phallic incarnation; with Pan, the male force of nature; with Dionysus, indestructible living energy" (65–6). By this reasoning, he goes on to say that access to creativity is more natural for men: "For a woman it requires an addition to her female identity; she has to bring it out of herself, give birth to it." This "masculine Eros of the creative principle" is a transcendent "upward" motion away from the earth: "Therefore we find in eros literature the recurrent symbols of the fallen sparks, the ladder, the ascending fire, the wings, the Olympian goal of immortality" (83). What Hillman highlights is not only the strength of the taboo that Psyche has broken but also the way that interpretations have encoded male sexuality to obscure the possibility of female creativity and, in this story specifically, of Psyche's experience. Women's intellectual creativity has been conflated with physical pregnancy. Rejecting her, Eros "straightaway flew up from the hugs and kisses" (293). Psyche clings for a time to his right leg, but "exhausted fell to the ground" (295). Within this configuration, earthbound Psyche cannot hold a place.

The Grounded Journey

Psyche's transformation has its mystic qualities, but it is, at the same time, human and earthbound. (Even paradisal experience brought "constant habituation" and knowledge of her own and another's body.) Throughout her experiences, the betrayals and tasks, she is depicted as walking. Hers is a journey in time, grounded – with the significant exception of its conclusion in marriage and ascendance to immortality. This is a kind of time that Julia Kristeva refers to as "project, teleology, linear and prospective unfolding: time as departure, progression and arrival." Kristeva writes that it is the "time of history" and "of language" and "of that enunciation – death" (192). In her argument, Kristeva is pointing out that this description of time is less associated with female life, but here, the narrative structure places Psyche fully within it.

Psyche makes her way on foot. If hers is a soul's journey, it is also conducted on the soles of her feet and is solitary. In the connection of soul and sole, Nor Hall says that soul-feet are the way through which we enact "the interrelationship between human beings and green-life, rock-life, animal-life and planet-life" (166). Walker adds that "stones dedicated to Isis and [Aphrodite] were marked with footprints, meaning 'I have been here'" (*Dictionary*, 309). Footsteps mark a moment-by-moment measurement of time, a linear and incremental timekeeping, a logical and even "scientific" time measurement. Footsteps suggest destination and the possibility of an ending, a goal, death.

Psyche learns to track this time's passage in a path already marked by Aphrodite.

Learning as Listening

Psyche's rejection by Eros emphasizes the focus on learning acquired through listening and illustrates what *Ways* designates as received knowledge: "women in this position listen to others for directions as well as for information" (40). Their ideas and ideals are dualistic and simplistically absolute and separate: "Paradox is inconceivable" (41). Belenky et al. also note that in such situations women do not see themselves as possessing authority or as being linked in any way with authority; authority is "they" (44). These women and Psyche do not understand that advice, too, may be weighed and evaluated.

In fact, following rejection by one authority, Eros, Psyche listens to and seems to accept the advice of another, Pan. For Psyche, there is no irony in Pan's description of Eros as the "greatest of the gods" and a "soft hearted youth." Eros has not been especially soft-hearted in his rejection of Psyche, and in his rage against the sisters, retribution, not forgiveness, follows from his wound. Neither is Eros, precisely speaking, the greatest of the gods; he inspires fear of a different sort – the fear of one's own innermost desires unleashed.

Psyche turns next to the goddesses, Demeter and Hera, who firmly and politely refuse to assist her because Aphrodite "is making an intense investigation to track you down" (315). Psyche's inability to interpret Pan's advice, to see the truth concealed behind his words, her deference to others (her father, her sisters, Eros, the goddesses) and her failures of judgment identify her as a received knower.

The received knower assumes that by empowering others, she, herself, may gain what she wants because these others will take care of her (*Ways,* 47). At the same time and like the women interviewed in *Ways,* Psyche's behaviour implies her understanding "that she must begin to listen to her own voice if she is to become clear and confident and to move on in her life" (*Ways,* 51). By her own decision and in her own best interests, Psyche turns to Aphrodite and accepts her as mistress and mentor.

Subjective Knowing

In just such a manner, the third "way of knowing" indicates a shift from seeing the source of truth as residing in an external authority to seeing its source by way of an "inner voice and infallible gut" of intuition (*Ways,* 54). Although there are still "right" answers, an inner source of certainty guides the growth of self-confidence and presupposes the growth of judgment. For women, this shift to subjective knowing arises out of an awareness of "*failed* male authority. Society teaches women to put their trust in men as defenders, suppliers of the economic necessities, interpreters of the public will, and liaisons with the larger community"; because there is an absence of "stable male authority," the "sense of disappointment and outrage" is "pervasive" (*Ways*, 57–8).

Keeping this in mind, it is possible to interpret Pan and Eros as representing failed male authority, representatives who remind us of the father and priest who similarly failed to protect her. Psyche's suicide attempts can be regarded as reactions to this loss of support from an all-powerful external authority and as reactions to a pervasive psyche-shattering disappointment. Women who are subjective knowers are characterized by a distrust of "logic, analysis, abstraction, and even language" and in addition lack "grounding in a secure, integrated, and enduring self concept" (*Ways* 71, 81). Psyche's acquiescence in being "sacrificed" following her father's "betrayal" and the suicide attempts following Eros's defection and Pan's advice all accurately reflect such a lack of self-esteem.

This absence of a firm self-concept has, at the same time, a positive aspect: an openness to growth, a desire for change. Such women use "the imagery of birth, rebirth and childhood to describe the experience of a nascent self" (*Ways*, 82). Psyche is pregnant and so portrays this "nascent self" powerfully. Watching and listening continue as important learning tools, but such women now begin to make comparisons, learning from others' experiences as well as their own (*Ways*, 84).

In her first task, Psyche reproduces the movement from the perceptions and understandings of the received knower towards the tasks of the subjective knower. Confronted with a "motley mass of seeds," she is instructed by Aphrodite to "put each grain properly in its pile" (329). The seeds can be read as facts, as received "grains" of knowledge and information; they do not need translation or interpretation; they need sorting, categorization. As noted earlier, the seeds may depict, literally, the content of agricultural and herbal lore necessary to the provision of food and naturopathic medicines. Metaphorically, the process of sorting allows Psyche to know herself capable of recognizing differences in type, of making comparisons, and of organizing similarities and differences categorically; she discriminates and classifies.

In the sorting, Psyche's helpers are ants. According to Erich Neumann, ants are "symbols of the instinct world" or the "vegetative" nervous system (95); to Robert A. Johnson, they are servants of Eros (48); to Mary Anne Ferguson, they are "the cooperation of natural forces" (61); to Christine Downing, they are "siblings in their helpful aspect" (*Sisters*, 50). Bringing all these views together, I see the ants as epitomizing Psyche's own intuitive powers, continuing the sisters' influence, and recalling the power of the natural world and sexual pleasure. Psyche brings intuitive, sensory, and affective awareness together with the cognitive aspects of previous events to confront this new task. As instincts, as servants, as helpful siblings, the ants re-enforce Psyche's ownership of all the abilities needed to guarantee successful completion of the task.

Procedural Reasoning

The second task set by Aphrodite enlarges on the capabilities of the first by introducing a greater complexity. Aphrodite tells Psyche, "Pro-cure a hank of ... fleece of precious wool in any way [you] please, and bring it to me at once" (333). The fleece is from "[s]heep whose fleeces shine with the pure hue of gold" (333). Upon hearing the task, Psyche again attempts suicide but is prevented by the "green reed," who advises, "Do not approach these fearsome wild sheep at this time of day, when they borrow heat from the burning sun and often break out in fierce madness ... But until the afternoon allays the sun's heat ... you can hide ... And then ... if you shake the foliage in the adjacent woods, you will find some of the woolly gold" (333). Attending to advice direct from the natural world, Psyche is successful: "Once she had been carefully instructed she never faltered or had reason to regret obeying" (335).

Procedural knowing, the fourth category according to *Ways*, arises out of the perception of conflict (the confrontation with "fearsome sheep") and through meeting authorities that are benign and knowl-edgable (as in Psyche's "green and gentle reed"). Also, Aphrodite by her associations, in her words and actions, is both benign and knowl-edgable as well as confrontational and exacting; by setting the tasks, she has provided the opportunities and the helpers that allow Psyche to recognize her own power and knowledge and to expand her self-knowledge. This second task and category emphasize the acquisition of more complex procedures, skills, and techniques. Psyche has exer-cised reason in interpreting the "kind and simple reed"; she does not need others to decipher this advice for her; and she collects the fleece successfully because she pays attention to the language of the natural world itself.

As symbol, the fleece is variously called "male solar spirit" (Neu-mann, 101), masculine power and courage (Johnson, 54), and female "sexual power ... the recognition of potency" (DuPlessis, "Psyche," 86). There are, however, other interpretations that fit more easily into this examination of women's learning experience. Marija Gimbutas tells us that sheep were sacred to the Bird Goddess, as well as being a food source in Neolithic settlements, and that the Bird Goddess was associated with spinning and weaving (75, 67). She also notes that the Bird Goddess was the precursor of Aphrodite, Hera and Isis (318). Nor Hall makes a more direct link with the goddess, the sheep, and knowledge: "Delphi means 'womb.' A small herd of mountain goats discovered the womblike cleft in the earth that later became the Delphic temple site" (177). Although in the divisions of labour of the classical goddesses, Athena bestowed the gifts of weaving, in Elizabeth Wayland Barber's account of the history of women's work, we are given information that links attitudes towards Aphrodite as a goddess of procreation with the craft of spinning. Barber describes how the remaining musculature of the famous and ancient armless Greek statue of (Aphrodite) Venus de Milo in the Louvre suggests that the goddess is actually spinning thread (236–8). The sexual/reproductive goddess who is spinning, making thread magically, is likened to the pregnant woman who creates a child also as if by magic. Moreover, this associates Psyche with the Three Fates, the spinners of life and death, "aspects of the archaic Triple Aphrodite" (Walker, *Dictionary,* 302) whom she will meet in the fourth task. In this manner, then, Psyche is indeed Aphrodite's initiate, and the collecting of fleece may be interpreted as a preliminary chore to spinning and appropriate to her pregnant condition.

As prelude and companion task to carding, spinning, and weaving, the gathering of fleece implies these traditional and domestic female crafts. If, as Hillman notes, creativity involves an ordering process, then here, gathering fleece, carding, and spinning are both process and metaphor, representing images for creativity as well as problem solving. In just this way, again according to Hillman, Psyche reasons: "while eros burns, psyche figures out, does its duties, depressed" (94). (Certainly, there is much in traditional female responsibilities to learn or "figure out.") Gathering, carding, spinning, and weaving all imply those important systems of order, pattern, and procedure that are similar to theoretical and even "logical" thought.

Like the learning entailed in the provision of food and medicines symbolized by the first task, the supply and maintenance of clothing and household furnishings continue through time as a designated and endless female obligation and duty. Through the collection of the skeins of "woolly fleece" and (by implication and projection) through the carding and spinning of threads and finally to the weaving of patterned cloth, this image of collecting strands of fleece grounds a reading that suggests that Psyche has moved into procedural knowing.

Procedural knowledge comprehends the world as increasingly complicated; it integrates or synthesizes objectivity with subjective experience and circumstance and emphasizes attending to, and waiting for, meaning that emerges from the object rather than from the self alone. Such an understanding consists of the ability to fore-see, to see ahead, to plan out and forward. Likewise, in procedural knowing the resolution of conflict does not involve violence and aggression but hinges on the acquisition of techniques for conflict resolution/avoidance. That Psyche must postpone until evening the gathering of the strands of golden fleece indicates the importance of judging context and the significance of foresight, forbearance, and the ability to wait.

Connected Knowing

As Belenky et al. describe it, procedural knowledge may be of two forms: separate and connected. Separate knowing is measured in knowledge itself, is based on "impersonal procedures for establishing truth," and is most at ease in doubt and distance. Connected knowing is measured in understanding, is based on "truth emerg[ing] through care," and begins with belief and compassion (102). Psyche's experiences, her desires for connection and reconnection to her family and to Eros, her submission to Aphrodite, and her trust in and reliance on helpers strongly suggest that her learning takes the connected form.

Psyche's second task also involves a particular and "connected" perception of time. This time sense is one that is integral to housekeeping and empathy (a seeing out into, a seeing within), forbearance and waiting. In *The Sacred and the Feminine,* Kathryn Allen Rabuzzi characterizes this kind of time as mythic, experiential, and subjective, and "radically at odds with the more accepted time patterns of Western culture. Though we know better, we often act as though linear, quantifiable time (associated with masculine questing) were given in nature" (145). In traditional cultures and agricultural societies, time is seasonal, but this time sense can be directly linked to housekeeping chores that "are so obviously circular that their completion can scarcely be experienced" (149). Similarly, Kristeva joins together "*repetition* and *eternity*" in their perceived closeness to female life; these are perceived as cycles, gestation, recurring biological rhythms in a kind of cosmic time (191). Psyche's tasks enact this second seasonal time sense, which is present in the natural and domestic worlds.

As I understand it, however, this time sense is more cyclic than circular; it is open-ended. In this way, there is a sense of returning to the same chore or season, but passing time means that difference is accounted for and included. To be accurate, the image must contain the idea of return-with-a-difference. There is not the stop/ending of an implied return. Mary O'Brien extends the relationship between temporal or seasonal consciousness and gendered reproductive consciousness to emphasize movement or flow: "Female temporal consciousness is continuous" (32). Psyche, waiting to collect the fleece and then gathering it, encodes a second time sense as well as connected procedural knowledge.

This inclusion of difference into the cyclical round introduces the possibility of looking backward; memory links sense experience, time, and awareness or consciousness. Knowledge is transformed into memory; remembered experience into understanding. The process is akin to Psyche's first task, the sorting of seeds, but enlarges its significance.

Self-Constructed Knowledge

Psyche's third task, collecting water in a crystal jar, presents not only a concise symbolic representation of an experiential view of consciousness and time, but adds a movement outward into a more personal and self-constructed knowledge and understanding. For women, self-constructed knowledge promotes the integration of (paradoxical) opposites and dualities. *Ways* describes this as a healing of the split between emotion and intellect (179), a healing that takes place in a "connected" mode (186). Aphrodite sets the third task as a test of Psyche's "courageous spirit and singular intelligence" (335). Although "singular intelligence" denotes Psyche's own uniqueness, what the task also involves is the recovery of connections lost through dualistic thinking – what Mary O'Brien calls a "male-stream" thinking that she conjectures may be linked to the "gap" in male reproductive consciousness (34).

In this third task, Aphrodite gives Psyche a list of clear but complicated instructions. "Do you see that steep mountain-peak standing above the towering cliff?" asks Aphrodite. She goes on to tell Psyche: "Dark waves flow down from a black spring on that peak and are enclosed by the reservoir formed by the valley nearby, to water the swamps of Styx and feed the rasping current of Cocytus. Draw me some of the freezing liquid from there, from the innermost bubbling at the top of the spring, and bring it to me quickly in this phial." Then, "she handed her a small vessel hewn out of quartz" (335).

Confronted with the enormity of the task, faced with the dangerous snakes lining the streams and preventing her ascent to the peak, Psyche is "transformed to stone" (337), returned again to stasis and silence.

At this point, she is aided by the "royal bird" of Zeus, "the rapacious eagle," who takes the phial, "alleging [to the spring] that he was making his petition at [Aphrodite's] orders and acting as her agent" (339). The bird links together god and goddess, Zeus and Aphrodite: it belongs to Zeus and to Aphrodite, whose precursor, as Gimbutus tells us, was the Bird Goddess. (Perhaps it is even a Golden Eagle.) The eagle fills the vessel and returns it to Psyche, who then carries it to Aphrodite. In symbol (object) and metaphor (process) these elements define the "intellectual" nature of the task and the many other levels of female experience to which the task applies.

The water provides a profound image of connection and of connected knowing. Both Neumann and Johnson see this image as symbolizing the water of life; both Gimbutus and Walker describe the goddess's nature as being water-like. In addition, springs, birds, and snakes are associated with goddess shrines. In *The Woman's Dictionary*, Walker sees water as a metaphor for spirit and the unconscious, for fertility, creativity, rebirth, and baptism. Water is also life sustaining and suggests maternal nurturance: "The Goddess was shown holding either her own breasts or a jar with two streams" (357). If we remember that the Psyche who embarks on this transformational learning journey is pregnant and if we link these accumulated meanings of water symbolism to Walker's analysis of mountain symbolism, then the association is made particularly powerful: "The oldest deity in Greece was the Divine Mountain Mother ... called ... Deep-Breasted One ... The idea of universal breast milk flowing down from mountain peaks was common to both East and West" (346). The vital nature of the task might require not only the ability to contain water in a jar and life in the womb but also the ability to sustain life with breast milk subsequent to birth. Thus, the water and the task are female and feminine, doubly goddess inspired.

Gimbutus emphasizes the curative sacredness of water, links it to the Bird Goddess, and describes it as "Living Water which imparts strength, heals the sick, rejuvenates the old, restores sight, and reassembles dismembered bodies and brings them back to life" (43). On a more general though equally fundamental level, this third task recalls traditional women's tasks of nursing the sick, of healing and medicine. The care givers in the family and community were then primarily, and continue now to be, women. Furthermore, Sarah B. Pomeroy remarks the similarities between the ritual cleansing of the corpse and the care of infants: "the cycle of life takes us from the care of women and returns us to the care of women" (44). This imagery further sustains the connections and empathetic responses characteristic of connected knowing.

In Psyche's task, water/milk from the spring is to be contained in a small vessel. In his interpretation, Johnson remarks on the quantity contained: "a little of a quality, experienced in high consciousness is sufficient for us ... [W]e may see the world in a grain of sand" (62). The crystal container, Johnson describes as "very fragile and very precious" like the ego (62). Johnson also interprets this task as an admonition to women "to approach the vastness of life's responsibilities in a more orderly manner, to do one thing, take one crystal goblet at a time, concentrate on it, and do it well" (63). According to Neumann, Psyche's task is to function "as feminine vessel"; she is "a vessel of individuation" and a "mandala-urn" who gives "a configured unity" to "the flowing energy of life"(103). Here, both interpretations suggest Psyche's ability to give form to, to construct and take responsibility for, her own understanding.

Linking Polarities

Neumann recognizes that "the essential feature of this spring is that it unites the highest and lowest" (103), and consequently, the spring itself may be described as continuously bringing together these polarities (in a continuum). According to Neumann, the stream is "male generative" and "the paternal uroborus" and hence with this symbolism the vessel and water conjoin the dualities of masculine and feminine, male and female, as well as high and low. Indeed, with his interpretation of the eagle as a "masculine spirit aspect," Neumann sees this task as an integration of opposites: "The eagle holding the vessel profoundly symbolizes the already male-female spirituality of Psyche, who in one act 'receives' like a woman, that is, gathers like a vessel and conceives, but at the same time apprehends and knows like a man" (105). Neumann ties this to Psyche's earthbound nature: "Because Psyche is born of the earth, she can only receive and give form to a part of the infinite that is within her reach, but this precisely is what befits her and makes her human" (106). Neumann notes that this development, too, is double, but the doubled nature involves an accompanying increase: "This is the surprising thing about Psyche's development: it is a development *toward* consciousness that is accompanied throughout *by* consciousness" (106). Because this "duality" proceeds incrementally, however, it exceeds the idea of a "closed" binary union; it is the both/and, two/one. The "duality" becomes three and includes the continuum between.

The task transforms other dualities by the addition of object and process. The water is called "dark" and "black" (335). The container is of crystal or quartz, which was believed by the ancient Greeks to be "petrified ice" and suggests clarity and lightness (Walker, *Dictionary,* 508, 519). Of the eagle, Psyche's helper, Walker says that it "is traditionally associated with lightning, fire, and the sun as well as the hero who, like Prometheus, brought down fire from heaven for the benefit of humanity" (401). Thus, "black" water in a "petrified ice" container is carried by (golden Aphrodite's) bird of light, sun, and fire. In contrast to the Promethean theft, here the components are Psyche (human consciousness) and the dark waters (the unknown) brought by the eagle at the behest of the goddess Aphrodite. The eagle carries the water down from the mountain top where it had surfaced from deep in the earth's core, the source of the spring. The liquid stream contained by ice, the crystal container, is carried by fire, the eagle, and is "doubly" triple in temperature and substance.

The polarities are brought together and carried onward through space and time. The continuum between perceived opposites, the movement between and through the polarities, occurs with an accompanying growth. From a "spring," the water "flows down" to the underworld river, Cocytus; from earth's centre it flows up to the mountain top and down to the underworld again. Thus, lowest through highest becomes lowest again. Suggesting the triplicities in the nature of the goddess, the movement is not only through life to death and rebirth but reveals the goddess as life giving, life sustaining, and life destroying.

Ways comments that, analogous to this symbolism of Psyche's third task, women at the level of constructed knowledge integrate the dualities of subjective and objective knowledge, intuition and analysis, structure and procedure. The basic insight of this stage is an understanding that "[a]ll knowledge is constructed, and the knower is an intimate part of the known" (*Ways,* 137). Accomplishing her third task, Psyche is able to accept responsibility for her own knowledge – containing it; similarly, she becomes a passionate knower by joining – empathizing and connecting – with that which is to be known. With this containment of her own knowledge, with her "in-sight" or sight into all the connections of life, Psyche is prepared for her final task. As Robert Johnson observes: "A woman may not undertake the fourth task unless she has first gathered all the necessary strength from the first three" (65). Here, the task is an image of how women abandon either/or dualistic thinking, accept ambiguity, contradiction, and difference as inherent in life and human relationships, and recognize the full complexity of human life.

Choosing Insight

In the fourth task, Psyche encounters the second injunction against seeing. She is warned by the tower "not to open or look into the jar that you will be carrying, and in fact do not even think too inquisitively about the hidden treasure of divine beauty" (347). Recalling Johnson's description of the tower as "a construct, a convention, a set of rules, a tradition, a system" (65), I suggest that it represents Psyche's assimilation of a framework of values and knowledge.

Psyche pays heed and successfully completes her descent journey, but then she decides to "take out a tiny drop of [beauty] for myself." Her next observation, that this ointment "might *even* enable me to please my beautiful lover" (emphasis added), clearly indicates that pleasing her lover is not the primary consideration; rather, it is more of a beneficial side effect. Psyche opens the container, "but there was nothing there, not a drop of beauty, just sleep – deathlike and truly Stygian sleep. Revealed when the cover was removed, it attacked her instantly, enveloping her entire body in a dense cloud of slumber" (349).

The descent moves Psyche between the dualities and polarities of Persephone/death and Aphrodite/life and between being awake in the underworld and falling into deathlike sleep in the upper world. In processing these opposites and bringing them together within a psyche, Psyche creates an epistemology that defies polarities and dichotomized reasoning. As pregnant mortal woman, asleep above ground and awake below, Psyche symbolizes contradiction and the "paradoxical" facts of life: increase, nurturance, birth, and death exist beyond opposition. She gains an insight into the mysteries of life.

In her trance, Psyche experiences a third time sense – here, time is the timelessness that is a recognized part of creativity.[3] Like the creative process, this sense of time exists outside of measurement and quantification. This time sense, described by Betty Edwards in *Drawing on the Right Side of the Brain*, accompanies the "slightly altered state of consciousness of feeling transported" that is part of the experience of "any kind of art work" (4). Comparing the state to daydreaming, Edwards grants that it accompanies many other activities, such as jogging, needlework, or listening to music. What she further emphasizes is that we can set up these shifts and move into them to gain "access at a conscious level to ... inventive, intuitive, imaginative powers that have been largely untapped by our verbal, technological culture and educational system" (5). Realizing that this powerful problem-solving ability is unrecognized in much of Western educational practice, she notes that this trance-like space is where we develop an "ability to perceive things freshly and in their totality, to see underlying patterns and possibilities for new combinations." Creative problem solving "will be accessible through new modes of thinking" (5–6).

At the same time, because of the way that Apuleius has structured the events following Psyche's deathlike sleep, her trance might seem to be a punishment for disobeying the injunction against seeing. Her trance is something from which she must be wakened and rescued by Eros: "'See,' he said, 'you almost destroyed yourself again, poor girl, by your insatiable curiosity'" (349). Eros then seeks "to win support for his case" from Zeus, and Psyche's journey is taken over by Eros and by Zeus (351). She is returned to inactivity, and on a very elemental level, this has the appearance of punishment. According to Annis Pratt, women's descent or rebirth journeys "create transformed, androgynous, and powerful human personalities out of socially devalued beings and are therefore more likely to involve denouements punishing the quester for succeeding in her perilous, revolutionary journey" (142). In an epistemology that structures understanding in duality and opposition, in Western scientific and technological attitudes, and in the binary oppositions of Greek myth, transformations like Psyche's are unacceptable and must necessarily be subsumed and reabsorbed.

To emphasize the importance of this suppression in this world order, and unlike the injunction against supping in the underworld, Psyche's wedding in "heaven's summit" is sumptuous. She drinks ambrosia and is given "a rich wedding banquet" where all the gods attend and serve. And here we observe who is said to dance and what the tune: "[Aphrodite] danced gorgeously, stepping to the tune of the lovely music ... Thus in *proper* form Psyche *was given* in marriage to [Eros]" (355, emphasis added).

Shamanism

In the context of the learning journey, however, there is a more positive way to interpret the trance and understand the failure and passivity that follow it. By restoring the goddess as mentor, the locus of the understanding of the learning that she elicits in Psyche is extended. As goddess, Aphrodite's presence suggests that learning encompasses a spirituality within the natural world. Beyond what the twentieth-century Eurocentric tradition perceives as an education only of the intellect and beyond a view of spirituality as something only existing separate from nature, Psyche represents a more ancient pattern. In his advice about mentoring, Laurent A. Daloz notes that "both education and religion are centrally about growth of the spirit, and it is no accident that in less specialized societies healers, teachers, and priests are often the same person" (104). Teacher, healer, and priest work a similar soul transformation simultaneously. The journeys in life and in nature do not supersede each other; they coexist. As Mary Anne Ferguson observes, Psyche gains "competence and confidence both in the world and in herself" as she "symbolically encounters the full reality of the world – earth, water, sky, and finally underworld" (61).

Psyche's journey not only conjoins many learning journeys but also provides a window, back through Apuleius, into a more ancient heritage. In Apuleius's rendering, Psyche's ancient knowledge is subsumed and obscured by patriarchal culture and religion. By deciphering Psyche's journey as a shamanic initiation and quest, we gain a way of encoding the transformations of her tasks into both a personal empowerment and the possibility of a social empowerment that she may once have returned to her society, but which she cannot yet return to our own.

If Psyche is a shaman, then her "trance" is in itself the sign of her power. Only those who are not familiar with the inner experience would see the outer manifestation as deathlike sleep. Michael Harner describes the shaman as "a man or woman who enters an altered state of consciousness – at will – to contact and utilize an ordinarily hidden reality in order to acquire knowledge, power and to help other persons" (25). In his classic study of shamanism, Mircea Eliade especially emphasizes the significance of this deathlike sleep. He calls shamanism "one of the archaic techniques of ecstasy – at once mysticism, magic and 'religion' in the broadest sense of the word" (xix). It is during this ecstasy or trance that the shaman is able to ascend to the sky or descend to the underworld, to communicate with spirits or "nature spirits." The shaman, a "great specialist in the human soul," serves as a mediator who accesses kinds of information not readily available in everyday life and uses it to bring healing (8).

In Psyche's sacrifice and betrayal are encoded the ways of becoming a shaman. Eliade states that, together with what is termed "the call," shamans are "chosen" by heredity and the will of, or choice by, the clan. Psyche is a princess and therefore could be said to "inherit" her role as shaman; she is worshipped by her society and so "chosen" by the clan; the oracle has confirmed this choice with a "call."[4] The characteristics of shamanic initiation include "ascent" and "descent" to talk with spirits above and below and the revelation of professional secrets. The marriage of death, her experience of paradise, the tasks, and her ability to talk with the gods, all mark Psyche's journey as shamanic and the opening of the flask as the gift of "professional" secrets.

The final ascent and marriage bring what in other initiation journeys is called a representation of the metaphysical truth: "those who
know have wings" (Eliade, 479). Having wings marks Psyche as an
initiate of the ancient Bird Goddess. Further, supporting a view of
these shamanistic attributes, Eliade records that the Indo-European
variant for women who become "shamanesses" is a dream of marriage
with an underworld spirit who visits her nightly and with whom she
bears a child (422–3). Finally, in her discussion of the shaman as
wounded healer, Joan Halifax reminds us that, if the path is "traversed
with 'an obedience to awareness'" (30), the simple attainment of old
age provides a life-span shamanic initiation.

Psyche's journey also reveals a quest pattern that Western culture
has in common with other ancient and non-European cultures. In his
analysis of the inner experience of power, David C. McClelland lists
the characteristics of such an empowerment quest: the messenger
voice, the spiritual trip, the divine helpers, the surrender to spiritual
authority, the dangers, the four gifts of power, and the four evidences
of a spiritually guided life.[5] Clearly present in the story of Psyche are
the oracle, the journey, the helpers, and the surrender to Aphrodite.
Her four tasks are roughly equivalent to what McClelland describes
as the four gifts of the vision quest. The first gift, healing, comes with
the first task and the herbal knowledge it bestows. The second gift,
wisdom and foreknowledge, comes with the strands of golden fleece;
the third gift, supernatural strength, is evidenced in obtaining the
water; and the fourth gift, compassion, is integral to Persephone's
realm and the descent journey.

By McClelland's definition, the vision quest ends with the return of
the shaman to heal the community; the quest, both a journey and
acquired knowledge, is undertaken for oneself *and* for the benefit of
other people. What is absent in Apuleius's version of Psyche's journey
is the evidence that she utilizes her gifts of power; instead, she seems
to take them with her to Olympus and does not return with the
knowledge to benefit her people. This, indeed, is the way that Marie-
Louise von Franz interprets the outcome of the myth: Psyche's ascen-
sion to Olympus means that the knowledge she has gained is not made
available to her society; the happy ending is "tragic" because it occurs
in the "Beyond," the unconscious (106). What the situation suggests
is that there is no place for the "wise woman" or her knowledge in
Western culture.

This kind of shamanic learning, however, might play an important
role in our society, and in discussing the way that technology can be
reconciled with our roots in the earth itself, John A. Grim supplies a
direction for utilizing Psyche's power. "Shamans are important reli-

gious personalities," argues Grim, "because of their unique ability to give symbolic meaning to the forces that animate the cosmology." Because they are able to identify themselves "with primordial earth processes, they establish for their tribes a particular religious consciousness which they continually reassert during difficult transitional times" (207). Insofar as Psyche is a shamanic figure, she can be said to represent such a spiritual reconnection in difficult times. A woman and liminal to androcentric society, she symbolizes a lost consciousness; she moves from being a silent icon at the centre of her society to being an outcast in the wilderness, and in this wilderness, she is a learner who achieves a resolution of opposites and an integrative wisdom.

Eros, Psyche, and N(arr)ativity

The previous analysis of the journey and tasks undertaken by Psyche illustrates how familiar comparisons and relationships may augment the interpretation of human knowledge. An analysis that finds in metaphor the processes and relationships of female life and female reproductive consciousness enables us to see that learning in Psyche's story can be shown to arise out of real physical and material bases. If storytelling is an exercise of metaphor, then narrative structure too may be employed to represent reproductive consciousness. We make sense of our lives by the ways in which we structure the stories about ourselves and our experience, even before we use imagery to enhance this narrative frame. Identifying the ways that the stories of Eros and Psyche differ in their narrative bones allows for a recognition of gendered consciousness. At the same time, this identification may encourage a transformed understanding of the universal experience of nativity. What begins in difference can be resolved by an understanding of what is shared.

Narrativity

In structuring his interpretation of the tale, Erich Neumann describes Apuleius's telling of the Eros and Psyche myth as a narrative that "falls into five parts – the introduction, the marriage of death, the act, the four tasks, the happy end" (57). Such a five-part arrangement is familiar to every literature student as exposition, rising action, climax, falling action, and conclusion (Abrams, 141). Commenting on the pattern of rising, flying, and falling in the myth of Icarus and relating it also to the myth of Narcissus, David C. McClelland refers to the whole configuration as the "Icarus complex." He regards this complex as exclusively male and as originating from an intense relationship with the mother. In his evaluation, "ascensionism is an expression of the power drive" and "shows us a person engaged in an extreme form of asserting his independence of earthly ties, narcissistically insisting on his autonomy" (194–5).

In folk tales, McClelland observes the occurrence cross-culturally of some key elements in this model: rising, falling, fire, emphasis on the visual (gaze, look, perceive, stare, watch) and less emphasis on other sensory experience (smell, hearing, touch) or on interpersonal relationships. Such a sequence of rising, flying, falling, he specifies as "pleasure-pain" and contrasts it with the female story sequence which he tags "crisis-release" or "crisis-pleasure." For the female, he suggests, "[t]he sequence is pain-pleasure, the reverse of the male pleasure-pain" (101).

To McClelland, the myth that epitomizes this female psychology is of Demeter and Persephone, wherein he sees two motifs: *women are the source of life* and *going without brings increase*. Going down under (Persephone's submission) or going without (Demeter's loss of her daughter) is followed by a return which produces fertility and joy" (97). The psychological pattern that he describes, that "the woman submits, is taken advantage of, and triumphs" (96), is the narrative pattern of the passive and feminine heroine (female) rescued by the active and masculine hero (male). This pattern of female experience is the kind to be found in male quest stories, and the situation affirms the primacy granted the male and masculine view of experience.

Certainly Psyche's rescue by Eros and her subsequent elevation to Olympus would seem to place the story within such a masculine category; in Neumann's five-part breakdown of the Psyche story, moreover, we see that the introduction, marriage of death, the act, the four tasks, and the happy end do indeed follow exposition, rising action, climax, falling action, and conclusion. This would seem better to exemplify male experience than, as Neumann seems to assert, to depict the feminine and, thereby, female behaviour. The narrative pattern makes Eros and his experience, the masculine, the centre of the story even though much of the tale is about Psyche's ordeals and her experience of him and her own erotic pleasure. Indeed, Neumann's interpretation of the tasks does make Eros their centre: "With each of her labors she apprehends – without knowing it – a new category of *his* reality" (107; emphasis added).

In her analysis of Apuleius's *Metamorphoses*, Marie-Louise von Franz appears to agree. She interprets the tale of Psyche as a story of masculine psychology, as a story of a particular man, Lucius, and his anima. Consequently, Psyche is perceived more as an element of male consciousness than as woman herself. Of the *Metamorphoses*, she comments: "It concerns in particular the problem of the *incarnation of the feminine principle*, and of its 'reconnaissance' in a patriarchal Christian universe" (4). Like McClelland, she connects a son's intense closeness to his mother with an equally intense desire for escape, for freedom. This freedom is found in "the intellect where generally she cannot follow." Von Franz calls this "the escape over the stratosphere: one leaves the earth ... where the old lady cannot reach, and one feels a man and free, but this naturally has a disadvantage ... as soon as he wants to touch the earth ... there the old lady stands" (19). As she sees it, such a search for freedom can be recognized in the Socratic detachment of emotion from reason and the Platonic and neo-Platonic detachment of the material, the real, from the ideal. In addition, man may transcend the human – escape the connection with the mother – by rising to the realm of the gods, above the earth, or descending to the sphere of animal life, beneath consciousness and the human realm. Thereby she associates both ascent and descent journeys, rising and falling, with male experience.

Narrativity and the Metaphor of Union

Von Franz sees the goal of the ascent journey as the integration of the anima, but in the use of the *hieros gamos* to symbolize this goal, she finds difficulties: joining "the divine, elating, transpersonal and freeing aspect of the *hieros gamos*, the sacred marriage motif, with the incompleteness and disappointing narrowness and dirt of human life, is still, one might say, one of the greatest unsolved problems" (88). She recognizes the continuing difficulty for Western philosophy inherent in resolving human life with the spiritual – the profane and the sacred – by a symbol of marriage, but my own concern is with the negative and dependent valuations that this equation and the marriage motif stamp on nature, on female life, and coincidentally on any analysis of the female (feminine) role in the narrative pattern. This valuation allows male and masculine beings to be both male "god" to woman and feminine "woman" to god – all the while maintaining the denigration of actual female life and the world of nature.

Focusing specifically on the relationship between marriage and narrative plots in prose fiction, Evelyn J. Hinz has used the concept of hierogamy to distinguish the kind of relationship found in romance from that which characterizes the novel. As she sees it, the novel employs a "wedlock" marriage plot and is concerned with the assimilation of the couple into the social sphere; in contrast, romance features a sacred marriage and links the union of the couple to the union of the elements, earth and sky – thereby serving to reconnect the individual to the cosmos. In effect, the sacred union leads to a rebirth and renewal of the cosmos. Referring to the myth of Psyche and Eros as the paradigm for romance, Hinz observes that in modern romance only the tonalities have changed; the idea of sacred marriage remains the same: "all that has happened is that the locus of the divine has shifted from "up there" to "down here" (907). What Hinz makes clear is that the idea of the union is foregrounded and that, however the opposites are characterized, wherever the union transpires, sexual union/marriage is the means whereby opposites and difference are narratively bridged.

As I see it and would point out, what characterizes both von Franz's observations of the thought structure inherent in Western philosophy and Hinz's commentary on prose plot developments is the recourse to polarities that necessitates the reconciliation by union: falling/rising, descent/ascent, down/up, dark/light, human/transpersonal, disappointing/elating, dirt/divine. According to Mary O'Brien, such dualistic patterns are tied directly to an eroticized, male-defined sexuality and to what she refers to as male reproductive consciousness. She describes this consciousness as having at its core the recognition of the gap between the male role in conception and the resulting birthed child. Because of this gap, men must mediate or understand their role intellectually by a creation of "intransigent dualism," and this is "a specifically masculine experience" (67).

O'Brien regards the creation of an intellectual tradition of male dominance and superiority as a means by which men may compensate for an absence from the totality of the reproductive cycle: "sexuality represents the male moment of inclusion in genetic continuity" (75). Simultaneously, this intellectual mediation of the male gap in human reproduction has been employed to secure for men an exclusivity of power. "The experiential moments of female consciousness, confirmed in actual labour," she writes, "are thus denigrated and dehumanized, given a low value while they are quite frankly imitated in a 'higher' sphere, the creation of concepts in a male intercourse of spirit and thought" (132). Through this mediation, men are able to find power and superiority in absence by assuming the (sole) right to give birth to ideas.

A dualistic view of the world conjoined to a rational system grounded in an intellectually mediated paternity would logically resolve dualities within a metaphor of union, with an emphasis on marriage, intercourse, and conception. According to O'Brien, "Men value the moment of sexuality for more than the immediacy of sexual gratification and the pleasures of copulation. It has symbolic value in social terms; it confirms an inclusion in genetic continuity and access to the double freedoms which the idea of paternity translates historically into forms of male dominant society" (191). In this sense then, the sacred marriage is an especially appropriate metaphor of male experience. Even if the object is the new birth, the *hieros gamos* is a masculine ending, as the focus is on the sacred marriage and conception to obscure the import of the female role in pregnancy, birthing, and child care: "We have no philosophy of birth" (O'Brien, 198).

In contrast to men's reproductive consciousness, according to O'Brien, women's awareness of their reproductive role is experiential, continuous, visceral, and mediated in the physical act of giving birth. Accordingly, while conception is equally the locus of female genetic contribution, menarche/menstruation is the initiating and ongoing female reproductive experience, and pregnancy, childbirth, and lactation are major components in species reproduction. None of these are, very obviously, equivalent metaphors of union.

Leaving pregnancy aside for the time being, we can see that birth and breast-feeding are clearly indicative of growth, separation, and at least a partial dis-union, and hence birth is a metaphor of *transformation* and of partial – though certainly dramatic – change within a continuing relationship. Furthermore, marriage as union can readily be and is traditionally imaged in a ring and as a circle, closed and complete, while birth may be likened to a circle opened. Here I call on McClelland again, who notes just such a preference in males for the image of closed circle and in females for the circle "broken" (89). He also associates these images with a series of stylistic preferences: "Note how much easier it is to describe the male style: it shows a preference for the simple, the closed, the direct. In contrast, women are more interested in the complex, the open, the less defined" (88).

The Eros Plot

By returning now to Apuleius's story of Eros and Psyche, we may review how all these stylistic elements appear to describe the gendered reproductive consciousness of either Eros or Psyche and which of the elements consequently contribute to our understanding of their actions. Eros's story fits the Icarus complex: the emphasis on vision, flight, fire, the fall/wound, the intense relationship with the mother. Aphrodite is shown as unusually close to her son Eros, and the closeness between them is depicted as negative and extreme. Aphrodite pleads with Eros "by the bonds of maternal love" (243). As a projection-reflection, this exchange exists in the province of Narcissus and is encoded as transference: that is, the "bonds" of love are transferred to Aphrodite; they are not mutual or interactive; she is overpowering and she imprisons. Moreover, Apuleius emphasizes the intense and sexual nature of this love: "So saying she kissed her son long and intensely with parted lips" (243). Aphrodite's love for Eros, as a mother's love for her son, is sexualized into a problematic union of opposites and has overtones of the incestuous (Neumann, 91). Apuleius re-enforces the message of the unhealthy nature of this mother-son affection and stresses the visual aspect of Aphrodite's interference in her son's life by having Demeter and Hera both remonstrate with her: "Will you never stop spying inquisitively into your son's pastimes?" (311).

Lance Donaldson-Evans elucidates the association between vision and Cupid/Eros by saying that the eyes are directly associated with Cupid and are often the "means by which he casts his shafts" (21). This concern over issues of vision and sight is evident in the initiation of Eros's conflict with his mother. He does not choose Psyche openly – in the sight of Aphrodite. This emphasis on sight is re-enforced when he forbids Psyche to look at him and when he cautions her about her sisters: "But he warned her time and again, often with threats, never to yield to her sisters' pernicious advice to investigate her husband's appearance" (261).

With regard to flying and fire, Eros is, of course, the winged and fiery god. Moreover, it is in flight that he leaves Psyche upon her discovery of him: "And as his words ended he took wing and soared into the sky" (295). Likewise, he is wounded by fire, by Psyche's lamp: "O bold and reckless lamp, worthless servant of Love, to scorch the very god of all fire, when it must have been some lover who first invented you that even by night he might the longer enjoy the object of his desire" (293). Burned, "the very god of all fire" returns to his mother, Aphrodite.

The Eros plot line of the myth concludes in the "rescue" of Psyche and with their reunion, the *hieros gamos*, and the "proper form" of marriage. The progression from union to reunion to lawfully sanctioned union exists as only part of, yet nearly obfuscates the importance of, Psyche's journey and the profound physical and social responsibility that she "bears" for human continuity. To clinch this pattern as specifically male, Eros's absence following the conception of their child – during which time Psyche completes her tasks – and his return to her at a time that is nearly coincident with the birthed child, mimics exactly the pattern of male reproductive consciousness described by O'Brien.

To sum up, then, it is Eros's story that fits the "traditional" story pattern with its beginning in love at first sight, rising conflict over vision, climax in discovery and burning wound, falling action in recuperation and Psyche's rescue, closure in marriage and "happily ever after." In his description of the story as a quest for union, "for communion with the *anima mundi*, the mystic soul of the world" (240), Ben Edwin Perry uses language that emphasizes this male pattern in Apuleius's stylistic contributions. These are said to lie in the "wealth of concrete details which lengthen the description, or dialogue and make it more picturesque," and which, like the adding of new episodes, "prolong dramatic suspense by leading upward to a climax" (377). This description reiterates that progress for Eros may be recounted as a movement from pleasure and freedom to care and responsibility, and with the emphasis on sexual union to reunion, the action is imaged as complete, circular; its focus is on the male/daemon/ begetter.

The Psyche Plot

A very different narrative model informs Psyche's story. In the structure of her story there is a concurrence of ends and new beginnings, death with fertility, absence and renewed desire. Whereas the signal of a male journey pattern and its (successful or unsuccessful) conclusion might be considered the climax and sexual union, the signal of a female journey pattern might be evident in silences that signal another pattern, the renewal of growth and the beginnings of transformed connection. In contrast to the traditional male linear model, which may be called an "either/or" confrontational mode or mind set, the female model – although equally sequential – may be referred to as a "both/and" cooperative outlook, an outlook that combines differences within increasing awareness.

If the metaphor of union underscores the narrative pattern through which the figure of Eros passes, there lies within the figure itself the evocation of a wider interpretation. In her text, *Eros the Bittersweet*, Anne Carson notes that "the Greek word *eros* denotes 'want,' 'lack,' 'desire for that which is missing'"; she explores the notion of contradiction and paradox, which are so much a part of desire (10). For her, the epithets "limb-loosener" and "sweetbitter" that the poet Sappho bestows on Eros are suitably appropriate because they suggest the physicality of the pleasures and pains of erotic longing and include the sense of time-ordered experience (3). Lovers are "wedged between" paradoxical feelings like love and hate (117). For me, the way that paradox consistently seems to make up for the absence in emotional life, or the distance between the conflicting experiences of emotional life, illustrates the need, desire, or longing for a paradigm that might account for and include what is missing. Carson goes on to describe how even the act of reading presents the same kind of absence and duality. To her, reading is "almost like being in love" because as action, it sustains an emotional and cognitive "incongruence" (85); the reader must negotiate longing and detachment, reality and illusion, in the relationship between self and story.

In his description of Psyche's first sexual experience, Neumann comments on a similar disjunction of, or absence between, end and beginning in female sexual experience; her honeymoon and first sexual experience are both dual and threefold. For Psyche, "the act of defloration represents a truly mysterious bond between end and beginning, between ceasing to be and entering upon real life. To experience maidenhood, womanhood, and nascent motherhood in one, and in this transformation to plumb the depths of her own experience" (64). Because Psyche is pregnant, she is also a symbol of a biological transformation, and in this way, she makes her own rite of passage. This is reminiscent of the comment Neumann makes of Psyche's own development as being towards consciousness and accompanied by increased consciousness.

In an intellectual paradigm that resolves opposites in paradox and a metaphor of sexual union, Eros is doubly appropriate. He is both the absence and the figure of male-identified desire; the equation is both dual and triple. The separation of pattern from definition reveals how Eros and the erotic are significant in Psyche's story, but it also shows that the whole of her experience, the entirety of her reproductive consciousness, requires an inclusion of continuum; more is needed than the suggestion of erotic union and paradox to fully express her experience. The *hieros gamos* is not the most appropriate ending to the story of her experience; nor is the closed circle, union to reunion, the metaphor most applicable to the development of her story. The circle opened, continuity, transformation, and spiral movement are.

Repetitions-with-change constitute Psyche's plot. The betrayals and the tasks all reveal this difference in kind. The first betrayals are public and encompass the roles of the "Fathers" in the larger community; the second, private, include the sisters and her lover/husband; all represent "breaks" in what were enclosing circles of community. Each task, too, is of a different order, and each completion indicates change, a process of growth and maturation.

The Descent Movement and the Eleusinian Mysteries

To understand the implications of introducing the sequential connection between endings and transformation and to explain psychic renewal as it pertains specifically to female life, it is important to give close attention to the multiple meanings of Psyche's fourth task, carrying a jar down to Persephone in the underworld and returning with "beauty" for Aphrodite. The descent motif provides a direct connection with the Demeter/Persephone myth and recalls the unique value that the Mysteries have for Apuleius; the conclusion of the *Metamorphoses* deals with the initiation of his protagonist, Lucius, into the Mysteries and the cult of Isis.

Through an interpretation of the rites at Eleusis and relating what is known historically of the rites that took place there, McClelland notes the link between Demeter and the Mysteries and draws attention to the important element of secrecy. He concludes that the secrecy of these rites and the value placed on this secrecy result in the enhancement of the Mysteries. This secrecy he also relates to what he perceives as women's penchant for having and telling secrets. Jane Ellen Harrison advances a different interpretation. Secrecy was not "the main gist" of "a mystery"; purification was, "in order that you might safely eat and handle certain *sacra*. There was no revelation, no secret to be kept, only a mysterious *taboo* to be prepared for and overcome" (154). Harrison also notes that the sacra "were of trivial character" (157), and this in itself implies a less than total taboo against secrecy. Thus, to Harrison, secrecy does not play a dominant role in enhancement of the Mysteries and a taboo is *meant* to be broken – but only after proper preparation and purification, after initiation.

Harrison's argument informs my conviction that Psyche does not "fail" when she opens the jar, but rather completes the task as ritual passage within the opportunity for learning that is provided by the metaphor of exchange between Aphrodite and Persephone. Equally important, whatever the reasons provided by Apuleius for Psyche's decision, this choice itself, the action of choosing, acknowledges her initiation and acceptance of profound values and her own life responsibilities. There is also a difference in kind between the taboo of looking at Eros and that of looking at the "beauty" that is death. Looking at Eros (as male figure) upsets a cultural proscription; opening the jar (a womb symbol) signals a personal spiritual transformation. If there is an insistence on linking the descent journey to death, then the specific connotations for female life lie in the possible and very real dangers of (unlawful) sexual experience for women: cultural ostracism, male violence, illness or death in pregnancy or childbirth.

The Eleusinian Mysteries were rituals designed to bring mystical insight into the meaning of death – the role of death in life's experience.[1] In her discussion of ancient Greek representations of women, Page DuBois stresses that as rituals of harvest and planting, death and rebirth, these Mysteries occurred in the fall and preceded the sowing that took place at that time. One aspect of the rites involved the sacrifice of pigs. According to Walker, the pig was sacred to the goddess and was "taboo in the usual dual manner: both 'unclean' and 'holy' at the same time" (*Dictionary*, 385). Marija Gimbutus tells us that the pregnant sow was sacred to the "Pregnant Goddess," and DuBois goes on to describe how, in a later part of the sacrificial ritual, "the remains of piglets, which had been thrown into ditches ... in an earlier ceremony ... were placed on altars and mixed with the city's seed-corn and sprinkled in the fields to secure their fertility" (60). Stressing that these were rotted remains, Gimbutus reports that the remains "were mixed with the seeds used for sowing" and "were believed to increase the capacity of the seed to germinate" (147). For Paul Friedrich, Demeter and Persephone not only are "a Greek cultural metaphor for the agricultural cycle" but also show the very real and human concerns of grief for the dead and of fear and helplessness before the greater issues of life and death, "fertility and immortality" (157).

That this rite originated with an agricultural people gives an earthy, practical dimension to any interpretation of the spiritually ritualized idea of rebirth – to what Mircea Eliade (1954) refers to as "eternal return." What was hauled up from the "depths" was "trivial" and universally available; it was rotten pig flesh, decayed animal matter, and whatever its metaphoric purpose, it is fertilizer. What could be present in the Mysteries is not only the idea of individual resurrection – the stench and appearance of decay and corruption would make individual death only too vivid and real a concept – but also the acknowledgment of a particular kind of "beauty" essential to life.

Of the contents of the jar, Apuleius tells us, "there was nothing there, not a drop of beauty, just sleep – deathlike and truly Stygian sleep" (349). This "Stygian sleep" is related to the river of death, Styx, and may indicate the reality of death's stench, of corruption and decay.[2] Metaphorically speaking, death resides in the jar, and that the jar is a womb symbol intimates the knowledge that shadows maternity. The blood mysteries are mysteries of corruption and decay as much as they are mysteries of preservation and life. Mortal women birth mortal beings.

The energy that Aphrodite, as the representation of women's sexual and reproductive life, depletes in the care of Eros and which she must restore, comes from the realm of the Death Goddess, Persephone. The dead and decaying animal or vegetable matter is the process of life feeding from death; life growing out of death. Death transforms life to renew energy in life. Transferred to the human community, the spiritual realization is that death is an important and fitting continuity in life. As much as rain and sun, to be fertile, the earth requires the energy that decay provides. Rather than the going without that McClelland sees as bringing increase, death itself fosters growth and increase.

Psyche's fourth task involves a spiritual journey in which she meets and accepts a profound truth, that death is an essential part of the process of life, not its opposite. Her journey to the heart of life's mystery is not to meet her own death by "failing" her task, nor is it only a journey to reconcile opposites, to unify polarities; her journey is a passage that encompasses a spiritual and philosophical integration of the idea of death into its rite-full place within an understanding of life processes. As Christine Downing states: "The beauty to which Persephone but not Aphrodite has access is the beauty that comes with an intimate inner knowledge of death – the ultimate beauty of the psyche" (*Sisters*, 51).

Elizabeth Kubler-Ross phrases it thus: "Death is the key to the door of life" and "Death is the final stage of growth in this life" (164, 166). The meaning taken from the grief of loss can be spiritually and intel-lectually transformative, just as death itself is the final physical trans-formation of an individual life. This knowledge comes, as is fitting, before Psyche gives birth, during the time when she prepares to meet her responsibility for the care of new life. This awe-full beauty is not a paradox but the magnitude of coming to terms with, and making meaning from, consciousness of death. The good death, the best that any parent can hope for, is a death that precedes the child's. Life's profoundest grief may lie in surviving one's child, but Aphrodite's jar carries no promises and Persephone's gift brings no reprieve.

Nativity as Ending

This continuity provides a different conclusion from the idea of death as finality, as ultimate end. By focusing on death-as-process rather than death-as-end, the concerns shift from an obsession with death and transcendent union to an integration of death, development, and growth into connection and community. Psyche's story seems to end in death, in the sense of the immortality that she acquires through the *hieros gamos*, the marriage to Eros, but many have regarded this ending as unsatisfying, albeit for different reasons. Christine Downing identi-fies another relationship of mortal and immortal: "the real aim of [Psyche's] journey all along has been not the reunion with Eros, not her own divinization, but the meeting with Persephone and the discov-ery that they are sisters, sister doubles, one immortal, one mortal" (*Sisters*, 51). As she sees it, therefore, "[t]he given ending (with Psyche made an immortal resident of Olympus)" is unsatisfactory because it "returns Psyche to the unreal situation of the beginning where she is exalted above all mortal women" (50). Mary Anne Ferguson argues that the pattern for such an ending is "circular, rather than spiral," but sees it as true to life because women "are initiated through learning the rituals of human relationships at home, so that they may replicate the lives of their mothers" (59). This circularity accords with Annis Pratt's warning about the punishments suffered by women who have undertaken descent or rebirth journeys.

Despite the way that the emphasis on the *hieros gamos* seems to punish Psyche by returning her to passivity, however, the last words of the tale – stated almost as an afterthought – suggest an ending with a profoundly different import. Psyche's story ends in birth: "And when her time was come, a daughter was born to them, whom we call by the name of Pleasure" (355). Speaking generally of the symbolism of the child, Carl Jung tells us that the child is "both beginning and end, initial and terminal creature," and most often represents the "phallus, the symbol of the begetter" (*Introduction*, 134). As a female child, however, Psyche's daughter represents the rebirth, not of the begetter, but of the mother; crudely put, the daughter cannot be phallus, since she is both female and culturally powerless. Psyche's child is a new being who, like Psyche, represents the power of a continuous reproductive consciousness, the process of life's continuing possibility.

Furthermore, giving birth is equally a metaphor of conclusion and beginning, a metaphor of transformation in female life. Menstrual cycles, conception, and pregnancy may all be understood as a "before-the-beginning" as much as a "before-the-end" state of being. Pregnancy especially "carries" the "growing" awareness of life-before-birth, life-before-life, of increase. At the same time, birth carries within it the possibility of death for either mother or child. According to Kathryn Allen Rabuzzi, this aspect of childbirth has its own spiritual and mythical element: "During this instant, in which the laboring woman and the Mother Goddess are fully one, the great mystery that a woman discovers is that birth is simultaneously death" (204).

In actual reproductive biology and for species survival, the well-being of Psyche's daughter is actually more important than Psyche's own, and in what seems a paradox, the importance of Psyche's own survival as care giver has, conversely, increased. Because Psyche's story ends with the birthing of Voluptas, the narrative reifies all these seeming paradoxes. Birth is both/and, a threshold experience that carries both the potential of real, physical death and the reality of the psychological "death" of the old, unitary way of being-in-the-world. Along with the physical and psychological realities of birthing a child comes a new beginning, new responsibilities.

Virginity

Not only does childbirth carry the potential for a woman's physical death and/or the death of her infant, but even without these very real physical dangers, it carries the matching and equally real potential for the death of the unitary responsibility to the self, of psychological virginity. Just as during pregnancy Psyche is an image of one who carries another within her, an image of physical two-in-herself-ness (perhaps given the age-old admonition to "eat for two"), with the birth of her child, she represents an additional and psychological two-in-one. Thus, the loss of "virginity" that pregnancy and birth entail also brings an accumulation of competence in giving care and assuming responsibility, as well as an increase in experience and maturity.

There have been many definitions of "virginity" suggested by women scholars, all set forth with the desire for reclaiming an authenticity of female experience that is missing from the patriarchal meanings. M. Esther Harding introduces the term "one-in-herself" to suggest that ancient or more "primitive" societies viewed the virgin as a single woman belonging only to herself regardless of sexual behaviour or experience: "A girl belongs to herself while she is virgin – unwed – and may not be compelled either to maintain chastity or to yield to unwanted embrace" (103). Whereas both Harding and Marilyn Frye link their definitions to intercourse, acknowledging the power structures that confirm male hegemony, Frye goes on to say that the "word 'virgin' did not originally mean a woman whose vagina was untouched by any penis, but a free woman, one not betrothed, not married, not bound to, nor possessed by any man." She goes on to describe its meaning as "a woman sexually and hence socially her own person" but contends that in "any universe of patriarchy, there are no Virgins in this sense" (1992, 133).

Since the word "virgin" comes from the Latin *vir* meaning "man," menarche is also a signal that a woman is not *vir*-like. Not first sexual experience and "loss," but first menstruation and gain of an embodied power might signal the acquisition of reproductive power. The patriarchal sacrifice alluded to in Psyche's "man made" and "flame-red" bridal veil is "fiery" and external to Psyche, placed over her. So, too, the blood of first intercourse – if the hymen has not been broken in athletic or other physical activity – mimics the original dedication to female being and may, or may not, herald pleasure, however much it is another increase in experience. Such blood recalls Psyche's pricking of her own thumb on Eros's arrow.

Of "virgin birth," Barbara Walker states that it is a term evolving from the "virgin-born" designation given to children born of temple priestesses – those women, "holy virgins," dedicated to Aphrodite: "The Holy Virgins or temple-harlots were called 'soul-teachers' or 'soul-mothers' – the *alma mater*" (*Encyclopedia*, 1048). The joining together of all these views and definitions suggests a different definition of virginity that might be applied to Psyche. With first menses, as a mortal girl, she may *have acquired* virginity in a consecration to life lived as a woman. Psyche is dedicated, has dedicated herself to Aphrodite; her daughter is thus "virgin born"; her tasks encode knowledge, an embodied, incremental consciousness, and make her sacred wisdom an *alma mater*.

Beyond and Outside Nativity

There are other goddesses who figure in the background of Psyche's tale and who suggest the continuity that extends beyond and outside of female reproductive life. Via the Demeter and Persephone myth, we meet the nearly obscured goddess-as-crone, Hecate, who is intelligence and compassion (Hayes, 10–11).[3] Literally, Hecate is not grandmother as her ancient origins and place in the trio might suggest, but her association with Persephone and their underworld companionship suggest a disinterested motherliness and recall her role as "nurse of the young" (Zeitlin, 75). Giving an affection not compelled by biological connection or maternal love, she is a "tender-hearted" and "helping figure," the only one to have heard Persephone's screams as she was carried away (Friedrich, 165, 154).

The importance of this non-biological mothering quality is revealed by her role following the reunion of Demeter and Persephone: "After mother and daughter are reunited, Hecate once more appears in the hymn in order to receive the Kore and remain her companion for always: Hecate and Persephone are as inseparable as Persephone and Demeter" (Jung and Kerenyi, 154). Hecate and Persephone are also as inseparable as Hecate and Demeter, a situation reflected in the tendency of scholars to see "*Demeter and Hecate in one person*" (Jung and Kerenyi, 158). This, in effect and twice over, makes a doubled figure. Demeter and Persephone are almost always together, "thought of as a *double figure*." Without Persephone, "her *mother's* Kore," Demeter would not be mother, "*Meter*" (Jung and Kerenyi, 152).

According to C. Kerenyi, these two forms are, in reality, not two doubled figures, but "a triad of unmistakable individuals"; "the torch appears to be the attribute of each of them." Their communal epithet, "*phosphoros*" (bringer of light), emphasizes the kind of transformational consciousness this triplicity implies: a consciousness symbolized in "[o]ne torch, two torches held by the same goddess, three torches in a row" (Jung and Kerenyi, 154). Perhaps it is because she is not specifically associated with generativity that her representation in human form is made unfamiliar; as Kerenyi notes, this third goddess is lost in, or obscured by, the moon; in fact, she is its dark phase. The three goddess aspects become "maiden, mother, and moon" and are linked to the triple form as "the *three* realms of earth, heaven [sic], and sea" (Jung and Kerenyi, 156).

Other attributes associated with the figure of Hecate equally signal an enhancement of meaning in the metaphors of Psyche's journey. Charlene Spretnak tells us that ritually prescribed food, called "Hecate's suppers," was offered to the goddess as a means of ritual purification. Echoing Psyche's supper in the underworld, this gives resonance to an interpretation of the ritual import of Psyche's fourth task and the contention that Psyche is meant to open the jar; she has undergone the ritual purification that enables her to accept the increase of wisdom. Zeitlin also reveals that Hecate is an intermediary, an "intercessor" who became predominately associated with women (74–5); this might likewise account for the tower as lunar symbol and intercessor for Psyche. Hecate is a "divine guide of the mysteries" who signals "dangerous crossroads" and "mysterious feasts" (311).

In Hecate's moon connections, both Friedrich and Walker link her to Artemis, as midwife figure and huntress. Of Artemis specifically, Walker observes that she was called "Cutter" and, in her huntress-destroyer aspect, "Butcher" (58). Zeitlin notes that this constellation of goddesses – Demeter, Persephone, Hecate, Artemis – is hostile towards male sexual aggression. This suggests that in the Psyche myth the knife, like the torch, may evoke such a midwife figure's hostility, as well as the sisters', towards an Eros/eros who/that is not freely chosen. Thus, Hecate, appropriately enough, conjoins food, ritual, the torch, and the knife to female reproductive life. In this way, she is present in the background in Psyche's myth and, in her moon connections, she exerts a symbolic and metaphoric presence.

The Meaning in the Middle

In this model of female development, it is no longer necessary to see the middle only as a "detour" of struggles or imposed delay or simply as a means of creating (sexual) tension. The "middle" of the narrative becomes a place where transformations occur, a continuing transformation that makes meaning from life even as it enhances the meaningfullness of the life process. If Psyche's story begins "before-the-beginning" and ends with "no-ending," in birth, what is contained in the "middle" necessarily takes a different form; her story line relaxes from its original bindings, may lose "tension," and becomes increasingly complex by offering the possibility of including new meanings.

Her story emphasizes an incremental gathering-in as well as expansive action whose purpose is increase and transformation. Rather than progress to unitary, solitary ending, the "aim" of such a life story relaxes into the living of it; pleasure is celebrated in its very daily-ness. Each "episode" is as important as the next, no less important than the one preceding, and all three are joined. If there is a "goal" in this kind of narrative, then the goal incorporates what Peter Brooks refers to as "arabesques" (and I describe as spirals). In such a view, a life well lived tells, in an accumulation of sensory detail and description, about gains in experience and knowledge as they transform an individual human psyche. Relationships in their complexity become a source of richness; those encountered along the journey become interesting for the varieties of experience and attitudes they bring. At the same time, the spiral pattern lends itself to a description of embrace, a pattern of accretion, taking in, cooperation and accommodation; the emphasis is on care, continuity, and maintaining connections and reveals the interrelatedness of learning, of the journey and the narrative.

In the landscape of this narrative structure, the paths contain intense and sensory descriptions of voyages out from and back to, of heights negotiated and plains and valleys traversed. Each moment described leads always back to the psyche and to re-vision and growth. The process is continuous, both self- and other-referential. Within the spiral, the circle and line appear together, combined with the continuum as another both/and. Both circumference and plane change but sequential continuity is maintained. The journey is *both/and*, that is, *both* (deeper or higher *and* broader or narrower) */and* (ongoing). Foregrounding the second "and" implicit in "both" allows me to emphasize the shift beyond duality and into movement.

The dictionary confirms the multiplicity of meanings of the spiral and introduces yet another – an element of fixity at the centre within the movement. Defined variously as a "locus in a plane of a point moving around a fixed centre," as a "three dimensional locus of a point moving parallel to and about a central axis at a constant or continuously varying distance," and as a "coiling in a constantly changing plane," the spiral links transformative change and centred being.

To reiterate: Psyche's story begins before the meeting with Eros; it begins in context and relationship, within a family, and continues through disconnection (betrayal and violence) to new connections encoded as marriage and conception. The first betrayal with the attendant losses of family, community, choice, and self-esteem is followed by the honeymoon with Eros, other betrayals, by her sisters, by Eros, followed by connection to Aphrodite, renewed and self-chosen connection to Eros, the birth of Voluptas. The initial pattern, of connection and betrayal repeated, evolves to integrate a wider life experience through the four tasks. Each task brings growth and new understanding in a repeating pattern that involves accumulation and assimilation, a move "away from" followed by movement "back towards" a different experience, a different level, a different plane: physical, psychological, emotional, spiritual. In each experience and task, what presages Psyche's new growth is silence.

Voluptas beyond the Ending

Erich Neumann presents Psyche and Eros as metaphoric figures in psychic integration. Their union and reunion include sexual and spiritual components and result in the conjunction of human and divine, female and male. He notes the strength and lasting power of this religious mystery: it "has occupied the centre of psychic development and of culture, art and religion" and "has brought both good and evil, but in any event it has been an essential ferment of the psychic and spiritual life of the West down to the present day." Clearly, Neumann's analysis of the potency of this image is accurate; as a general rule, the culture of the West has conceptualized both the spiritual mystery and its metaphoric expression by way of an image of heterosexual love.

Moreover, this Western tradition has used a reproductive metaphor in a way that classifies female experience under (someone else's) sexual pleasure and under self-sacrifice, and devalues authentic and powerful female being. The male/masculine figure is regarded as the agent-saviour, and the female figure and the feminine are subsumed under and consumed in a (sexualized) union of dualities. Neumann goes on to say: "This love of Psyche for her divine lover is a central motif in the love mysticism of all times, and Psyche's failure, her final self abandonment, and the god who approaches as a saviour at this very moment correspond exactly to the highest phase of mystical ecstasy, in which the soul commends itself to the godhead" (139–40). It is this attitude towards spirituality that has in part prompted my own revisioning. By emphasizing Psyche's earthbound and specifically female nature and reinterpreting the metaphors of her journey, I argue that Psyche's is neither a failed journey nor one that involves a self abandoned. Furthermore, a female reproductive consciousness includes pregnancy and birth as well as sexual union and conception; therefore, in her embodiment, Psyche represents the possibility for a different metaphor of relationship, learning, and spirituality in this different life journey. I should also point out that such a biologically grounded exploration will be inescapably literal, but this very explicitness provides provocative yet fundamental and even profound imagery for reinterpreting the self in relation to the world.

Birth as Maternal Transition

Psyche's relationship to her own sensuality, to Eros and the erotic, is a process of transformation; in her pregnancy and in giving birth, she continues to flourish and evolve. Throughout her journey, she sustains and supports a pregnancy; in giving birth to a daughter, she recreates the mother-daughter bond and the ties of sisterhood that were lost to her. What seems less apt, however, is the conclusion that leaves both Psyche and her daughter in the realm of the father gods, back within the patriarchal fold; this immortality is one that implies an assimilation back into a patriarchal pantheon, not one that brings new knowledge back to, or changes, the community.

Embedded in Apuleius's story is an allegory of the shift in values necessary in a patriarchally ordered continuity. That the worship of a young and mortal virgin, the controlled female and dependent feminine, replaces the engagement in what Neumann calls the "primordial feminine mysteries," those of "birth and rebirth" (148), signals a paradigm shift of incalculable significance for Western society, for what is deemed intellectual pursuit, and for women's roles. That Psyche should be rescued by Eros, that Zeus should step in and "fix everything," is a reflection of those power dynamics. That Psyche has not been viewed as completing heroic labours signifying her own agency further emphasizes an androcentric cultural imperative. This shift turns away from community values and an understanding of the life energies that include and value female being and turns towards a male empowerment, a power over and exploitation of both the natural world and female life.

Apuleius tells us that Psyche's daughter is named Voluptas, a name that various editors and commentators (Hanson, Adlington, Hillman, Johnson, Neumann) translate as "Pleasure."[1] This identifying of pleasure with voluptuousness emphasizes a sexually luxurious sensuality appropriate to conception; in effect, however, the continuity of sense experience in Psyche's journey, her labours, and the birth are downplayed or ignored. Certainly, ancient Greek or Roman society did not value physical life or the natural world, and this perspective partially accounts for the absence of an ongoing, post-birthing experience of motherhood within Psyche's story. This absence is similar to that implied in the "beyond the ending" that Rachel Blau DuPlessis explores in her analysis of twentieth-century narratives by women writers. Like Carol Pearson and Katherine Pope, who conclude that female quest patterns are *heroic*, and Lee R. Edwards, who interprets Psyche as a *hero*, DuPlessis names as hero the female protagonist whose activity, growth, and insight are central to the story. Conversely, a heroine is one who needs attention or rescue. Whereas the usual narrative ending takes over female being in a rescue like Psyche's, the "magical" unlaboured birth of a child and the absence of any continuation of story equally inhibit female agency and reinstate her as heroine. The birth of a daughter (and not a son) in this ancient story highlights a continuity fundamental to women's individual lives and across generations: a transgenerational reproductive consciousness.

Motherhood has never been viewed as heroic or grounds for philosophic meditation because it is regarded as biologically impelled and therefore "natural" (O'Brien; Okin). Likewise, Adrienne Rich's analysis shows how motherhood has been negatively interpreted and "institutionalized" to the detriment of the actual experience of mothering. Along with this negative opinion comes a corresponding (and paradoxical) absence of the mother from psychological theory; as Jessica Benjamin observes, "No psychological theory has adequately articulated the mother's independent existence" (23). This absence is as (paradoxically) vivid as that of Psyche's own mother. Clearly, the work of motherhood has been interpreted in ways that are inimical to its definition as a cultural activity. Benjamin's and Rich's observations about motherhood echo O'Brien's observation that we have no philosophy of birth, and all three serve to underscore how this aspect of female life has been left out of what is understood as human experience. It is equally clear, then, that any articulation of a philosophy of female being must include a revisioning of birth and birthing. As a way of articulating such a philosophy and considering the entailments of this experientially grounded metaphor, I include Psyche's pregnancy and the birth of Voluptas, along with the idea of "conception" as sexual union, to ground in physical life a revisioned sense of self, of self in community and within the spiritual mysteries of life.

Because I see birth as a metaphor for the self in relationship, it might seem that I am substituting an image of an unequal dyad in the mother-child relationship for an image of union encoded as a duality of opposites in marriage/intercourse. To address the concern that the birth metaphor simply substitutes a profoundly unequal dyadic relationship for an ideal of equality – and obscured inequality – of opposites requires a careful examination of the facts of the birthing experience.

Even though my approach is a woman-centred revisioning and my concern is with the ways in which women are culturally disadvantaged, I re-emphasize that the experience that all human beings, male and female, share, whatever their other differences, is that profound and original transition from uterine life, however it may be differently labelled – "natural," technological, breech, caesarian. What female life may *add* is the experience of giving birth. That experience certainly does not take away from being born, nor does it negate life that does not include physical birth giving; it merely brings one more experience to the many others possible in life. And, as *one* aspect of Psyche's journey, pregnancy and birthing are as intellectual, as hazardous, and as spiritually fulfilling as any other. Above all, the physical labour involved in giving birth is a transitional labour: Psyche's labours of child-rearing have yet to begin; the tasks are training rather than culmination.

Birth as Species Survival

Although I have already noted that the birth experience is dangerous for both mother and infant, Wenda R. Trevathan helps us contextualize this danger through her discussion of the evolutionary significance, the survival benefits, of human birth and mother-infant bonding: "Darwin argued survival, but today we know that reproduction is what evolution is all about. But indeed, reproduction cannot occur unless survival has preceded it." She describes the anthropological heritage of the mother-child dyad in clear scientific terms that are especially useful as a way of removing any sentimental imagery. Each woman who gives birth is "a sexually reproducing mammal with the characteristic features of viviparity and mammary glands." Each has "an endocrine repertoire from ancestors as remote as reptiles, a placenta from earliest viviparous mammals, and a birth canal from her earliest hominid ancestors." At the same time, the "newborn infant enters the world with its own set of hormones, a large brain inherited from remote hominid ancestors, and a state of helplessness unusual in the primate order" (ix). Trevathan discusses reproductive survival within this context and underscores the increased potential for failure (death) because of the intricate, complicated nature of the adaptations that have made *homo sapiens* so successful a species.

These adaptations include two genetically contributing parents and (usually) the necessity of sexual intercourse; a placenta for the transfers of nutrients and waste; a birth canal of a shape and size limited by bipedalism or upright walking; and, because of this last, the birth of dependent and immature offspring requiring constant, intensive care giving. Furthermore, encephalization, or the skull enlargement that is the outcome of the larger brain – a tremendous asset in survival terms – also adds to the danger inherent in birthing. Trevathan emphasizes that these compromises and modifications for survival have resulted in heavy and unequal burdens for the human female; these modifications, like metaphors, have their "entailments."

The Entailments of Birth

Trevathan states that the first entailment of this complex of behaviours making up the human reproductive capacity is that "the human female cannot carry to term a fetus phenotypically greatly different from herself, and she must be more selective in choosing her mate" than other primates (34). In other words, for ease (read success) of birth, the reproductive partner should be of similar physical size. In the myth of Psyche, Eros is an ancient god/ daemon, but Psyche's own choosing and the ultimate success of the birth of Voluptas, however, assume their equality. (As well, both represent, at times, a human couple.) Theirs is in this way a union grounded in (literal) biological reproductive reality as well as mythic significance.

In affective terms, as Trevathan notes, the father's presence at the birth contributes to the mother's more "positive" immediate attitude to the child, a response important for the survival and flourishing of the live but immature offspring (114). Eros, as we have noted, does return before the birth. The dyad is immediately "opened" to include an essential third – both in terms of genetic input and in terms of postpartum psychological and emotional support; the dyad becomes a triad in which the presence of the third contributes, optimally in a positive and affirmative way, to the "original" two. Seeing this twosome as either mother/father or mother/child makes clear the "essential" triplicity in reproductive terms.[2]

A second entailment of human birth that Trevathan argues "is that birth is routinely performed with assistance in our species" (108). Her emphasis that this is routine in the lengthy history of human birth is both surprising and significant for our understanding of women's experience of birthing: "Assistance at childbirth has probably been a normal part of parturition in human beings for more than a million years." Clearly, she does not mean the kind of technological intervention for which North American medical practice has been criticized (Davis-Floyd; Kitzinger; Greer, *Sex*). While women can and have given birth alone, she goes on to state that "having that assistance and support would have made the difference between life and death for many mothers and infants" (110). Whereas now, in present-day Western societies, such birth attendants are more likely to be professionally trained doctors and midwives, historically they have most often been older female relatives who have already given birth (111).

Historically, therefore, success in birthing has depended upon the bonds between women, and I believe it would be safe to assume that such bonding behaviours would be self-selective with assisted birth; that is, women who formed close bonds with women experienced in birthing would have access to the knowledge, physical aid, and emotional support that would ensure successful birth and in that way would pass on a genetic predisposition for affective connection. Thereby, the triad "opens" further to include reliance upon a community – historically of women – a significant reliance given the unarguably complex and difficult nature of human birth processes.

Another of Trevathan's details – one that might be considered peripheral but which is noteworthy for my interpretation of Psyche's story – is that "there is a statistical bias toward nocturnal birth."[3] Trevathan explains this by suggesting "that this non-random distribution reflects a time in our past when it was advantageous to deliver at a time when fellow band members were available to assist and provide protection" (95–6). Again, such behaviour accentuates the historic and anthropological importance of the community to the birthing female and downplays what has been perceived as a closed mother-child relationship or even the mother-child-father nuclear family.

Symbols in the Birth Community

These last two entailments indicate real and experiential – even essential and historically female – reasons for the presence of Psyche's sisters and for the lamp and the razor/knife that they bring her. However phallic in symbol or connotation, the lamp and the knife/razor would be useful (even essential?) utensils for midwifery and thus quite within the purview of the female and domestic realm. Certainly too, as Friedrich notes, women's ritual objects in the Mysteries included not only seed cakes, serpents, pomegranates, and poppies but also lamps and swords (209). Here, again, the successful birthing of Voluptas argues for the survival of the sisters through to the end of the tale.

The Physiological Role of the Placenta

The knife, of course, is necessary to sever the umbilical cord, and the umbilical cord accentuates the issue of mother-child "unity" and Apuleius's emphasis on the "bonds" of mother love. Trevathan describes the placenta as an adaptive strategy allowing for greater diversity in the gene pool. It permits, within the maternal "environment," the development of a fetus that is not identical with the mother, that in fact shares less than half her genetic make-up (13). In this day of implants and transplants, we are made very aware of what happens to foreign tissue in the human body unless strong intervention occurs. The placenta-as-barrier offers this powerful intervention and protection from the destruction or expulsion that would otherwise occur. The placenta permits the coexistence of two different entities and allows an intrinsically distinct and separate creature to exist within a maternal body. The already-released ovum is fertilized – thus consisting of transformed cell(s) – and exists within, both part of and separate from, the maternal body: and/both. As a product of union, the zygote is a self-contained assembly of cells that is different from each of the contributing parents; it is immediately more than and different from the union of its two parents. In this sense, the zygote-fetus does not come directly from either contributing parent but is a combination of genetic input "out from" the genetic heritage of each. In a rudimentary way, the contributing ovum and sperm, as well as the zygote, are already separate from each parent.

Further, the placenta, in connecting fetal cells to the mother, may be described as transformational; it is an outgrowth of fetal tissue, not an outgrowth of the maternal body. Placental operation is a function of fetal development and attachment to the uterine wall. The three layers of tissue or membrane that separate the uterus and fetus are likewise all fetal in origin (Trevathan, 7). This does not imply that the maternal "environment" is passive, however; it receives, sustains, nourishes, and, in due course, labours to release.

The Psychological Self at Birth

At the same time that fetal existence may be described as physiologically separate from the maternal body, fetal separateness (self-ness) may also be psychologically comprehended. Daniel L. Stern, working as a psychoanalyst and developmentalist, suggests that at birth there is at least an "emergent self" present. Acknowledging that there is no consensus on what constitutes the sense of self or the corresponding sense of other, he nonetheless states that we are all aware that such a thing as "selfness" exists and changes throughout life. Centring his theory on this innate sense of self, he states that "some senses of the self do exist long prior to self-awareness and language" and include the sense "of agency, of physical cohesion, of continuity in time, of having intensions in mind and other such experiences" (6).

Beginning with the presumption that "some preverbal senses of the self start to form at birth (if not before)" while others need differing levels of maturity, he suggests that the task of understanding this sense of self is one which must be concerned with "the developmental continuities and changes" that occur throughout life (6, 7). Offering his theory of identity formation as a "metaphor for clinical practice," he clarifies the significance of the changes that result when the child is seen as a distinct being: "Once parents see a different infant, that infant starts to become transformed by their new 'sight' and ultimately becomes a new adult" (276).

A perception of individuals who are already "selves" at birth makes relationships with them immediately interactive; as well, these relationships hold the potential for increasing complexity. A changed perception of the infant as a separate being compels a parallel change in our perceptions of the mother, the mother-child bond, and mother work. In this context, then, at-one-ness, the sharing of the maternal body by fetus and mother, does not imply union and the loss of the infant self or the submerging of the infant's self in the "greater" environment; neither does it suggest passivity or loss of self in the mother. At the same time that the pregnant woman's bones, blood, and tissue cradle and sustain fetal development, the fetus may be said to initiate a connection that maintains separation even as it sustains life. This interaction provides a metaphor of agency, receptivity, and nurturing, a metaphor for an interactive community of (at least) two that encourages and enables separate co-responsive growth and individuality.

That the fetus exhibits a developmentally appropriate agency also erases the proscriptions of gender from concepts of the origins of human agency. From our earliest cellular beginnings, there seems to exist a powerful intention for both connection to and individuation from community or environment. Such an agency may be described as encompassing an "inherent" sense of self that demands – for *survival* – both connection and separation within relationship, within an interactive biosphere. Fetal agency in prenatal biological development moderates our perceptions of the symbiotic existence, dependency, and absence of intention ascribed to the newborn. Other behaviours of the newly born infant suggest that, as Stern argues, the infant is neither passive nor without a sense of self. Trevathan, too, notes that interactive communication occurs immediately after birth and that these "bonding" actions are multi-sensory and include vision, olfaction, and touch (150).

All of this together encourages a recognition that in the unity of mother and child usually ascribed to pregnancy there is also a very distinct triplicity because of the separation of fetus and mother that is implemented by the placenta. Thus, the placenta is barrier, connection, and conduit allowing the passage of nutrients and waste between the maternal environment and the fetus through the umbilical cord. The cord itself is biologically and physiologically triple, for it "carries the fetal blood from the fetus to the placenta via the two umbilical arteries, and the returning blood via the single umbilical vein." Its blood vessels are coiled in a spiral fashion, and finally, both cord and placenta ensure that the "maternal and fetal circulations are entirely independent" (Bourne, 90, 85).

The Post-Birth Gap

Physiologically, the placenta and umbilical cord bridge a "gap" between different beings, allowing them to coexist by providing a barrier, a connection, and a process for sustenance. This important and physical "thirdness" of intrauterine life is recognized in many cultures. Commenting on the disposal of the placenta and afterbirth, Trevathan observes: "if there is a childbirth practice that comes close to universal incidence, it may be with the proper disposal of the placenta and umbilical cord" (106). Several cultures ascribe "personness" to it, and some consider it a friend or younger sibling; it "has its own metabolism, its own life span, and it can live in the absence of a fetus" (107).

If we accept that the placenta and umbilical cord are an outgrowth of the fetus and fetal development, and if we likewise accept that the sense of self very early encompasses body boundaries, then we can understand how the removal of the umbilical cord may in fact be experienced by the newborn as like an amputation. If this amputation is metonymically transferred to the male sense of body cohesion, then it is also not surprising that Western culture has placed so much stock in Freud's castration theory. Indeed, this concern may be further exacerbated by the practice of circumcision, which constitutes a repetition of that original cut. In the context of the placental role as connection, it is even less surprising that the metonymic transfer of castration is from its "rightful" anxiety (the loss of the testes, the source of genetic potency) to the erect penis, the phallus, the means of male sexual connection.

For female experience, such an amputation-like occurrence might account for what is perceived as an equivalent feeling of absence or sense of loss that is intensified by patriarchal betrayal and the general cultural message of being "born wrong." That this loss may be exorcised in the care of and affective connection to others and in the historic responsibility for infant care has without a doubt effectively served the grand imperative of species survival.

Metaphoric Ground and Mediating Intelligence

By grounding the metaphor of loss to placental amputation, by reinscribing this ground as the means and metaphoric process of connection and separation, there arises a wealth of new and transformative meanings about the ways in which we connect to others, to the environment. What the placental metaphor brings into focus is the means of analysing how a human concept or an intellectual or social system is a self-generated construction that both connects us to each other and provides a barrier that nurtures and protects the self even as it manages relationship. The placenta as metaphor includes the awareness that the construct itself is a conduit – it grows out of the self, connects infant self to mother/environment, and carries blood and waste between them. The placenta as an object is necessarily and immediately available to interpretation.

Metaphorically, the placenta is the site of continuity. That which is absent in dualistic thinking – the gap or third in dichotomy – thus becomes available as a metaphor in any enquiry, and any enquiry may be said to be faulty if it does not examine this essential third element. By this process of reasoning (inscribed metaphoric), a debate that has only two sides and finishes with a winner and a loser provides a less than adequate way of seeking or seeing truth. The conduit – the form – has conditioned the results, but it has also obscured the process. Absence conditions the nature of the (failed) understanding.

The placenta metaphor enables a revised image of the mind as well. The placenta is the third that operates as a mediator between self and experience, between self and other. The mind, too, can be shown to have a physiological triple nature in its mediative function. In *The Right Brain and the Unconscious*, R. Joseph uses the binary brain model, but his interpretation can equally suggest a three-part brain. In describing the responsibilities of the dual mind, for example, he also portrays the limbic system as "so ancient and, in some respects, primitive that some have referred to it as the *reptilian brain*" (110). When he contrasts this "old brain" with the "new brain" and describes the right and left hemispheres, he illustrates again the tendency to "dualize." At the same time, however, he observes that the "old limbic brain has not been replaced, for it remains buried within the depths of the cerebral hemispheres, where it continues to exert its influence much as it has for the last million years" (110).

Joseph tells us that the "limbic level of the mind could be referred to as the *primary unconscious*, as its appearance precedes all other aspects of mental functioning" (118–19). In his revaluation of the role of the right brain and the unconscious, Joseph also recognizes "the constraints of language" and argues for a greater reliance on context, the "way things are said, the body language and facial expressions" (375, 376). Such a view of the brain as a mediator of experience and of language as a metaphor in that process of mediation enables us to change the way we understand and analyse humans' interactions with the world and each other. Understanding language and intellectual, social, and cultural constructions as metaphoric placental systems can also lead to changes in ways of thinking. What this third of placental connection/barrier offers is a way of including continuum in analysis and contextual understanding in meaning.

The Discourse of Relationship

Focusing on the social nature of the relationship between infant and mother and on the ability of the infant to make an impact on his/her environment changes the way that we regard that relationship. To return infant behaviour to its own and real agency restores to maternal behaviour the complex affective and intellectual behaviours that interactive social functioning and responsive infant care demand. The ongoing labour of mothering requires an ability to perceive similarity and difference and to recognize what is best for the self as well as understand what is appropriate for the well-being of a different-though-similar and dependent other.

Equally evident within this metaphor is the understanding that, at an affective and relationship level, (an age-appropriate) distance and separation are as fundamental to well-being as is connection. Writing about mothers' awareness of "ambivalence," their contradictory feelings of love and hate for their children, psychotherapist Rozsika Parker decries the taboo against expressing negative feelings that makes mothering unnecessarily difficult. Whereas she explores, in *Mother Love/Mother Hate*, the presence of conflicting feelings from the perspectives of mothers who contend with the representations of idealized motherhood, I would further argue that only when there is emotional space between individuals, between mothers and children, does there appear room for development. Psyche grows within the tasks as much from Aphrodite's setting of them as from her provision of helpers. A redefinition of the mother (parent)/child relationship that acknowledges differences and separations (or failures) describes a transformative, good-enough mothering (parenting).

Because of their prominence in male life and masculine values, mastery and agency are easy to understand as important ingredients in the well-lived life, but the feminine relationship values have equally played their part despite their devaluation. Recognizing that relationship is an important life goal and that interconnection is a fundamental psychological aim, Ruthellen Josselson presents a scheme for the "development that takes place within, through, and for relatedness" (2). She underscores the need for developing a theory of "self-in-relation" that could "postulate individuation toward greater belonging and sharing, and see development as moving not toward separation but toward increasingly complex relatedness" (16).

Locating this development in "the space between us," she explains psychological growth as an enlarged perception of the individual security that results from a recognition of barrier and boundary, coupled with an increased comprehension of interconnection, what she terms "recursive processes": "The clearer we are about who we ourselves are, the more we are able to risk ourselves with another. The more certain we are about our own boundaries, the freer we become to experience a range of affect and interconnection with others" (19). Josselson describes "the discourse of relatedness" as consisting of eight ways, each of which constitutes "actually or metaphorically, a way of reaching through space (or being reached) and being in contact with each other" (6). These eight are holding, attachment, passionate experience, eye-to-eye validation, idealization and identification, mutuality and resonance, embeddedness, and tending or care. Josselson also acknowledges the importance of context: "Relationships always occur in existing systems, enhancing, counterpointing, or clashing with what is already there" (27).

Part of Josselson's concern is with the absence of a language to describe relationship – the discourse of "we" – and she stresses the need for metaphor: "Our limited language of relatedness requires that we rely on metaphor to grasp its various phenomena." Seeing the "physical and the psychological as metaphorically interchangeable" (5–6), she uses some metaphors already familiar through this examination of Psyche's story: clarification as "candle" (20), holding as "invisible threads" (29), security as a "container" (30), death as "abyss" and "fall" (33). Stating also that "[r]elatedness and individuality are not dichotomous" (15), she continues with the observation that the growth of the one is accompanied by growth in the other. Recognizing this, Josselson uses paradox to suggest this mutuality and to explain each of the eight dimensions of relationship that she identifies.[4]

As my analysis suggests, I see a more concise rendering in a threefold process combining difference with accretion (the both/and). Similarly, I see a physical birth-base for conditioning our psychological (metaphorical) understanding of relationship in the placental connection. In the self-cord/placenta-mother and the mother-placenta/cord-child triplicities lie the physiological bases for a more accurate analysis of the psychological and philosophical complexities that characterize subjectivity, relationship, agency (selfhood), and community.[5] The umbilicus is a passage, a "cord," a "belt," which "ties" two together, can "knot" and "buckle," is finally "cut." In the loss of the physical connection of the pre-birth state lies the metaphoric space – gap, fissure, slit – to be "transcended" – bridged, reached over, through, across.

In the umbilical cord originate the metaphors of ties, paths, bonds, belts that link us together. In the placenta and cord lie the ways of grounding our consciousness in metaphoric process. The feelings of/in attachment prevent incorporation (symbiosis) as well as give energy and sustain life; beings do not merge – they relate. This (absent) third, seen and named as space, is the means and constituent text of connection; it is as fundamental to relationship as the two (or more) who are connected. As mediator, as barrier/threshold and path, the fluid-filled birth sac, the placenta, and the umbilical cord exist to protect difference and self-ness as much as they further connection and survival.

With conception and the fertilization of the egg comes the drive for biological, physical attachment to the mother/womb as a survival imperative. With birth comes the need for affective connection as a way of ensuring physical nurturance and continued survival. With maturity comes the desire to find one's place, to connect in community. Thus, the four more basic of Josselson's eight dimensions – holding, attachment, eye-to-eye contact, and embeddedness – are followed by an increasing complexity of connection in mutuality, idealization and identity, passionate experience, and tending.

Liminality and the Gap

The navel centre to cord to placental threshold is the child-path to connection; here is the self-as-agent that is impelled to connection out from the self to threshold, the place of border, barrier, and attachment, to community. The placental threshold to cord to developing fetus is, in turn, a mother-path: receptive agency, response-ability, and energy willed to move out through borders and in(on)to paths that end in new creation. This threshold crossing has frequently been imaged as a movement, like Psyche's, into the wilderness and the natural world, away from community.

The sign or mark of this process is, conceivably (and whimsically), the navel, signifying both connection and separation and, as well, identifying the process of growth and change. As semiotic scar, it marks community at the same time as it signs uniqueness and is as individual as a fingerprint. Coherency of separation, loss, connection, agency, and context exist and are distinguished in this centre. Aspects of Victor Turner's inquiry into ritual activity lends credence to the idea that we may have a very real consciousness of placental nature and function: a placental consciousness. In *The Ritual Process*, he describes and likens liminality to "being in the womb" and as a "betwixt and between position" (95). In "Variations on a Theme of Liminality," Turner acknowledges that the source of the term is Arnold Van Gennep's examination of rites of passage. What Van Gennep found was that these rites "have basically a tripartite processual structure" that is "marked by three phases: separation; margin (or *limen*); and re-aggregation" (36). Turner represents the *limen* as gap, as an absence and a separation.

This middle is called an "interesting problem" by Turner and variously described as threshold, corridor, tunnel, and pilgrim's road (37). The pilgrims or "liminaries" are also middle and "evade ordinary cognitive classification, too, for they are neither-this-nor-that, here-nor-there, one-thing-not-the-other. Out of their mundane context, they are in a sense 'dead' to the world and liminality has many symbols of death" (370). He goes on to say that gestation, parturition, lactation, and weaning are all present with the symbols of death: "But the most characteristic midliminal symbolism is that of paradox, or being *both* this *and* that ... both living *and* dead, at once ghosts and babes, both cultural and natural, human *and* animal" (37). Turner notes the effect of liminality on social conditions and community connections: "certain kinds of liminality may be conducive to the emergence of communitas" (47). This communitas is also characterized as requiring "flow" and a "merging of action and awareness" (51). The symbols of such a connection to community are described as "transitional processional, liminal, and transformative" (52).

Psyche's journey has been marked by an awareness of the both(two)/and(one) understanding that indicates a coexistence of (perceived or preconceived) opposites with process as the continuity and the path between. Female life, female reproductive consciousness, and a philosophy of birth provide images and metaphors of similarity and difference, agency and accretion, that are present in Psyche's story and echo in Turner's description of liminality and ritual process. What is represented is that which constitutes process. The gap is the absent third, the placental connector. This gives the basis for a new metaphor of being, and a new way of reinterpreting old metaphors, for the transforming psyche.

Liminality and the Goddesses

Using the term "liminality" to discuss how Aphrodite as a figure is able to bridge the physical and the mystical, Paul Friedrich identifies seven antagonistic categories: sex/purity, mortal/immortal, female/male, passive/active, prostitution/marriage, nature/culture, curse/blessing. Noting that her role is one of "emotional assertion" rather than of "systematic, logical rules," he goes on to reiterate that all gods are liminal in some way but, together with the related figure of Eros, Aphrodite is identified with sexual love as the great leveller of "grids and paradigms" (148). A swift review of the categories shows how, in the story of Psyche and Eros, several of the equations are represented in each figure and, in my interpretation at least, how Aphrodite can be seen as a mediating figure who stands between them.

Introducing two more categories, sensuousness/sex and motherliness/maternity, Friedrich speculates about the erasure of the connection between sexuality and maternalism. This, he suggests, accounts for the division of powers between Demeter and Aphrodite, and he further hypothesizes that the Mysteries are representative of "the mystic union of the complexes of sexuality and maternalism, of Aphrodite and Demeter-Persephone." In the androcentric culture of ancient Greece, the Greater Mysteries of Eleusis were marked by a "symbolism of incest" and "a categorical and successful taboo" (210). Again, given my own interpretation of the pervasiveness of the image of heterosexual union and recalling my explication of the belief in incest inspired by narcissism and patrilineal family structures, both incest and taboo reveal more about male social control than truth about maternal behaviour. In the same way, divisions created among goddess representations reify stages or aspects of female life but obscure process.

What I do infer from the matrix of implications surrounding the myths of Narcissus, Demeter, and Persephone and the symbolism of Aphrodite as a sexual goddess is another set of reasons for Aphrodite as Psyche's mentor. Her liminality and her sponsorship allow for a full integration of sexuality and maternal behaviour, an integration that exists outside of long-held definitions. Acknowledging similarity, difference and the mediation-between of Aphrodite (as the representation of a female-initiated and -inspired sexuality and sensuality) implies the possibility of a relationship between lovers and between parent and child that is capable of change and growth with an acceptance of the responsibilities in relationships and kinship networks. As a goddess, Aphrodite makes explicit what androcentric cultures have kept obscene, off screen: sensuality, sexuality, and motherhood exist on a continuum, change over time, and reflect circumstance. A fully sexualized goddess who is also a mother implies full female reproductive consciousness, one that may include pregnancy, birth, and motherhood as well as sexual union and conception. Psyche's journey represents the possibility of a different metaphor of relationship, learning and spirituality in a differently interpreted life journey. Aphrodite's liminality marks that gap, as the navel marks the absence of a once-necessary physical link.

Ancient Metaphors of Centredness

Whereas I have come to think of it as a marker of both real and absent metaphoric process, the navel is generally regarded as one of the most ancient symbols. In his analysis of the significance of archaic man's "symbolism of the Centre" and concern with the "centre of the world," Mircea Eliade notes the biological terms used in ancient texts about the "Holy One" who creates "the world like an embryo" that "proceeds from the navel onwards" spreading "out in different directions" (*Myth*, 16). The centre is described as the earth's navel, where creation began. An omphalos, it is "pre-eminently the zone of the sacred, the zone of absolute reality" and "all other symbols of absolute reality (trees of life and immortality, Fountain of Youth, etc.) are also situated at a centre" (17–18). The symbol of the sacred is embryo, world, creation – child.

As Eliade tells us, the path to this omphalos or centre is a "difficult road," a "pilgrimage," a "danger-ridden" voyage, "because it is, in fact, a rite of passage from the profane to the sacred, from the ephemeral and illusory to reality and eternity, from death to life, from man to the divinity" (18). Here the journey is a reversal of the physiology of the symbol. This interpretation of the "centre" and the path that leads "to" it, is a complex representation with different layers of meaning. Now, it is a source of creative energy for the transmission of inspiration, a threshold-centre and path, the centre as divinity, the Other-centre, and finally, it is the self, the centre-within and originating agent of the journey.

The navel as centre symbolizes not only how the varied subjects/individuals are represented as circles of being but also mark the scar where they were connected by moments (movements) of the arduous journey. These concentric circles of being conflate distance and deny or reverse the journey, even as they emphasize the absent link.[6] The journey as the metaphoric line that brings the circles together would necessarily be spiral.[7] The restoration of a physical base to the metaphor causes a different emphasis in the interpretation of journey and centre. According to Eliade, we become ontologically real by the repetition or imitation of an archetype; when we use the archetype of birth, which emphasizes connection as well as conception and includes separation, ontology is re-rooted in the original placental connection. Whereas Eliade calls the centre "the navel of the earth" (13), "where man was formed" (16), it may be more appropriate to see the centre as the place of human intent and a source of the will to join with the womb, the mother, the family, the world, the spiritual.

For Eliade, a "meaningful act" can be "any repetition of an arche-typal gesture" that "suspends duration, abolishes profane time, and participates in mythical time" (36). He goes on to distinguish male from female initiations by focusing on the cultural disruption of the male: an act of rupture, a separation from the mother carried out within an age group.[8] In this way, male initiation is an entrance into male society that enforces a total separation from the mother and from female society; sexuality becomes an important part of the "eternal return" because it is the only (culturally acceptable) way of returning to a family community. The anxiety over relationship with an "other" is a culturally created fear.

Female initiation, as Eliade notes, is physical and individual. A young woman is removed from her family and instructed by an older woman in "the secrets of sexuality and fertility" (42). In addition, he sees menstruation, pregnancy, and birth as sacred and so rightfully argues that they constitute initiatory ordeals equal to that of young men. In his discussion of the Hellenic Mysteries at Eleusis, Eliade also makes several observations that fit with Psyche's tasks. The initiate becomes "he [*sic*] who sees" (111), and in the association of initiation with spirituality, Eliade identifies the "maieutic procedure (from the root *maia*, 'midwife')," which ties initiation and spirituality directly to childbirth (114).[9] Psyche, through her desire "to see" Eros and in conceiving, in her pregnancy, and later in giving birth, images a pri-mordial understanding that vivifies individual change and transforma-tion even as it repeats an ancient gesture. She participates in an action that renews life even as it brings a profound and personal psychic renewal.

Female Being and the Sacred

I have described Psyche's journey of self-reflection and self-analysis, of growth in knowledge and understanding, as being shamanic. Now, in the shamanic experience, as Eliade describes it, there is also acknowl-edged centre and connection: "The shaman knows the mystery of the break-through in plane" (*Shamanism*, 259). The breakthrough place is described as central, as a sacred space, as the navel or "umbilicus" of the earth. These planes are not transcended but instead are "linked together by a central axis" (259) and represent an intelligence or understanding of metaphysical truth: "Those who know have wings" (479).[10] "For the Shaman in ecstasy," observes Eliade, "the bridge or the tree, the vine, the cord, and so on – which *in illo tempore*, con-nected earth with heaven – once again, for the space of an instant, becomes present reality" (486). In spite of a description of the centre as existing in space, Eliade accounts for a very umbilical connection.

This depiction of connection presents an image of the sacred, the spiritual, the numinous, that is different from Rudolf Otto's definition. For Otto, the numinous is a creature consciousness, "the emotion of a creature, submerged and overwhelmed by its own nothingness" and characterized by "overpowering, absolute, might" (10). The feelings associated with this numinous are described variously as tidal, bursting, spasmodic, convulsive, daemonic, horrible. The mysterious is also described as daunting, fascinating, and "wholly other" (26). The threat and profound fear are of loss of self, of absorption and drowning. The language employed by Otto, with its implication of rise and fall, corresponds to the expressions used to describe the structure of male narratives, the patterns perceived in Eros's experience, the male erotic or reproductive experience, and the Icarus complex. That the other in this case is not female in no way detracts from the language that characterizes the experience.

My examination of Psyche's experience, however, suggests that her journey could allow for a different language of relationship to the spiritual – one that includes nature. This language would recognize difference as integral to connection and nurturing. The expression of the spiritual, in a way more in keeping with embodied experience, would include a recognition of the centrality of process to human life and would see its continuities as well as contraries. An emphasis on embodied life within the biosphere, a return to understanding our sense of community with all things, a vision of at-one-ness and integration in the whole pattern, brings with it a heightened awareness of how we contribute to, as well as take from, the whole. Recalling the child-to-mother bond and their placental connector, the image of the sacred as an embodied mother goddess of the natural world includes the ways in which we are dependent and individual even as we are agents and responsible for our willful actions.

Lifeprints

Earlier, I described Psyche's journey as a soul's journey on the soles of her feet in the footprints of the goddess Aphrodite; it is not a single life prescription, but rather a pattern of possibility, one that emphasizes a conscious awareness of intellectual, emotional, and spiritual growth. In *Lifeprints: New Patterns of Life and Work for Today's Women*, Grace Baruch, Rosalind Barnett and Caryl Rivers give a timely reminder about how dangerous it is to limit our lives to one role: "no one pattern fits all women, no one lifeprint guarantees well-being and no one path leads inevitably to misery" (viii). As in the case of Psyche, however, what is common to all "walks of life" is the importance of both meaningful work *and* affective relationships to well-being. As *Lifeprints* puts it, in order to have a feeling of well-being (joy), women require both a sense of mastery (agency) and pleasure (satisfaction): "Doing and achieving are at least as important to the lives of women as are relationships and feelings" (15). Placing all Psyche's relationships and tasks within the context of redefined female life reveals how, as *Lifeprints* expresses it, in the context of love relationships, they "can only enrich and deepen a life – they cannot transform who a person is" (20). Redefining the tasks to highlight Psyche's intellectual and spiritual achievements and placing these in the context of a revalued physical experience account for the possibilities of transformation.

Just as I see in the Psyche myth a fruitful interpretive instrument, I see in women's autobiographies a way to test my own hypotheses about the Psychean experience.[1] Women's autobiographical writings are a way for women to reflect on their own life experiences. Being able to show that the structures, themes and motifs uncovered in the myth are also present in some autobiographies will initially confirm a pattern for possibility and difference even as it provides an underlying metaphoric unity. In the juxtaposition of ancient myth with modern women's stories, there may be revealed what Keith Louise Fulton has called an "authentic voice," one that does not "set aside parts or even most of ourselves" (426). In contemporary women's autobiographies one can find the many ways to differently print and re-print aspects of this ancient pattern, corroborating the richness and complexity of Psyche's tale. In this chapter, I take the opportunity to suggest some general outlines.

Contouring Autobiography

In his theory of (men's) autobiography, *Metaphors of Self*, James Olney reminds us of, and rightfully emphasizes, the importance of metaphor to our ways of knowing and as a way of producing order. He also emphasizes that this impulse to order is "closely related to soul and essential being, is not of the order of facts but of the order of process: an activity exercised continuously out from a centre." Like Eliade, however, he goes on to interpret process as a movement outside of the self, "back from manifestation to source." In this out-from-centre and back-from-manifestation movement, by my metaphoric ground, placental consciousness, there is a confusion of author-ity. So described, source and manifestation become image reflections – like Narcissus and his mirror self – forever imposed and imposing on the world. To Olney, this obliges an analysis that sees "the mind of man, a great shape-maker impelled forever to find order in himself and give it back to the universe" (17).

Olney himself is aware of the dilemma that this solipsistic attitude towards subjectivity presents: "If all selves are unique and, in their uniqueness, only subjectively experienced (ie., we may only experience other selves, but then only as objects, not as proper selves), and if all selves are constantly evolving, transforming, and becoming different from themselves, then how is it at all possible to comprehend or define the self or to give anyone else any sense of it?" He continues with his answer: "It may be that the nearest one can come to definition is to look not straight to the self, which is invisible anyway, but sidewise to an experience of the self ... that can reflect or evoke it and that may appeal to another individual's experience of the self" (29). This sidewise experience is by metaphor: "The self expresses itself by the metaphors it creates and projects" (34). That Olney regards the self as isolated and solitary leads him to perceive autobiography as singular or, with the author, as a mirror double, a stand-in substitute that is static, or a series of images and image-reflections.

Many women's biographical writings, in contrast, are specifically concerned with challenging what Sidonie Smith calls the "metaphysical or universal subject."[2] In particular they take part in the "[r]adical challenges to the notion of a unified and unitary core of selfhood [that] wrenched the ideology of the universal subject out of its ontological, teleological, and topographical boundaries" (55). She identifies Marx, Freud, Derrida, and Lacan as among those who contribute to the deconstruction of this concept of self: "Site of fractures, splittings, maskings, dislocations, vulnerabilities, absences, and subjections of all kinds, the architecture of selfhood seems to have collapsed into a pile of twentieth-century rubble." The "self" has become "one" and "not-one." The mirror has broken; "the very grounds of representation soften, break apart, and disperse" (57).[3] Again, by my reckoning, the site, splitting, absence, subjection, and architecture exist over the absent third, the placental consciousness, and have more to do with self constructions than with being – unitary or otherwise.

As Smith sees it, however, the deconstruction of the unified self does not seem to have affected the male perception of female being or the confrontational aspects of identity boundaries that ensure women's marginality. Women are still seen as having an "embodied subjectivity"; "woman remains the object of, and in, contestatory male discourses." She warns that this changed perception of male subjectivity, accompanied by an unchanged view of women's being, "threatens another kind of subjection that would erase real women outside the 'text,' silence the heterogenous specifics of their experiences, including the experiences of oppression, in service to the impersonal and homogenizing technologies of rampant textuality" (59). Any ability to cause change, to transform, and any capability to see multiplicity and difference are immediately curtailed by this post-modern view of subjective experience.

In Smith's analysis, because of its "tremendous elasticity," autobiography becomes the area where this concept of selfhood may be challenged. She uses some twentieth-century women's autobiographies, such as Gertrude Stein's, to describe the "generic engagement" that allows "the entry into language and self-narrative of culturally marginalized peoples through which they recapitulate the contours of subjectivity" (61). As she describes it, "they fashion and refashion, then fine tune various identities through which they make meaning out of their experiences" (62). If I conjoin her insights with my revisioning of the birthing metaphors, autobiography is a (placental/journey) place-process for the transformative connections from older to younger selves, from self to (a specific) other, self to society, self to reader. Placing autobiography in a triple connection brings a way to transform the mirror and the gap, brings a metaphor that demands difference and connection, and foregrounds context and time as elements in any analysis of individual life. Clearly, seeing the self as originating in a triple connection, continuously sustained and limited by that connection, makes autobiography into a process of transformation and growth even as, as process, it transforms with growth.

This concern with evolution accounts for what Estelle C. Jelinek describes as the "irregularity" of women's narratives: "The narratives of their lives are often not chronological and progressive but disconnected, fragmentary, or organized into self-sustained units rather than connecting chapters" (17). She relates this feature to "the multidimensionality of women's socially conditioned roles" and also sees it as the cause of the relegation of women's autobiographies to "non-artistic" categories. In her analysis of Lillian Hellman's style, she suggests why such a circumferential style is important: "Had she forced an orderly and linear narrative on the events and persons that affected the development of her personality and values, she would have destroyed the achievement of the cumulative, three-dimensional portrait of herself" (18). While women's autobiographies might be called anecdotal and self-contained, one could also argue that the deliberate re-membering, building up, and sequencing of narrative carry the possibility of seeing each event as evoking change, as "pregnant" and "bearing" on the next in cumulative meaning-full life experience.

Features of a Psychean Text

A comprehensive explanation of the Psyche features in women's autobiographies is obviously beyond the scope of this study. What is possible, however, is to provide a skeleton framework of the tendencies in a Psychean text. What is intended is a framework that acknowledges a complexity and diversity much in keeping with the individual lives lived. I likewise give fair warning: the choices (of both autobiographies and critiques) are intended to be as wide-ranging as the references must be cursory.

The configurations of Psyche's story are present in women's autobiographies if they have any of the following features:

1 The story begins "before-the-beginning" of the individual's birth, in origins and ancestry, and seems concerned with context, with the author's life in the family, the larger community, in the matrix of life or within a personal philosophy; the ending is "no-ending" but spirals onward, intending an opening out to another stage, another

reading, a new reality; the narration shares experience as well as "secrets" and catalogues achievement.

2 There is a real consciousness of threshold, of a place that is an early transition; this "placental" place is both barrier and way out; it is metaphorically described as, for instance, window-, door-, or passage-through; this transition is articulated in its completeness, as a process "out-from/through/in-to," a threefold movement; this movement is accompanied by a sense of "Call."

3 Beginnings indicate both a move out as well as the awareness of loss, of connections "cut" or "severed" on social or personal levels or on a combination of both levels; grief is necessarily "passed through" to new connections or re-connections – with life itself, perhaps; there is an awareness of a betrayal as inherent in patriarchy and the particular price women have paid in cultural suppression, repression, or abuse; there is a realization of "split"; cultural failure is a cause for grief, growth and action.

4 The narratives are experiential, sequential, and concerned with process, with crises that are moments of passage and psychological growth, of recognition and transformation contextualized as intense moments in a life journey; "digressions," as they appear in women's writing, turn out to be spirals out and back to re-collect experience that "adds to" narrative; such "digressions" might have a "circumferential" aspect and involve the moving out to "encircle" the experience/information in order to "ferry" it back to the narrative; there is an awareness of three different sensations of time: linear, seasonal and creative time or timeless-ness.

5 The awareness of the "gaps" of life, of the coincidence of expectation and discrepant outcome, is made explicit by the use of humour, a sense of irony, and paradox; these devices and this sense of humour may be seen to arise from a recognition of the incongruities of awareness between values held in a life-lived-as-a-woman (or as part of a marginalized group) within a social, intellectual, and cultural community defined by men and male concerns, the dominant cultural group; this outlook corresponds with an optimism that looks towards new being in life in spite of hardships, grief, and loss; this is congruent with a philosophy of death as necessary ending, as threshold rather than as ultimate end, "tragic fall," or transcendent union.

6 Human relationships of all kinds, including but not exclusively focusing on the male-female courtship dance, are viewed as enriching and predominate in the narrative; the mother/mother figure or mentor has a pre-eminent place; the sister-sister bond, the community of women, is regarded as supportive, fulfilling, and vital; relationship/s

with child/ren figure as relationships of change and interaction, important in mutual growth rather than as clone-like extensions of the self; there is a consciousness of the richness of the third phase of life, the life of female being beyond the reproductive phase, in a wider, socially expansive "mothering."

7 Relationships are seen as being processes of connection that recognize differences and see separation as the way of growth; they are seen as having a triplicity, emphasizing the growth and change in relationship between two (or more) individuals in context and through time.

8 The accumulation of sensory detail indicates an awareness of the richness of life as it is lived physically; all of the senses are evoked: hearing, movement, smell, taste, touch, and vision; this acute awareness of the physicality of life brings with it a heightened awareness of the natural world; this natural world is felt to have a being, an energy, that appeals emotionally to the spirit.

9 The spiritual aspects of the life journey are expressed outside cultural contexts; spirituality is registered in an affinity for the earth, the earth as home or place of at-one-ness; this bond, this communion-with, brings a heightened sense of self and agency and is self-energizing rather than symbiotic or self-obliterating; spirituality is expressed in ways that suggest the redefined and tripartite prebirth connection.

Entitling Lifeprints

From even a brief glance over some titles of women's autobiographies, Psychean motifs emerge.[4] Mary Daly's *Outercourse* is described as backgrounded in patriarchal suppression and a voyage into the "Clusters of Moments," "the Realm of Wild Reality," and the "Homeland of Women's Selves and of All Others" (1). In her Introduction, Daly herself notes the importance of these moments as she comments on the first word in the title of Virginia Woolf's *Moments of Being*; she describes them as moments of seeing beyond – into context and into wholeness (Daly 3–4). Emily Carr's *Growing Pains: An Autobiography* integrates growth and pain, the positive and negative aspects of life inherent in growing up. Similarly, Gabrielle Roy's *Enchantment and Sorrow* proposes their coexistence, that life consists of both, that they are inseparable, just as Fredelle Bruser Maynard's *Raisins and Almonds* includes the sweet with the bitter. Movement on a path within the landscape materializes in the title of Zora Neale Hurston's *Dust Tracks on a Road* and L.M. Montgomery's *The Alpine Path*. These titles also suggest physical discomfort and struggle, but the struggle is tempered by the community that is intimated in "path" and "road."

Path and road indicate a recognition of connection to those who have gone before and those who will come after, of being part of this larger procession. Margaret Laurence's *Dance on the Earth*, which can be read either as a descriptive or imperative phrase, celebrates an embodied movement of life in the world of nature, in the world of here and now, and is all the more remarkable a title in view of the fact that her memoir was completed during her final illness. Maya Angelou symbolizes her struggle to find personal freedom within the cage of racial intolerance in *I Know Why the Caged Bird Sings*. That she "sings" evokes a joyful attitude in keeping with life-as-celebration in spite of limitation and restriction.

Maria Campbell's title, *Half-breed,* suggests both the social betrayal of racism and bigotry and the creation of a new community in her search for personal dignity. The bitter irony of the epithet is turned into a banner of survival and new being. Equally critical and harsh are the titles *Don't: A Woman's Word* by Elly Danica and *Daddy's Girl* by Charlotte Vale Allen. Both give the lie to the patriarchal myth with all the painful intensity of the betrayed. The sense of process beyond displacement and attachment to a home newly found is suggested in Laura Goodman Salverson's *Confessions of an Immigrant's Daughter.* One of the most amusing of the titles is *The Autobiography of Alice B. Toklas* by Gertrude Stein, since title and author seem to contradict one another. What is not at all contradictory, however, is what such a paradox implies about the strength and importance of the relationship of each to the other in both lives.

Gertrude Stein: Circumferential Sequencing

In his analysis of Stein's *The Autobiography of Alice B. Toklas,* James E. Breslin makes several observations about style in this unorthodox work. Blending "the domestic particularity, whimsical humour, and ironic precision of Toklas with some of the leading features of Stein's writing – e.g., stylized repetition, digression, a language that continuously points up its own artifice" – means that the "reader is not sure who he is listening to; nor is he meant to be" [*sic*] (152). The building up of particulars and the stylized repetitions foreground the accumulation of knowledge. As readers we have returned to not-quite-the-same-point in the narrative and with new knowledge. These signals begin immediately in Stein's narrative: "There are a great many things to tell" (6), "I must tell a little about" (7), "Before I tell" (8), "But to return to" (9), "As I say" (10). Such "digressive" passages, however, do not seem to be mere forays out from the text or observations that serve no purpose and which can be ignored without loss; rather, the movement is out and back, and these passages are best described as circumferential. Stein's method is to spiral out from the narrative in order to gather in more memories and then to come back with them in tow, to enhance and add to the narrative.

Wendy Steiner suggests a similar way of interpreting Stein's narrative structure: "Stein believed that the old-style story with beginning, middle, and end was inappropriate to the twentieth century, because of the high pitched intensity of modern media-filled life. Instead of projecting one forward in time to a final resolution, a modern narrative should force one into the fullness and depth of each moment, and should proceed as a succession of such moments. Each should be a copy of the last, with only minimal differences" (176). Steiner notes that such repetition with a difference is not the same as design that involves exact repetition (177). Breslin also describes the book as having "an elusive centre and discontinuous design" (152) and observes that this circularity suggests a lack of progressive linear movement.

Breslin continues by comparing Stein's style as a writer with Picasso's as a painter: "Like Picasso's portrait, *The Autobiography* gives the inside by way of the outside; it plays down psychology and sticks to the surface, recording externals ... in a way that clearly manifests deliberate and idiosyncratic acts of selection and stylization ... *The Autobiography*, in short, gives us Gertrude Stein being" (154). The inside/outside paradox, the accumulation of the details of context, and the interrelationship of Alice and Gertrude suggest a consciousness of relationship based on connections.

In Stein's "disembodied strategy" of writing through Alice, Sidonie Smith sees "a subversive return of the repressed body." This paradoxical achievement is the result of appropriating "bourgeois heterosexuality" to "lesbian pleasure" (78-9), of writing through the body of her lover, making the text "an act of erotic union" (80). Stein does this by employing the forms of marriage: "Through the camouflage of normative gender arrangements of heterosexuality she encodes the 'abnormative' alignment of desire." By inscribing the heterosexual-union-as-marriage beside lesbian relationship, Stein has disrupted "paternal narrative" (81-2).

I would argue further that this reflects a reproductive placental consciousness and exists beyond the notion of heterosexual union and culturally prescribed concepts of sexuality. By speaking through Alice, by using the triplicities of "placental" shadow – lover, and sister-self, she has evoked both the self and other, the like and unlike complexities of the sister-sister/lover and of the relationship itself. By announcing this device at the end of the autobiography, Stein invites us back to a transformed reading of it. In his discussion of the conclusion of the text, Breslin emphasizes a vision of ending as no-ending, of new awareness, birth, and spiral: "The autobiography ends by folding back on itself; and a reader is invited to re-read the book in the light of the revelation that Stein is the author ... Yet the book's conclusion also reveals Stein to be on a quest that is not completed; the book's ending is also open. The end of the book closes off and frames a life at the same time that it breaks out of its frame, its artificial closure, to affirm the ongoing process of the author's life" (161). Thus, the impression is one of an ending that spirals out into another reading.

Mary Daly: Context, Spiral, and Threshold

Mary Daly's *Outercourse* shows the spiral as the informing structure of her autobiography and in the process provides insight into her reasons for that choice. She describes the spiral as an "accumulated Gynergy of Moments," and a "Qualitative Leap" to a "New Galaxy," and gives evidence of the desire to contextualize the life story, to give a base to the spiral (5). Daly recreates language to emphasize process and movement. Mentioning the importance of verb tense to an understanding of spirals, she presents actions as occurring in time: "were" and "are" and "will continue to be" (6). She writes of making verbs from nouns (be-ing, re-call, dis-covery) to focus on process and movement.[5] Although her training in dichotomous argument is clearly evident, she, existing Echo-like outside the argument, is conscious of a "patriarchally inflicted *aphasia*" and chooses to leap into the "Background" as a way of bringing in context, as a way of jumping over what is perceived as missing and into something new. "Qualitative Leaping is," as she says, "not merely 'beyond' but toward and into something else, which I have named *Spinning*" (8).

Emphasizing sequence as part of the spiral, she accentuates the interconnections of the moments of her autobiographical voyage by calling them "organic" (10). Daly stresses that both autobiography and philosophy are "interwoven" and "fit together" into a quest (12). The metaphors she uses – of light, the sea, volcanoes, the galaxies, planets, sun, moon, and stars, and of pollution – place this before-the-beginning squarely in a consciousness of earth, even as she writes of "space" travel.

Daly also writes of breaking taboos, repeating "Calls," intuitions of nothingness, patriarchal betrayals, "The Dream of Green," the expulsion from paradise, and opening the "Third Eye/I" of intuitive understanding.

Her voyage in a "craft" on a "subliminal sea" holds "contrapuntal movements," the coexisting and contradictory directions in her quest. Indeed, she also articulates a threshold moment, an "Exodus" from organized religion (138–9). This articulation of "Be-Falling" is reminiscent of Psyche's "Stygian sleep," the mark of the shaman's return, and her responsibility for bringing new awareness to the community.

This exodus is close followed by the breaking of another taboo – movement into lesbian sexuality. "From that moment nothing was ever the same again," and, she reveals, "the transformation was permanent" (144). Even in her joy at finding her own way to sexual expression, however, lies the tolerance of difference that is basic to (maternal) response-ability, to an understanding of the physical, psychological, and affective lives of others' lifeprints: "In my view, then and Now, there are many dimensions of woman identification" (145). For Daly, difference, deviation, and connection are "*Spinning*" and creation is "Dis-covering the lost thread of connectedness" (195). As a way of knowing, undertaken "with other Spinning Voyagers," she "Dis-covered more about our connectedness with each other and with the cosmos" (196).

Even her relationship with her mother is recounted as a nexus of conflict, difference, and deepened understanding: "My mother and I had been very close during my childhood, but adolescence and early adulthood had brought years of grief and struggle between us." Their "time of living together in Brighton" and their "great reunion" brought "a transcendence of that conflict." For Daly, the "reunion recaptured the early ecstatic dimensions of our communication" and a "deeper understanding between us." She goes on to assert: "We had not merely come 'full circle.' Rather our progress was spiral-shaped. My mother was not simply my mother, but also my sister and friend" (91). Although she uses the term "transcendence" to describe the reunion with her mother, the description itself provides a clear articulation of the transformative nature of the experience.

Her response to her mother's death is revealing: "I remember the way I said the word 'No' when I saw that my mother had died. It was No to the unspeakable loss that I had dreaded since childhood. It was the ancient awful No that countless other daughters had gasped at such a Moment throughout thousands of years. Now it was my turn to say it." That she can recognize both timelessness and seasonal time's continuity, the eternal returns of a life experience that exists in an intensity that is out of time, in no way obviates the individual and personal loss. This anguish of loss – the existential "No" – has not, likewise, obscured the irony in her use of "Luckily" to describe the too late arrival of the ambulance whereby her mother "was spared

the horror of returning to the hospital and suffering prolonged 'treat-
ment'" (93).

Virginia Woolf: Loss and Grief

In *Moments of Being*, Virginia Woolf marks her own mother's untimely
death as "the greatest disaster that could happen; it was as though on
some brilliant day of spring the racing clouds of a sudden stood still,
grew dark, and massed themselves; the wind flagged, and all creatures
on earth moaned or wandered seeking aimlessly" (40). The images that
she uses to convey the sense of loss for her sisters and herself speak
of an awareness of sensory experience. Yet, this is immediately followed by her sense of irony in being unable to remember her mother
through words. The mother remains a real presence nonetheless: "there
she is ... familiar ... closer than any of the living are, lighting our
random lives as with a burning torch" (40). The positive "light" Woolf
associates with her mother and the torch continue in her association
of the metaphor with "womanly virtues" (47–8).

In describing the relationship between her eldest sister, Stella, and
their mother, Woolf indicates the dangers of the loss of difference that
is possible in mother-daughter relationships – the threat of "constant
preoccupation": "It was beautiful, it was almost excessive; for it had
something of the morbid nature of an affection between two people
too closely allied for the proper amount of reflection to take place
between them; what her mother felt passed almost instantly through
Stella's mind; there was no need for the brain to ponder and criticize
what the soul knew" (43). Both separation and difference are integral
to relationship. For Woolf, these differences-in-connection must be
supplied by the process of reasoning, a reflective ability that recognizes
differences as other than an adversarial concept of self.

At her mother's death, Stella took up their mother's responsibilities
in the family: "no one ever again was to serve her for prop" and she
"never again, perhaps," cared "for anyone as she had cared for her
mother. That, whatever gain is to be set beside it, was the permanent
loss" (44). Loss and gain are inextricably linked in this view of a
transformative moment, but interconnection is irretrievably dichotomized for Stella. She may regard herself as dependent or as strong and
selfless; there is no recognition that we are always both.

In "A Sketch of the Past," Woolf acknowledges the "number of
different ways in which memoirs can be written," but chooses to begin
with "the first memory." She writes of not consciously choosing a way,
feeling certain "that it will find itself" (64). Mother consciousness,
female reproductive/placental consciousness, might explain this as,

metaphorically, a sense that the newly conceived will either find the appropriate connecting path "or if not it will not matter" (64), echoing (age-old and clichéd) mother-comfort words: "There, there, it's okay, it's alright."

Woolf further records the difficulty of locating in the memoir the self, "the person to whom things happened" (65). Like Psyche, she is compelled to act in a culture that allows her only to be acted upon; she is perceived as passive, and there is no language to express a female agency that is responsive to environment. Feeling is described as linked to an awareness of any change in physical circumstance, as a heightened sensory perception, and as "lying in a grape and seeing through a film of semi-transparent yellow" (65). Shapes and sounds are elastic and gummy and air-like; all are tangible and at the same time illusory, ecstatic. Another memory is described as rapturous and tangible, pressed and humming around her (66). Intertwining sight, touch, and sound, memory seems "more real than the present moment." Also tangible is the past, "an avenue lying behind, a long ribbon of scenes, emotions," ending in "the garden and nursery" (67).

Woolf even describes listening as a tactile connection to the past, using the metaphor of fitting "a plug into a wall." Wall and cord are tactile and concrete ways of presenting the reality of emotion and remembering it. If "strong emotion" leaves "its trace," the problem is "how we can get ourselves attached to it" (67). One such strong emotion ties her "looking-glass shame" and sense of betrayal to the social constructs of femininity and beauty. The memory of Gerald Duckworth's violation of her "private parts" and her resentment and dislike are tied to an age-old taboo of body and link her to "thousands of ancestresses in the past" (69). She suggests that what is not remembered is as important to memoir as what is; a memoir does not just present a chronology of events but must also account for the changing self within the process; a memoir must account for the equally important moments between. In what she calls a digression, she notes the same problem for the writer of fiction: "how to describe ... non-being" (70). What visual artists learn to see and explore as "negative space" is as essential as matter delineated; both "matter" in the process of the whole. They are the interconnective bits: "These separate moments of being were however embedded in many more moments of non-being" (70).

Angelica Garnett: Secrets and New Beginnings

Woolf's chapter titled "Reminiscences" was intended as a life of her sister, Vanessa. In the memoir of her own childhood, Angelica Garnett,

Vanessa's daughter, brings another generation's perspective on family relationships and secrets. She writes through to an understanding of the influence that her unusual origins exerted on her life. Of Woolf's feelings about Vanessa, she writes: "love, admiration and understanding played their part but were inextricably mixed with jealousy and envy" (22). In a passage reminiscent of Psyche's sisters, Garnett describes the rift that developed between the sisters when "Virginia took it into her head to flirt with Clive": "It was not however, Clive's attention that Virginia wanted to attract, but Vanessa's: her behaviour constituted an appeal for help addressed to Vanessa over Clive's body" (26–7). Garnett records her own ambivalence towards Vanessa: "Her image and personality had always obsessed me: on the one hand I felt compelled to imitate her, while on the other I resented her dominance" (2).

In this complex relationship lurks the "kindly" deceit. Garnett's biological father is not acknowledged openly, and the person she calls her father, believes to be her father, is not: "Owing to my likeness to Duncan, even my grandmother Ethel must have had her suspicions. I was the only person successfully kept in the dark" (38). One wonders just how successfully when she also states: "With [friends of my parents] I always felt secure, but also ill at ease, sensing that there was some profound inadequacy in me to which, in their kindness, they did not allude" (1).

Of Vanessa's death, Garnett writes about her feelings of ambivalence: "the thought that she might die was unbelievable, terrible and at the same time inadmissibly exhilarating. Like the disappearance of some familiar monument, her absence would reveal a new perspective in which I might be able to find freedom" (171). She cannot realize this potential for a new beginning, however, without one of her daughters, who faced a turning point of her own: "Her crisis had a deep emotional impact and brought me to life – it also taught me much; but I have learnt many precious lessons from all my children" (175). The intensity and complexity of this intergenerational chronicle are summed up in an observation about aging: "And yet it seems to me that one's maturity should be a better time than one's childhood, however wonderful that may have been. Mine has only just begun" (176).

Margaret Laurence: Sensory Richness and Metaphor

Margaret Laurence's *Dance on the Earth* combines the view of closure as an invitation to go on and back with an emphasis on the dance of life itself. Persisting even in the face of death's seeming finality, her memoir ends with: "I know now, as I did not know when I wrote the first draft of these memoirs, that my own dance of life has not much longer to last. It will continue in my children, and perhaps for a while in my books. It has been varied, sometimes anguished, always inter- esting. I rejoice in having been given it. May the dance go on" (222). And the book itself continues with "Afterwords" that are "after" only in the sense of following in page sequence; the entries are of poems, letters, and speeches written earlier in her life, before the memoir. *Dance* is also an exploration of movement as metaphoric connection: "I know there are many ways of dancing other than the literal ones. These other ways, of friendships, of work, of stubborn hoping in a terrifying world" (17).

By using this metaphor of physical movement through life as a means of connecting with memory, she describes her own three mother-mentors and how they influenced her life; in doing so, she affirms, too, the special and close bond between women in the com- munity of women, even in the isolated nuclear family of the twentieth century. In the silences, we recognize the grief that shadows joyful relationship and signals the need for learning and transformation in women's lives. She writes of learning at five: "My mother is dead. I might not have known precisely what 'never' meant. But I think I under- stood I would never see her again. After that, I have no conscious memories for about a year" (25). She links two aspects of her person- ality to this mother and to this moment: "The part of me that remains young and clowning ... I probably owe to her. How much of the other side ... may have begun to grow in my spirit at my mother's death, I can never know" (26). The substance of joy and grief bound together in memory's process and in memory's absence accumulates into the person she has become, the one in the act of writing her memoir.

Gloria Steinem: Self-Worth and Consciousness

Feminist and activist Gloria Steinem articulates the importance of self- worth to any truly revolutionary project. In the examination of her own life and in the recognition of her own losses and experiences of injustice, she writes of her desire to create a new being and in this way a new society of transformed beings. Part of this new consciousness is what she describes as a "Universal I." This universality is expressed through reconnections: with nature, with animals, with the body, and in a differently articulated spirituality. She gives a vision of the self that encompasses a "universe in microcosm": "We are so many selves ... What draws together these ever-shifting selves of infinite reactions and returning is this: There is one true inner voice" (323). Her chal- lenge is to hear her own authentic voice through the displacements of cultural betrayal.

Steinem writes about coming to terms with aging and with the stages of life. Because of her active career and the choice not to have children, because she "didn't have their growth as a measure of time," she "had been behaving as if the long plateau of activist middle life went on forever" (243). Describing her passage through denial and defiance as stages of dealing with age, she writes of finally recognizing that "I needed a model not of being old, but of aging," and "that my denial and defiance were related to giving up a way of being, not ceasing to be" (244, 245). One aspect of aging that continues to disappoint her recalls Psyche's original burden: "It hasn't liberated me from that epithet of 'the pretty one.'" She clarifies what makes this an annoying burden: "If that sounds odd, think about working as hard as you can, then discovering that whatever you accomplish is attributed to your looks" (247).

Zora Neale Hurston: Time and Timelessness

In her autobiography, Zora Neale Hurston describes a personal philosophy that summarizes her convictions in phrases that reverberate with compelling and sensual images, before-beginnings and after-endings, of her own sense of power, of personal integrity. "I do not pretend to read god's mind," she says: "Somebody else may have my rapturous glance at the archangels." What Hurston values is daily life, connection, and evolution woven together by a sense of creative timelessness: "The springing of the yellow line of morning out of the misty deep of dawn, is glory enough for me." Affirming that "nothing is destructible; things merely change forms," she declares: "When the consciousness we know as life ceases, I know that I shall still be part and parcel of the world. I was a part before the sun rolled into shape and burst forth in the glory of change. I was, when the earth was hurled out from its fiery rim. I shall return with the earth to Father Sun, and still exist in substance when the sun has lost its fire, and disintegrated in infinity to perhaps become a part of the whirling rubble in space." This sense of the spiritual is not one based on fear. She includes a rhetorical question to heighten her emphatic pronouncement: "Why fear? The stuff of my being is matter, ever changing, ever moving, but never lost; so what need of denominations and creeds to deny myself the comfort of all my fellow men? The wide belt of the universe has no need of finger rings. I am one with the infinite and need no other assurance" (202–3). As the allusion to Aphrodite's girdle mocks the legality of "finger rings," Hurston's expression of connection as a return "with the sun" expresses a consciousness of a seasonal continuity beyond cultural convention. Her description of being at "one" with the infinite and yet uniquely individual expresses a personal understanding that accords with placental consciousness.

Maya Angelou: Betrayal and Racism

Betrayal as a specific kind of loss is a central ingredient in African-American women's autobiographical writing, and it has been recognized as a signal of the loss of self-worth. As Regina Blackburn writes, "Most African-American female autobiographies confess to one incident in their early years that awakened them to their colour; this recognition scene evoked an awareness of their blackness and of its significance, and it had a lasting influence on their lives" (134). What is signified in such a "recognition scene" is the internalization of self-hatred because of an entrenched social hierarchy of privilege, an entrenched context. Blackburn contrasts the autobiographies of Hurston and Angelou in their responses to this betrayal as it is expressed in feelings about the South. According to Blackburn, "At an early age, Angelou recognized her hatred of self and allowed it to grow in the southern climate," whereas Hurston found comfort there: "Unlike so many who wrote about the South, she always considered the region home. She never desired to escape from it, and she was spiritually revived upon returning to it" (144, 138).

Angelou's betrayal experience initiates her autobiography, and the echoes of Psyche's sacrifice are clear: "Wouldn't they be surprised when one day I woke out of my black ugly dream ... Because I was really white and because a cruel fairy stepmother, who was understandably jealous of my beauty, had turned me into a too-big Negro girl, with nappy black hair, broad feet and a space between her teeth that would hold a number two pencil" (2). The description of this incident, with its bitterness of shame and humiliation lit with ironic humour, prefaces the narrative and thus implies its importance to the whole of the remembered life. This view encompasses "not only what the white world has done," according to Blackburn, "but also the black world" (134), and this double betrayal is re-enforced in the account of her rape by her stepfather. The style of the subsequent chapters is circumferential; each adds to, and is read through, this incident.

Although Hurston's moment of betrayal is equally complex, it does not involve racism specifically. Instead she records her inability to influence, her failure to make others act on her behalf. She writes of being unable to keep a promise to her dying mother – a failure brought about by her father's physical restraint and through her own inability to make others understand what her mother wanted: "I was to agonize over that moment for years to come. In the midst of play, in the wakeful moments after midnight, on the way home from parties, and even in the classroom during lectures. Now I know that I could not have had my way against the world. The world we lived in required those acts. Anything else would have been sacrilege, and no nine year old voice was going to thwart them. My father was with the mores" (64). Both Hurston and Angelou experienced betrayal in poignant, personal, and public ways and record the way that it affected them for long years after. Angelou's account of childhood sexual abuse and racial betrayal indicates the multiple levels of punishment present in a patriarchal society that treats difference in terms of value and heightens the double jeopardy of being black and female into an almost assured sexual betrayal as well.

Elly Danica and Charlotte Vale Allen: Betrayal and Incest

The sexual betrayal that occurs in the midst of the family can be as profoundly debilitating as racial intolerance. Elly Danica's *Don't: A Woman's Word* chronicles the painful intensity of the journey to recovery that such a sexual trauma necessitates. Danica makes specific use of the six gates of Inanna's descent pattern, which is similar to the descent in Psyche's fourth task. What Danica illustrates is the healing potential to be found in the creative process, in writing: "I thought I had no future until I wrote this book" (97). The recuperation is inherent in the process of remembering and revealing secrets that are layered with patriarchal power structures: "And I begin to see as well, how incredibly vital and urgent is the telling of what has been done to us; how we can come to use the truth about our pain to change the world for ourselves and each other" (99).

Similarly, Charlotte Vale Allen's *Daddy's Girl*, in both title and narrative, exposes the illusion and the dark depravity that can exist within the unquestioned patriarchal myth. Both Danica and Allen have mothers who were complicit in the betrayals. Danica recalls her mother as a woman who abandoned and condemned her: "Years of searching bring me to the woman who could not help me that night in the basement. The woman who walked away because that was the only choice she had." Whereas Danica says that she "can forgive that," she goes on to say that "I have more trouble forgiving her this: she said he told her I liked it and she believed him. Again. She believes still I was born liking rape. I was born female. I was born a prostitute" (69). The sense of being born wrong and being alienated from other women is pervasive, but still does not prevent her from finding mother-mentor and sister relationships. Danica finds such an older woman friend and acknowledges her mentorship, her companionship: "She teaches me about survival, living alone, and poverty with dignity. She is fifty years older than I am. She understands" (90).

Allen depicts the complex sense of responsibility that remains with daughters. When her mother refuses to wave goodbye, to send her daughter off "with gladness," Allen sees that "it hadn't occurred to me that I was abandoning my mother to Daddy. She'd be all alone with no one to stand between her and his murderous rage" (256, 257). Allen says that her own daughter, Jossie, is crucial to her well-being and keeps her "firmly anchored to life" (176). She directly confronts the issue of sexuality that seems to be ever present in our patriarchally inspired concepts of self-other relationships, including same-sex friendship. When editors raised the possibility that her friendship with Helen might conceal a lesbian attraction, she writes: "I reacted with some surprise and dismay, because what I was writing about wasn't a sexual relationship but one based on *love*." Allen's emphasis is dramatic: "I *loved* her. I wanted to *be* her. To my mind this was a great compliment: the wish to emulate what is good, wise and mature in an adult." Her reasoning is specific: "We were friends. It was the first time in my life that someone gave me equal status, placed me on a secure, recognizable footing. I've had few gifts in my lifetime of like quality" (177). The distinction she makes between love and sexuality registers the complex and loving relationships that exist between women. So often obscured and denied in a culture that pretends that women find all their emotional needs met in heterosexual relationship, these relationships continue to be meaningful despite being culturally silenced.

Maxine Hong Kingston and Fredelle Bruser Maynard: Humour and Consciousness

Although Apuleius's rendering of the Psyche myth contains little humour, one can see the potential if Pan's advice is considered ironic and therefore a basis of misunderstanding or at least of different understandings, which is required for humour. There is evidence in Kingston's and Maynard's autobiographical writings that this consciousness is often accompanied with a (more or less) bitter irony. Kingston comments on the discrepancies of growing up within a Chinese-American family and its traditions. Combining a remembrance of an aunt – who committed suicide because of an "illicit" sexual encounter and pregnancy – with the traditional practice of plucking the hairline, she says: "I hope that the man my aunt loved appreciated a smooth brow, that he wasn't a tits-and-ass man" (9). This same irony is directed towards incomprehensible cultural expectations and her own attempts to fit into American culture: "Walking erect (knees straight, toes pointed forward, not pigeon-toed which is Chinese-feminine) and speaking in an inaudible voice I have tried to turn myself American-feminine" (11).

Maynard displays a similar humorous outlook on her remembered life when she tells about growing up Jewish – "chosen and abandoned" – within a small prairie town in Canada: "Bounded in a nutshell, I created myself king of infinite space" (29, 14). Writing of her decision to marry a gentile and her father's reaction, she gives another dimension to the issues of marriage and culture that figured in my discussion of Psyche's myth: "I think he was not surprised when I told him I had fallen in love with a gentile. Devastated, but not surprised" (166). And of her choice of husband, she says that "he was obviously unsuitable so I married him" (189).

Laura Goodman Salverson: Displacement and Reconnection

Salverson begins her autobiography with a memory of a night journey that vividly encapsulates her profound sense of displacement and contributes to her desire for a secure future: "That visit stamps the beginning of memory – the first of a chain of unrelated events, insignificant in themselves, and yet each one having its ineradicable, subtle effect upon my future reaction to life" (13). The constant search for an economically secure home, the upheavals and privations and strained family relationships, are all set forth in the opening, the "first horizon." In her initial description of fleeing through "an infinity of darkness" on the Dakota prairie, what comes into focus is the connection with the earth and "the green world": "Far ahead, in the midst of an ocean of darkness, two small jets of light stood out like candle flames braving the night. Why it should be so, I cannot say, but those wavering jets of light marked a division of time for the little girl at her father's feet. From that moment her little thoughts and starry impressions were distinctly individual, and she herself no longer just the little girl who existed as the small, obedient extension of her mother" (12). These perceptions of opposites existing within one another, of light within darkness and "in the midst" as "standing out," display a sense of individual nature arising from a strong sense of relationship and of individuality expressed as belonging comfortably even in darkness.

Salverson also expresses an awareness of place and of the natural world as home. Of her return to Winnipeg, she writes: "There was no one to meet me so I was free to experience what I always experience on coming back to the golden west: a quite irrational thrill, as though something in the air itself is a missing part of me, and that now I am complete. A queer sense of coming home that has nothing to do with houses or people, or any tangible thing acceptable to reason" (356). From her early immigration to Canada through her years in the United States, nothing has prepared her for the unreasonable feeling of being at home that is associated with "the golden west."

Emily Carr, Gabrielle Roy, and Maria Campbell: Spirit in Nature

Likewise, Emily Carr recalls an affinity for the forest. She writes of the place that she found with the help of her pony, Johnny: "Suddenly he would nose into the greenery finding a trail no one else could see, pressing forward so hard that the bushes parted, caressing him and me as we passed, and closing behind us shutting us from every 'towny' thing." At their arrival in "some mossy little clearing where soft shade-growing grass grew Johnny stopped with a satisfied sigh. I let down his bridle and we nibbled, he on the grass, I at the deep sacred beauty of Canada's still woods. Certainly I [owe a 'thank you'] to old Johnny for finding the deep lovely places that were the very foundation on which my work as a painter was to be built" (14). The combination here – of embodied movement registered into/from, forward/behind, of sensual imagery and things taken within, of outward landscape as a source of inner wealth – suggests a spirituality of transformation and energy rather than transcendence and power. Not depicted as a fall, the "deep" is presented as something into which one goes, a connection to something within, not a way down.

Gabrielle Roy expresses similar feelings of psychic energy restored when she describes walking into prairie vistas. Significantly, she begins by expressing a sense of homelessness – "There's no longer anything to make me feel at home in Manitoba" – but then goes on – "except the little section roads that stretch away beneath the endless sky." And she is grateful for a sense of community and empathy: "There are some who understand, who'll take me to the edge of the open prairie and release me ... So, I set off ... walking towards the red glow low down in the sky where the prairie ends, because for the magic to work I need not only the illusion of infinite space but also the gentle time of day just before nightfall. Then, for a few moments, my heart may soar once again" (105). What a profound "except" this is! She walks "off ... towards" where the prairie seems to end at a "gentle" time between night and day; her heart soars not in preparation for a fall but in a repeated moment of magic; her friends have an understanding that releases her.

Maria Campbell's Cheechum practised a spiritual attunement with nature and passed this kind of religion on to her granddaughter – which may account in large measure for Maria's ability to recover from the abuses inherent in a racist society: "She taught me to see beauty in all things around me; that inside everything a spirit lived, that it was vital too, regardless of whether it was only a leaf or a blade of grass, and by recognizing its life and beauty I was accepting God." This green world god is different from the supernatural deity defined by patriarchal religion. Seeing Judeo-Christian concepts as human constructions, Cheechum reinterprets death as a natural process, saying that "heaven and hell were man-made and here on earth, that there was no death, only that the body becomes old from life on earth and the soul must be reborn, because it is young." Cheechum "said God lives in you and looks like you" and "the Devil lives in you and all things." For Campbell, this "explanation made much more sense than Christianity had ever taught me" (82). To Cheechum, both "God" and the "Devil" are aspects of the individual, and this seems more truthful than to see them as external forces, as projections.

Lucy Maud Montgomery: Love and the Task

Though Lucy Maud Montgomery spent much of her life in Ontario, her writing of the *Anne* books links her indelibly to Prince Edward Island. Her account of the "story of my career" emphasizes the pleasure of the task. Whereas many interpretations of Psyche's myth have seen in the tasks the means for reconnecting with Eros, Montgomery shows how the love of the task itself brings transformation: "To write has always been my central purpose around which every effort and ambition of my life has grouped itself" (52). Describing the pleasure of seeing her work in print, she compares this joy to "some of the wonderful awe and delight that comes to a mother when she looks for the first time on the face of her first born" (59).

Combining a sense of humour and wry observations about human nature with a discussion of the inspiration for and creation of literary characters, she says: "[F]or my own part, I have never, during all the years I have studied human nature, met one human being who could, as a whole, be put into a book without injuring it." She goes on to describe the way the author's creation must exist behind the written character: "But the ideal, [her] ideal must be behind and beyond it all. The writer must *create* his characters, or they will not be life-like" (72, 73). Of her writing career, she sums up with: "The 'Alpine Path' has been climbed, after many years of toil and endeavour. It was not an easy ascent, but even in the struggle at its hardest there was a delight and a zest known only to those who aspire to the heights" (95). Her sense of achievement is pictured as the successful completion of a physical labouring over real, difficult, and mountainous terrain.

Patterning Life

In this necessarily brief survey of women's autobiographical writings, I have attempted to indicate the range and variety in the voices that articulate Psyche's pattern. Even as their lives differ in time and place, they share an affinity with the consciousness of relationship and growth that characterizes this myth. To suggest, as Montgomery does, that there is a pattern behind the individual lives in no way delimits the range or possibility of choice or outcome. What Psyche's pattern does is to inform the range of potential in individual women's lives; it grounds us in a history, in physical and spiritual being, and in the natural world as home.

Retelling Psyche

Could I have predicted? Things on the surface seemed well enough. Certainly, I never expected this. A blank, a wall, now and again flickering with shaded memories. Baffled, I watch and listen, too tired to find my way through.

In one, I am twelve. In the summer I spent with Mrs Livingstone – the last one that she spent at the lake. She was, after all, nearing eighty. I was there as usual with my parents. My brother, I ignored – and he, me – although we had reached some kind of truce that spring. The family often returned to the city. I didn't. I moped that summer. A lot, I think. So, for the most part, my parents let me be, only insisting that I spend the nights with Mrs Livingstone. I'm not sure who was keeping an eye on whom, but the arrangement suited us both.

Days were always mine, walking down the back gravel road on half a summer's worth of toughened soles. Sometimes swaying in the hammock strung between the birches, I watched the sun dapple through the leaves. Mostly, I remember the wind. In the wind at the edge of the lake, I spent the hours dreaming.

One weekend, warm and windy enough to keep the mosquitoes away, the weather again drew me out to the sandy beach. Because the cottages faced east and the lake spread wide to the horizon, only clouds could stop the moon and sun from rising clear and bright, each in its turn. That weekend coincided with one of Mrs Livingstone's "enthusiasms." At least that was what Mr Livingstone always used to call them – before his death – implying he had watched her through many in their years together.

"Nose to the wind again," he'd say. "Off on another scent. No stopping her now. Head for cover."

That year, Mrs Livingstone picked up the myth of Psyche. She read the story, then looked for all the information she could find about it. All winter and spring she rummaged through the piles of library books that she had carted out to litter every nook and cranny in her cottage. Then, one evening, she began to tell the tale to me. At least, she told me how she wanted it to be. The way it lived for her, she said.

Her storytelling suited me. That was, after all, my silent summer. At her cottage and on the point of land that was her beach, we sat on old and lumpy cushion-covered benches. I got to make a fire while she chattered. I really hadn't intended to listen. I was good at pretending to hear, yet letting my mind wander. But, in spite of myself, almost unknowingly, I found the story tempting and was drawn in.

She started by telling me that the tale was first written down by Lucius Apuleius, but almost everyone assumed he followed a number of much older stories. "He wrote it in Latin, of course," she said, "but there are several translations. It's famous as an allegory of Love and the Soul. Like a fairy tale," she explained, "like the Beast and Beauty."

Just as Mr Livingstone might have said it, Mrs Livingstone cut to the chase. Her story began with "long ago and not too far away, there lived a King, a Queen, and their three daughters. The eldest was Lillias and blond like her father, the King; the second, Berylla, raven-haired like her mother; and Psyche, the youngest, had hair of a colour some-where-in-between, a kind of middle brown with black and gold all tangled up together.

"These three were happy girls with food and love and adventure enough to keep them busy and content. Like all the sisters I have known, they played well together and fought well together. They were different enough to make you wonder if they belonged to the same parents, and sometimes so alike you'd think that they were one." Here, Mrs Livingstone looked at me and I slid down a little on my bench; I didn't want to be reminded of any siblings – especially if they sometimes got along, or worse, might be alike.

"Lillias was intense and energetic, loved books and learning, and spent much time with the King when he consulted scribes and astron-omers or ruled at court. Berylla was quieter and gentle; her passion was outdoors, for plants and animals, for every growing thing. She collected frogs and birds with broken wings and dogs, and children followed everywhere she went. She loved the fields and woods and went there often with the herbalists, the old women who taught her about the restorations hidden in the plants and how to make up healing salves.

"The youngest sister, Psyche, stayed longest with her mother, the Queen, but as she grew older, trailed after both her sisters, if and when they let her. The rest of the time she read a little – she was a princess and so she had a tutor – or gathered flowers, or generally just went about bestowing sunny curiosity on everything she saw and heard.

"Of course, all three daughters were beautiful and all in the kingdom called them so. Who could wonder at that? These were princesses, dressed in love and given the finest of everything.

"But when Lillias reached the age at which, customarily, young women were married, the King, again as was the custom, arranged a marriage. He hoped to ensure the support of his most powerful advisor by handing Lillias to this courtier's eldest son. He directed the Queen to make Lillias ready and to prepare the marriage feast.

"Well, Lillias was not impressed," said Mrs Livingstone. "She did not want to marry anyone – even someone young and rich whose father was that powerful. She protested. To no avail. She wept. That did nothing but make her eyes all red and puffy. The King, her father, did not listen. The Queen tried to calm her and suggested that she might find some useful work. At least she would be near, and they might visit often, said the Queen. Lillias was not moved. Like the King, she would not listen; unlike the King, she was not heard.

"One moonless night, just before dawn on a day shortly before this so-carefully-planned wedding, Lillias awakened Psyche and Berylla. They did not recognize her; only her voice assured them. Dressed as a boy and in a warm dark travelling cloak, Lillias warned them to keep silent and told them she must leave. 'I will not marry and so I can't stay here.'

"'Where will you go?' whispered Berylla. 'West,' replied Lillias. 'I have heard there is an island there, where women have gathered to live and work as they please. Where I can study the stars.' Quietly the sisters hugged and bid each other farewell. To light her way through the dark, Lillias took a torch from its sconce, and after one small wave and one backward glance, she left.

"The two remaining sisters kept silent, watching as the King and Queen discovered Lillias's absence. The King raged and sent his soldiers out to find his errant daughter. They returned each evening without her.

"Each day the Queen grew more grim and worried, the King more white and angry. Finally, the King recalled the searchers, retired to the throne room, and shut the door and himself in. The Queen grieved for a time, then turned to plan a library so that, when this lost daughter returned, she would find a place that suited her. Lillias did not return.

"Some time passed and everyone spoke of how the two princesses were the most beautiful in the kingdom. All who saw them praised them. Then Berylla became old enough to marry. This time the King chose an alliance with the neighbouring kingdom and its widowed ruler.

"Berylla wept and said she did not want to marry this old king; she loved someone else. She pleaded with the King; he did not listen. She pleaded with the Queen, but the Queen said that Berylla must be dutiful. An end to war, a lasting peace, would come from this alliance.

"The Queen arranged the wedding feast, sewed the bridal finery, and packed a stock of ointments and some ancient healing recipes, a pharmacopoeia for Berylla to take to this other kingdom. Berylla took her favourite knife, the one she used for mincing herbs, for separating measurements of seeds in piles. When it was time for her to leave, she hugged her sister Psyche. She turned back only once to wave.

"With Berylla's departure, the Queen grew more silent and the King grey; they missed this daughter, too. But after a time, the Queen put aside her grieving and set to work establishing a hospice. This seemed to bring some solace, and eventually they received news that Berylla had arrived and made herself a place in that other kingdom.

"Psyche was lonely for a time and wandered about the castle, but soon the resilience of youth and her own sunny nature returned, and she resumed a happy interest in all around her. She was curious about everyone, helped her mother with the library and hospice both, kept her father company at his tasks, and played with the children who missed Berylla.

"Without her sisters beside her, Psyche seemed all the more beautiful. Even strangers stopped to comment. Word of her astonishing attractions spread far beyond the kingdom and grew with every telling. People called her 'more beautiful than Aphrodite' and 'a new Aphrodite.' They turned to watch her everywhere she went, told stories of her dress and hair and every move, and seemed to worship her. More and more, the ancient goddess's shrines seemed old-fashioned. They were abandoned; her rites ignored; her wisdom disregarded. More and more, Psyche was the centre of the people's attention. Called a rare beauty, she was rarely left alone.

"Psyche was a sensible soul, however, and had a sense of humour besides. One day, passing one of the goddess's neglected shrines, her gaze touched upon a bit of old, worn, but highly polished obsidian. She took to carrying this small, flat triangular stone about with her, even attaching it with leather to her belt. When all the noise about her beauty got too tedious, she'd find a quiet corner, take up this polished mirror, and, gazing, find herself. She'd catch sight of that self that others slid and lost behind their awe and worship.

"'Indeed yes,' continued Mrs Livingstone, 'she was beautiful. Her bones were good, her smile a delight, and her teeth were straight. And she had that funny crooked eyebrow like her grandmother's, the hair that curled too wildly like her father's, and eyes as deep and dark as looked back from her sisters' faces. All in all, she was a sturdy, sunny soul.

"Now golden Aphrodite noted the neglect of all her shrines within that tiny kingdom. And how the people ceased the care of flocks yet overworked their fields. This lack of due regard for careful generation did indeed annoy her; it was no way to show a reverence for life."

Mrs L. explained: "Old Bird Goddess and ancient sea-born queen, Aphrodite was like a mother-protector of life in the sea, of the earth and air, and even more. She rules over generation in the natural world, and she knew the danger in her lost adoration, her lost wisdom, and what her replacement signified.

"She set out to see this Psyche. Her son, the so-delightful Eros, went along with her as he so often did. Travelling over the kingdom, they saw temples slighted and rites forsaken. Everywhere, they saw a kingdom slipped out from harmony, its people taking no care of their community and no responsibility for one another. Finally, they came upon Psyche surrounded and clutched at by a great crowd. Pulling at her, calling for her attention, the multitudes seemed set to destroy the terrified girl. Aphrodite motioned Eros near her.

"'Here,' she commanded her son, 'use your arrows to cause this maid to fall in love. Let her be mesmerized by a passionate love for the most ordinary of men, one who is without rank or wealth or even health. Make him so full of grief and woe that there is no other like him. Nothing else can teach these people how silly is the error of their worship. Or provide for her such quick relief.'

"Eros moved to do as his mother required. He, too, was saddened by the foolishness of that tiny kingdom and even felt some god-like pity as he contemplated Psyche's plight within it. Stretching back his hand to retrieve an arrow from his quiver, he fixed it to his bow and as he did this, carelessly, with the point of his own arrow, he scratched a line across his palm.

"Finished with her surveillance, Aphrodite turned away, out and into the open seas where, there among her attendants, she sought refreshment in her salty spa. Left behind, stayed Eros watching, his left hand clenched against his chest.

"Knowing nothing of this or what the future held for her, Psyche sank into misery. No longer had she any privacy or quiet. Hounded day and night, watched everywhere she went, she lost her sunny nature. Driven thin and weary, she wept for the return of her older sisters to share this burden, and then she wept anew for wishing this on them. She despised the self that others found so pleasing – what was not her, or only part of her – and wished for the days with her sisters when she was just another daughter among beautiful daughters.

"By now Psyche's appearance anywhere in the kingdom caused so much disruption and instability that the King resolved upon another marriage. Even this would not be an easy matter. With Psyche's fame and reputation, not just any bridegroom would do; the King must make a show of care in choosing some great prince. But all his overtures to other kingdoms brought him no response. No prince wanted so popular and troublesome a bride to rival his regard.

"Finally, the King in desperation was driven to consult the high priest of Apollo's oracle, asking him to make a pronouncement, to resolve this perplexing dilemma. The priest conducted a long and solemn ceremony and finally gave this prophecy:

> "As if for wedding or for requiem,
>   Apparel Psyche beautifully
> Set her out upon the kingdom's farthest mountain.
>   Your son-in-law is not of mortal stock,
> But fiery-wild and heartless; a snake-like monster
>   Who flies and vexes all your kingdom
> With arrows bright and sharp.

"Then the King enlisted the priest to return with him to tell the Queen. Grief-stricken once again, she wept even as she carried out their strategy. The kingdom, uncomprehending, joined her in that sadness. But since their very adoration obliged the fate of Psyche, their grief and lamentations benefited nothing.

"Sewn up in finery for the day, hidden by a veil of red, dry-eyed Psyche bitterly spoke her feelings. 'Why are you torturing yourselves with this weeping and wailing?' she asked. 'It will do me no good just as it availed my sisters nothing. Lead me wherever you will. The time that might have saved me has long passed. No one can save me now.' Then she withdrew to silence and looking straight ahead. She was placed in the procession that made its way to the summit of the mountain and there abandoned in the cold."

I discovered I wasn't much warmer than Psyche right then. It was now close to midnight and northern summer nights may be long and light, but still they pack a chill, especially by the lake. Mrs Livingstone shivered too, so we went into the cabin for some hot chocolate.

We settled on the beach again the next evening. I was to set the wood ready and then light it when it grew dark enough. Mrs L. continued her story.

"Psyche's parents returned to the palace, where the King, in his council chambers and staring blindly into the cold hearth, was gripped by an attack to his heart's core so crippling that he slumped dead there upon his throne. The Queen, turned away to the tower, shut and bolted the door, locked herself in and every other person out. The kingdom fell further into disarray, the population quarrelling and fighting amongst one another.

"Psyche did not stop long on that cold mountain; carefully and gently, she was carried down into a beautiful green valley. There, she settled upon a bed of fragrant and velvet flower petals. Immediately calmed, she fell asleep to awaken sometime later, rested and serene. With her natural inquisitiveness somewhat restored, and holding the shining obsidian, she began the exploration of her new place. Surrounded by a crystal stream, a waterfall, singing birds, a multitude of animals, great tall trees and tiny flowers and shrubs of every kind, she saw that all these were a rich and beautiful setting for a palace of exquisite grace and intricate beauty – a manor that fit perfectly within so wonderful a site.

"This dwelling place, she thought, must be residence to some sacred being, constructed as it is with such marvellous skill. Beautifully grained and fragrant woods, precious and glittering metals, flower-drenched carpets, saffron pillows, and mosaics of precious jewels, all give their splendour to this uncommon dwelling. Following a brilliant blue butterfly, she ventured further into this remarkable place. Once there, Psyche could not help exclaiming – marvelling at such wealth and promise. Even more astonishing, she saw that there were neither locks nor guards; there was nothing to protect this 'treasurehouse of all the world.'

"A soft voice at her elbow questioned why she was so astonished. 'All this wealth belongs to you,' breathed the airy voice. 'Rest, bathe, dine, find ease; all this is yours,' it said again and softly faded. 'All this is yours. All this is yours.'

"That night it was Eros who came to Psyche, but he departed swiftly again before the morning. Such sun-filled days and silky nights continued for so long a time that Psyche grew used to her new home and this new lover, too. She took pleasure in the comfort of his voice, in the contentment of their quiet conversations, and in the textured darkness of his nighttime nearness. Although she could not see him, she knew his rich and honeyed voice and all his body's strength and grace.

"The story of Psyche's misfortune, the King's sudden death, and the Queen's seclusion had spread throughout the land and let loose a flood of weeping, rage, and violence. Eventually the news even reached the far away sisters. Lillias, wrenched from her studies by the plight of her childhood home, left her sanctuary and journeyed to Berylla in the south. Together, they decided to collect Psyche's remains for proper burial. Perhaps in the timeless rituals of grief, they all might find some solace. Worried and weary, they wept in one another's arms.

"One dark evening, Eros brought Psyche news of what transpired back in her old kingdom. Psyche's lover warned that her sisters soon would come nearby, searching for her remains. 'Do not answer their cries or look in their direction,' he cautioned his new wife. 'Otherwise you will cause me anguish and yourself great trouble.'

"Hearing a warning phrased just this way, Psyche, of course, agreed. But left alone the following day, she thought on what she heard and in this daytime loneliness, she longed to visit with her sisters and comfort them with the knowledge of her well-being. That evening, Eros found her listless, tired, and weeping quietly.

"He scolded her, saying that it looked as if he could no longer trust her and that she would be sorry if she persisted, but then, when her weeping only increased, he concluded that, of course, she could do as she pleased. 'Only,' he added, 'don't come to me when you get into trouble and are sorry. I've done my best and you can't say I didn't warn you.'

"Psyche continued pleading to see her sisters. Eros grudgingly agreed, warning her not to listen to her sisters' advice or dare to look at him or try to investigate his appearance. Then he made a great show of relenting, gave the west wind to her command, and set aside gifts for Psyche to give her sisters. Psyche thanked him by exclaiming her passionate devotion.

"When the sisters found the place of Psyche's sacrifice, they wept over remembered betrayals and loudly lamented that Psyche could not escape this fate. Hearing the noise they made, Psyche sent the west wind to carry them into her valley. Now the tears flowed from astonishment and joy.

"Quite the watery threesome," muttered Mrs Livingstone. "But it is after all a myth, and we should grant a little excess." She paused. "Oh well," she shrugged, "a lot."

"'Come,' said Psyche, 'let me show you my new home. Refresh yourselves, bathe and banquet here with me.' Laughing, the sisters started to tell their lives and what had happened to each since parting. Exuding that remembered nervous energy, Lillias told amusing stories that played down the hardships of her long and trying journey, the many paths she followed before she reached the island and her work. She spoke of peace and the contentment she found in study and in her community and how much work there was to do.

"Spreading square and capable hands before her, Berylla quietly spoke of learning to heal the ill and comfort the dying. She smiled as she recounted stories of her own children, adopted where she found them in the streets, and chuckled over the silly things they did. She grew sombre as she told of wars and famine and all the needless pain and hardship that her skill in healing brought her to witness but often failed to cure. It was the children, she said, that gave her daily strength. They gave so much with such a little kindness.

"Then, the elder sisters turned to Psyche and asked about this new husband and her new life. Was she happy? Did he treat her well? What life work had these new opportunities brought with them?

"Taken unaware by their questions, Psyche grew confused and mumbled out a story of her husband's youth and kindness, how she was happy, and how he spent much time in hunting. Quickly, she changed the subject, gave them gifts and sent them back upon the wind. How odd, the sisters thought together, and when they were set down again, reviewed the visit to find some reason for her sudden change. Finding none, they resolved to seek another visit before revealing her whereabouts to their old, despondent kingdom.

"That night, Psyche told Eros of the visit with her sisters. Again he warned her that her sisters would lead her on to look at him. 'They will try to get you to look at me, but if you see me, I will never come to you this way again. And you know you should be careful. You said we will be parents. Now is an especially risky time. If you guard my secret in silence, this child will be a god. If not, then mortal.'

"Psyche beamed and nodded pleasure at the reference to the coming child, but in spite of this anticipated joy, she confessed an anxiety deeper than she could hide. She longed for the comfort of someone to answer her questions, and so just before he turned away to sleep, Eros told her she would be fine – just so long as she listened to him. Psyche persisted. She asked again if her sisters might come to visit just once more. They always brought her strength, and Berylla surely would have something to say to help her. Eros promised that they could.

"When the sisters met again, Psyche poured out fragrant coffee and served sweet cakes (but left hers cooling in the cup and couldn't touch the food). The sisters, as they had planned, led the conversation to Psyche's absent husband. 'What does he do and where does he carry out his work?' asked Lillias. 'Who is his family and where do they come from?' inquired Berylla. Psyche ignored the questions and instead told about the coming baby, and in their excitement, the sisters promptly forgot the absent father.

"That is, the sisters forgot until, returning, they found themselves once more upon the mountain and no more sure of who he was than they had been before. Since Berylla had promised to return with some herbal teas, plain bread, and soothing remedies for Psyche's present discomforts, they saw one more opportunity to question Psyche.

"That night even as he promised that the west wind would once more do her bidding, Eros warned Psyche of the danger that any sight of him might bring. And Psyche, in the reassurance of his embrace, didn't even bother to agree so heavy were her sleepy eyes.

"The next day, the sisters did return and discussed Psyche's well-being and the child to be. Berylla brought out her teas and ointments and Lillias encouraged Psyche to eat 'just a little more.' Then both began to question Psyche about her absent husband, asking when they should meet and was he gentle. 'Do you think that he will be a kindly father?' they asked.

"Distraught and unhappy, Psyche confessed she did not have answers for any of these questions. 'I have never seen my husband,' she wailed. 'I am forbidden. Though what I do know of him is kind and generous, he threatens me with an unspeakable loss should I ever disobey.'

"'We can see the evidence of his generosity', replied Lillias. 'But there is a world of difference between a good husband and a good father,' added Berylla. 'Do you think he might also learn to be a gentle father?'

"'How would I know? How can I judge?' asked Psyche.

"'When you see him,' said Lillias, 'that will help you know. Why don't you put a lighted lamp under an inverted basket near your bed? And when this husband is asleep, take out the lamp and look at him. Then you may see if his nature and his disposition will bear his new responsibility.'

"'Take a knife, too, and conceal it by the bed,' added the ever practical Berylla. She had seen a little too much of the world and men to trust too eagerly. 'It will give you some protection if he wakes and is the kind of monster who would harm both you and this unborn child. Hurry, it grows late, and we must leave. Remember,' she added fiercely, 'even if we must leave you, if you do need help, do not hesitate to come to us.'

"Lillias nodded her agreement and the sisters hugged Psyche once again, and then, looking back only once to wave, they left.

"Psyche was understandably upset. By turns anxious, despairing, and fearful, she nonetheless hid the candle and knife in a safe place by her bed. At one and the same time, wishing never to see this husband again and in the next minute anxiously awaiting his return, she worried over what the night would reveal.

"Later, when Eros fell asleep beside her, Psyche slowly eased herself from her warm bed and carefully lifted the cover from the lamp. Picking up the knife in one hand and the lamp in the other, she turned to look upon her husband. There carelessly sprawled before her lay her love. Golden brown and rose, velvet and sinew, Eros lay deep asleep. And he was beautiful!" sighed Mrs L.

"Overcome with relief and a sense of being safe, Psyche put down her knife even as she continued gazing. Then, by the end of the bed, she noticed the bow, the quiver and arrows. Gently Psyche touched these arms and plucked an arrow from the quiver itself. Thoughtfully, she tested its sharpness with her thumb, turning yet again to look on Eros. She pricked herself.

"Startled, she looked at her thumb and saw bright drops of blood appear. At once she bent to show her love. So much in a hurry, she shook a drop of burning oil out from her lamp upon his right shoulder.

"Burned, Eros leaped up, reached for his weapons even as he saw Psyche reach for him and flew up without a word. As he arose, Psyche flung herself upon him, clasping tightly to him. Until she grew too weary, she clung there as he flew, then slipped and dropped upon the earth below.

"So freed, Eros touched down upon a nearby cypress tree and wept in rage: 'How thoughtlessly and unaware have I fulfilled my mother's wish; I am punished with my own arrow, and now you disobey me. I will leave you here. Loneliness be your lot and fortune both.' Eros took wing again and left.

"Psyche lay shivering in anxious fear. Desolate, she watched her love until he disappeared. With one long piercing wail, she threw herself over the bank of a nearby river. This river, Lethe and forgetfulness, would have nothing to do with this lovers' quarrel and threw her out upon the bank. A brief hiccup later, out splashed her mirror.

"Now, beside this stream rested the wilderness god, Pan, and on his lap sat Echo. 'Now, let me guess,' he mused as he spied Psyche. 'A suicidal leap, a pale complexion, those constant sighs, a ruinous digestion, and woeful ever-tired eyes – why, this must be an overdose of love.' 'An overdose of love,' sighed Echo.

"'Since I am an old man with countless, varied, and sundry affairs of love,' winked Pan, 'fear not my advice.' 'Not my advice,' repeated Echo. Frowning at his lap's companion, Pan persevered along his lengthy counsel. 'Pray to Eros. Ask his forgiveness. Flatter him. Defer to him. He is a kindly, pleasure-loving, and soft-hearted youth. Be sure to coax and plead and wait on him. Especially,' he firmly warned, 'do not seek blessing and consolation elsewhere!' Then echoed Echo, 'Seek blessing and consolation elsewhere!'

"Psyche gazed silently on Pan and his companion, but they had already forgotten her and turned away. She picked up her mirror, and forcing one foot before the other, she started out upon the rough and unfamiliar trail.

"Not stopping until she reached Berylla's palace, Psyche sought shelter in her sister's arms and poured out her sorry tale. In grief, Berylla tore her hair, lamenting the outcome of her well-meant advice. 'Rest here,' she said to Psyche. 'I will travel back to the mountain and heal this rift with Eros. Surely when he knows of my contrivances, he'll see the knife was only for protection and not to do him harm. Relenting, he'll then perceive just how important is his presence to you and to his unborn child.'

"Leaving her work, her family, and Psyche resting, Berylla sped back up the mountain. Calling to Eros, she threw herself upon a passing breeze – only to fall crashing on the rocks below. Bashed and battered, weaving in and out of consciousness from shock and loss of blood, Berylla crawled to a nearby road where she was discovered, recognized, and carted back to her palace.

"Psyche's grief doubled as she looked upon her sister. I need a knowledge greater than my own to meet this crisis, she thought. Perhaps from Lillias I may gather what I need. Coming to her eldest sister's garden observatory, Psyche retold her tale, adding what had happened to Berylla. Lillias jumped up immediately and said, 'I will convince him that the lamp was my idea and that if anyone should be punished, it must be me.'

"With that she left her studies and handed Psyche over to her friends for care. She herself went off to the mountain, planning so strong and rational a speech that it could move even the god of love. Throwing herself headlong into the wind, Lillias tumbled over and over down the mountainside until she, too, was picked up and carted back to the healing hands in Berylla's palace.

"Hearing of this second failed attempt, Psyche saw no other choice but to set out alone upon her path. Eros, meanwhile, had sought refuge in the darkness of the forest and retreated spent and sighing from his painful feelings and his wounded shoulder.

"A seagull watching all that had transpired was now annoyed past patience. She dipped and darted out across the rolling ocean's wide expanse until she came to where the goddess bathed. Settling down upon the waves, she proceeded to tell Aphrodite about Eros and

Psyche and what, since her visit last, had transpired within her far-flung realms.

"'The world has gone to wrack and ruin. Your shrines and sanctuaries continue empty and unused or fouled and stinking with pollution. One king is dead, the others old and sick beyond death and blind to what their greedy creed has wrought. Their consort queens languish ailing in their towers. Everything is crude and rude and violent. There is no happiness, no lasting solace, no care for family bonds, and certainly no love for little children or other wild things.'

"Hearing all this, Aphrodite grew furious. 'And my own son contributes to this woe and flees his obligations and the love he chose himself.' She shrieked and howled down the wind. Baleful, wearing a sea-raven's guise, she rose above the sea. Unerringly she flew towards her son's sequestered sickroom. Perching on a branch above his heart, she spit and raged her fury, sparing no thought for the burning fever he already felt.

"'What is this behaviour! How can this be appropriate to me or fitting to your ancient role?' Her wings outflung in anger spoke her tripled form. 'This carelessness does me no honour and brings to you no credit. What of your obligations? What of your choice and consequence?' And then relenting with some understanding of his inexperience of any loving but the kindling of a hot desire, Aphrodite spoke more kindly, 'Recover your good health here as is needful, but then redeem yourself and your desire.'

"She touched his brow and traced his cheek and added these last words: 'No one, my dear – especially you or I – escapes the burdens of their gifts.' With that, she smiled and flicked his chin and left him there alone.

"Finished with her son's part in all that had gone on, but shaking yet in anger at other and more profound betrayals, Aphrodite flew out over her world to seek solace in its diversity. But the gull had spoken truly. Everywhere she looked, the lands lay more wasted, bleak, and troubled than they ever were before. Stunned by the desolation she discovered, Aphrodite shimmered a momentary stillness.

"Her sister goddesses, Demeter and Artemis, found her in this glittering silence. Knowing full well the power of what would come, they sought to share their own concerns with her. 'How opportune,' said Aphrodite into the quiet all about her. 'I suppose you wish me to desist.'

"'No! No! We don't presume to tell you what to do or give advice,' the goddesses replied. 'But please, I ask, leave seeds enough to start afresh,' said Demeter. 'And let the blameless birds and animals, the faultless ones in nature, still survive,' added wild Artemis. Then ravening

Aphrodite wheeled against the sky and out again towards the sea. Behind her, the awful stillness broke into a thousand hurricanes, and earthquakes stormed across the land."

Mrs Livingstone struggled up from the bench and made her way across the beach. This was no place to leave a story, but she wasn't persuaded. I kicked sand over the smouldering ashes and followed after, up the rise into the cottage.

I remember the exhilaration of "dark and stormy" nights and all those summer thunderstorms when waves hammered in against the shore and lightning crackled the darkness. Such memories fit the tale and my own present pain, but that night in Mrs L.'s cabin, I was safe. She pushed aside some books and settled in her favourite chair and, to my pleasure, relented and continued with our story.

"In the strange stillness, Psyche, for a time, found walking easier. Coming upon an old, abandoned, and misused temple near a mountain well, she paused a moment to drink and rest and then began to tidy up the disarray. The broken jars of grain, a fan, a top, and woolly fleece all spoke of Demeter, as did the torch-ends left within the walls. To her it was that Psyche appealed.

"Demeter appeared. 'Your prayers are moving and I wish I might assist, but Aphrodite is my elder and we are bound by ancient ties of duty and respect. I cannot interfere. And yet, you have my blessing.'

"Psyche, disappointed, walked on and, passing into the next valley, came upon a woodland shrine. Here were many offerings and evidence of recent sacrifice. Animal skins, antlers, and a still-warm blood-stained altar marked the shrine to Artemis. Nearby the door the sacrificial knife lay clean and shining. Perhaps this is the goddess to assist me, thought Psyche, and so she meditated once again.

"Artemis appeared. 'I wish I might reward your gentle prayers, but my offices are to offer an assistance more specific than you require. Great Aphrodite is my elder; I cannot trespass in her realm. I cannot interfere, nor will I help. And yet, you have my blessing.'

"Out again upon the path, Psyche stopped a moment to sort her thoughts and rested her back against a rock. 'Eros has turned from me. My sisters cannot help. No other goddesses will save me. I can only face the worst that fate delivers and hand myself to what will be. I will submit to Aphrodite. A face to face encounter can't be worse than what has thus far happened.'

"So saying, Psyche turned towards the east just as all about her broke the raging gales of Aphrodite's earthbound promise. Buffeted by the tempest, wounded in this hail of trouble and sadness, Psyche leaned the fullness of her weight into the tumult and pushed a slow way into Aphrodite's presence.

"So suddenly did Psyche find herself again in stillness that she collapsed upon the ground. Aphrodite rose before her. With wide unblinking stare, the goddess stalked silently around the fallen Psyche. This way and that, the golden eyes missed nothing of the lonely Psyche's whole condition. Ruffling double her already awesome presence, the goddess pointed out a mound of seeds piled to her left. Jumbled together were apple and pomegranate, barley, wheat and millet, poppyseeds, sesame, lentils and beans.

"'There is your first task,' said Aphrodite, 'If you would be mine and earn your own life's work and love, sort out that motley mass of seeds and properly put each grain into its own and separate pile. Finish before moonrise.'

"Psyche lay silent and dumbfounded by the enormity of the task. An ant came by and, pitying her stricken figure, convened her sister-workers to sort the seeds into their separate piles. Grain by grain and one by one, they carried, sorted, and distributed. The one pile disappearing reappeared again in its nine constituent parts. Finished, the ants once more vanished below the ground.

"When Aphrodite reappeared, she casually and carelessly surveyed the careful industry and orderly accomplishment, and throwing Psyche a crust of bread, herself retired to the night, leaving the young Psyche curled up upon the rocky coast – warm despite the coolness of the night.

"The next morning, Aphrodite pointed to the pastures far inland and said, 'See by that river; there graze the sheep whose fleeces shine bright gold. Only their wool is fine enough for my shrine. Procure it, comb and spin a filet fit for a sanctuary entrance.'

"Psyche set out towards the stream. Once there, she knelt to drink before embarking on this complex task. Beside her and between the bank and stream, stirred into music by a breeze, the green reeds softly sang: 'Dear Psyche, you cannot move so quickly anymore, so do not go directly to those wild and powerful sheep, for they are fierce and will not let you near. Wait until they have grazed and tired. They will seek evening rest back in the forest. Then gather all the strands caught in the branches of the bushes round about the meadow.'

"Psyche waited through the day until the well-fed sheep moved out beyond the thickets to rest in the cool depths of the trees. She went to find what woolly gold was clinging to the branches. Among the shrubbery, all at once, she came upon the strands already neatly carded, spun into a web so delicate and strong it seemed no human could imagine its design. Behind this net, an ancient spider, squat and fat, cut free the filet from its place and disappeared.

"Gently Psyche caught the drifting fleece and carried it back to Aphrodite's shrine. And if her eyes had not been carefully cast down, she might have then detected the smile beginning so far back within those fierce and golden eyes.

"Certainly Aphrodite's voice betrayed no tender feeling. 'You sat about today and so this evening you must do another task. A steep mountain peak lies high above a towering cliff,' spoke Aphrodite into the gathering dusk. 'Dark water flows down from a heated spring that bubbles up from deep inside that peak. The neighbouring valley catches in a reservoir liquid enough for all the swamps of Styx and the swift currents of Cocytus together. In this crystal vessel, catch some of that rich rivulet and bring it back to me.'

"Taking the vial, Psyche willingly set off towards the mountain, but when she reached the plateau near the ridge, she saw the danger in the task and stood transfixed in silence.

"A cave high up slipped forth in brackish streams that then slid downward and into a valley through a chasm where they were guarded left and right and roundabout by fearsome snakes who kept unblinking watchfulness. 'Beware the darting tongues! Look out! You will die!' the slithering and red-brown reptiles hissed.

"Silent and swift beside her appeared a golden eagle. 'Give me the vial,' came an order from the gathering gloom. Swift and bright, the eagle swept the crystal container up the mountain valley, flying through the snakes. At the topmost spring, she announced that this was for the goddess Aphrodite and, unhindered, filled the crystal, which, returning down the selfsame valley, she handed full to Psyche.

"Psyche once again returned to Aphrodite with this token, but even completing that third task could not entirely appease the goddess. 'There is one other task for you to do. Take this casket down to Persephone, hand it to her and say, 'Aphrodite requests a little of your beauty, since she has exhausted what she has repairing all the damage in her realm.'

"Psyche shivered in fear. As if a veil had lifted from her eyes, she understood. She was being sent into the underworld of death. Psyche trudged towards the great and ancient standing stone so she might lie beneath it. By fasting there, she would conduct herself to death directly.

"Once settled against the giant megalith, Psyche was startled to hear the towering stone speak hoarsely in her ear: 'Cease this useless fasting. That is not how to approach death's gate. Get up, take two corn-cakes, soak them well in mead, and then go upwards to the Vent of Dis. Begin your journey there by walking downward through its opening and don't forget to take two copper coins within your mouth.'

"'When you have travelled a long way down the path,' continued the towering stone, 'you will meet a limping driver with a lame ass carting wood. He will ask you to hand him twigs that have fallen from his load. Do not lend your assistance, but pass them by in silence; his tasks are his alone.

"'Then you will come to the river of the dead where you must pay Charon the passage money. Let him take one coin out of your mouth by his own hand. While you are being ferried across, a dead old man floating on the surface will lift his rotting hands and beg you to pull him into the boat. Turn away; do not pity him.

"'A little beyond the river, you will come upon three old women weaving at a loom. They will ask you to weave a bit, but do not help them. If you put down one cake, you will never find your way back again.

"'There is a huge three-headed dog, the fierce and monstrous keeper of the gates. Split one cake in three to buy safe passage beyond those jaws. Once past, you will meet Persephone and her companion, Hecate. Only then may you beg your favour.

"'Persephone will bid you welcome and ask you to sit beside her to eat a sumptuous banquet, but you must sit upon the bare floor and request only a little of Hecate's bread and water. When you have supped, return with the filled casket, remembering to buy off the dog and sailor once again.

"Psyche hurried to complete this task. She did all that she had been told to do, and returning above ground with the casket, she sank down with exhaustion and relief. Aching limb by limb, worn beyond endurance from so much grief, she gazed upon the gift she carried. Remembering what Aphrodite had said of restoration held within, Psyche thought this: 'I have endured an awful journey and even willingly and with a good heart have undergone my tasks. My legs ache, my back is killing me, and soon I'll have a child. Here before me is the energy I'll need to meet the cares to come. If it restores a goddess, will not a drop be just enough for me?'

"Raising the casket lid, Psyche was overwhelmed. With blank dark eyes she gazed down into the casket; a stench of death's decay enveloped her entirely.

"Within his forest far away, Eros woke and looked about for Psyche. At once remembering, he stretched his wings and flew to find her. And finding her again was certainly no problem; his nose directly led him where she knelt there at the Vent of Dis.

"Quickly he folded up the stench into the casket and waved his wings to clear the air. He settled down in front of Psyche until she looked at him again. He hadn't long to wait. With silly smiling ear to ear and weeping tears that washed remaining hurts away, they each forgave and loved and reunited."

That's such a lovely ending, I thought then, but Mrs Livingstone wasn't finished yet. "What he had to forgive, I can't imagine, but Psyche always was a generous soul and certainly she loved him dearly.

"'Come,' said Eros, 'we both have tasks left incomplete. You must …,' and here he stopped as Psyche once again sat spellbound. A moment passed and then she looked at him.

"'Not quite now,' said Psyche wryly as she shook her head. 'Call my mother; bring my sisters to me. I need them. I want them with me.'

"Eros said, 'There, there,' a little nervously and in a hurry. 'Yes. Everything will be alright. But of course … your mother. And your sisters … Well … if you must.' And he was in such haste that he sent three winds abroad: the north wind to the Queen, the west wind to Lillias, and the south wind to Berylla.

"With Eros braced supporting at her back, Psyche's one more labour birthed a daughter she named Joy. Lillias held a lamp; Berylla knotted and cut the cord; and the Queen lifted the infant and carried her to the ocean shore nearby. There, while the sisters tended Psyche, she gave this newest grandchild into Aphrodite's arms.

"Borne gently out to sea, there Joy was bathed and dried and softly wrapped in down. Trailing laughter, like seaweed and morning sunlight, Aphrodite then returned the twice-blessed task of Joy to Psyche's arms, and Eros wrapped them both in wings as light and warm and strong as love can sometimes be."

I sat awhile with Mrs Livingstone. Not exactly tired, but more at ease and resting, just watching our reflections in the cottage's night window.

When I was young, I knew that Joy was mortal, a fleeting thing that came and went, and just assumed that Psyche was a goddess or at least a daemon like Eros. Or an immortal. But none of that is so important. If they come and go it's at our whim or in our need and not their own. I hear the story and the voice of Mrs Livingstone and have enough to make an answer out of darkness. I know a different Psyche now.

She has at times appeared with Aphrodite: bright in golden sunlight at the ocean's edge, in the fear and elation of a raging gale or flood, or tranquil by a moonlit mountain lake, or in the damp and earthy forest. For me especially in the green and level-to-the-skyline fields of home.

She has arrived together with her sisters: woven up in squabbles and older and more bitter life-betrayals, in nursing's care, or anywhere that people gather talking of work or family or even politics and what's gone wrong. And always friendship's kitchen carries tracings of her presence.

With Eros, too, in warm embrace of eye and arm and thigh, in loves lost or found again, in all the rages and betrayals a body's heat can generate. Or coldness. In first love and last love and all that are between.

With Joy and all new promise: in new buds and spring flowers, in children's laughter, in any species' infant playfulness, in bliss of work well done, and in the day's achievements task by task.

But in this moment Psyche walks alone. In the darkness between moonset and sunrise, I see her, there, smiling and patient, on the other side of the rain.

Apuleius's Cupid and Psyche

BOOK IV

...

[237] "Once upon a time in a certain city there lived a king and queen. They had three daughters of remarkable beauty. Yet the older two, although of very pleasing appearance, could still, it was thought, be worthily celebrated with mortal praise. But the youngest girl's beauty was so dazzling and glorious that it could not be described nor even adequately praised for the sheer poverty of human speech. Many citizens, as well as multitudes of visitors, whom the rumour of an extraordinary spectacle was attracting in eager throngs, were dumbfounded in their wonderment at her unapproachable loveliness and would move their right hands to their lips, forefinger resting upon outstretched thumb,[1] and venerate her with pious prayers as if she were the very goddess Venus herself. Soon the report had spread through nearby cities and neighbouring lands that the goddess born of the blue depths of the sea and brought forth of the spray of the foaming waves was now distributing her deity's grace far and wide and mingling amid human gatherings; or, if that was not so, that in a new germination of skyborn drops, not the ocean[2] but the earth had sprouted another Venus, this one endowed with the [239] bloom of virginity.

---

[1] A common gesture of admiration.

[2] The name of Venus's Greek counterpart, Aphrodite, was believed to derive from *aphros* "foam."

Reprinted by permission of the publishers and the Loeb Classical Library from APULEIUS: METAMORPHOSES, VOL I, translated by J. Arthur Hanson, Cambridge, Mass.: Harvard University Press, 1989. Original page numbers are given in square brackets in the text.

"Day by day the story spread by leaps and bounds, and her fame stretched out and ranged through the nearby islands and much of the mainland and most of the provinces. Many mortals travelled far by land and journeyed over the deep seas, flocking together to see the famous sight of the age. No one sailed to Paphos or Cnidos or even Cythera[1] to behold the goddess Venus. Her rites were postponed, her temples fell into disrepair, her cushions were tradden under foot, her ceremonies neglected, her statues ungarlanded, and her abandoned altars marred by cold ashes. It was the girl that people worshipped: they sought to appease the mighty goddess's power in a human face. When the maiden walked out in the morning, people would invoke the name of the absent Venus with feast and sacrifice, and when she walked through the streets, crowds would worship her with garlands and flowers.

"This extravagant transfer of heavenly honours to the cult of a mortal girl inflamed the real Venus to violent wrath. In uncontrolled indignation she shook her head, gave forth a deep groan, and thus she spoke with herself:

"'Look at me, the primal mother of all that exists, the original source of the elements, the bountiful [241] mother of the whole world,[1] driven to divide my majesty's honours with a mortal girl! My name, which is founded in heaven, is being profaned with earthly pollution. Am I to endure the uncertain position of vicarious veneration by sharing our deity's worship, and is a girl subject to death to walk around bearing my likeness? So it meant nothing when that shepherd,[2] whose justice and trustworthiness were confirmed by great Jupiter, preferred me for my surpassing beauty to such mighty goddesses. But, whoever she is, she will certainly get no joy out of having usurped my honours: I will soon make her regret that illegitimate beauty of hers!'

"She quickly sent for her son, that winged and headstrong boy who, with his bad character and his disdain for law and order, goes running about at night through other folk's houses armed with flames and arrows, ruining everyone's marriages, and commits the most shameful acts with impunity and accomplishes absolutely no good.[3] Even though he was naturally unrestrained and impudent, Venus verbally goaded him on even further. She took him to that city and showed him

---

[1] Sites of the most famous shrines of Venus in antiquity. Paphos is on Cyprus, Cnidos on the coast of Asia Minor, and Cythera an island south of the Peloponnese.
[1] Perhaps a reference to Lucretius 1 2.
[2] Paris.
[3] His Latin name is either Cupido or Amor, his Greek name Eros; all are also common nouns meaning "erotic passion" or "desire."

Psyche[4] in person – that was the girl's name – and related the whole tale of her rival's loveliness, moaning and groaning [243] with indignation. 'I beseech you,' she said, 'by the bonds of maternal love, by your arrows' sweet wounds, by your flame's honey-sweet scorchings, avenge your mother and avenge her totally, and exact condign punishment from defiant beauty. Accomplish this one act with a good will and it will take care of everything: let that girl be gripped with a violent, flaming passion for the meanest man, a man whom Fortune has condemned to lack rank, wealth, and even health, a man so lowly that he could not find his equal in misery in the whole world.'

"So saying she kissed her son long and intensely with parted lips. Then she sought the nearest beach on the tide-swept shore, stepped out with rosy feet over the topmost foam of the quivering waves, and – lo! – she sat down upon the clear surface of the deep sea. What she began to desire happened at once, as if she had given orders in advance: the instant obeisance of the seas. Nereus' daughters came singing a choral song, and shaggy Portunus with his sea-green beard, and Salacia with her womb teeming with fish, and Palaemon the little dolphin-charioteer. Now troops of Tritons bounded helter-skelter through the sea-water: one blew gently on a tuneful conch shell; another shielded her from the hostile sun's blaze with a silken awning; another carried a mirror before his mistress's eyes; others swam along yoked in pairs to the chariot. Such was the army escorting Venus as she moved [245] out toward Ocean.

"Meanwhile Psyche, for all her manifest beauty, reaped no profit from her charms. Everyone gazed at her, everyone praised her, but no one, neither king nor prince nor even commoner, desired to marry her and came to seek her hand. They admired her heavenly beauty, of course, but as people admire an exquisitely finished statue. Long ago her two older sisters, whose more moderate beauty had not been broadcast throughout the world, had been engaged to royal suitors and had already made fine marriages. But Psyche stayed at home, a husbandless virgin, weeping over her forlorn loneliness, sick in body and wounded in heart. She hated in herself that beauty of hers which the world found so pleasing.

"The unfortunate girl's wretched father, suspecting divine hostility and fearing the gods' anger, consulted the ancient oracle of the Milesian god.[1] With prayers and sacrifice he asked the powerful deity for

---

[4] Greek for "soul." The Latin word is *anima*, and the story which follows is full of word-play on the names of the two principal characters, Psyche and Cupid.

[1] At Didyma near Miletus.

a marriage and a husband for the hapless maiden. Apollo, although a Greek and an Ionic Greek at that, answered with an oracle in Latin to show favour to the author of this Milesian tale.[2]

[247] "'Set out thy daughter, king, on a lofty mountain crag,
    Decked out in finery for a funeral wedding.
Hope not for a son-in-law born of mortal stock,
    But a cruel and wild and snaky monster,
That flies on wings above the ether and vexes all,
    And harries the world with fire and sword,
Makes Jove himself quake and the gods tremble,
    And rivers shudder and the shades of Styx.'

"The king, once a fortunate man, upon hearing the holy prophecy's pronouncement returned home slowly and sorrowfully, and unravelled for his wife the ill-omened oracle's instructions. For several days they moaned and wept and wailed. But soon the hideous execution of this dreadful lot approached. Now the scene was set for the wretched maiden's funeral wedding. Now the light of the wedding torch grew dim with black, sooty ashes. Now the tune of the conjugal flute changed into the plaintive Lydian mode and the happy song of the marriage-hymn ended in a mournful wail. The bride-to-be was wiping tears away with her own flame-red bridal veil. The whole city joined in grief over the harsh fate of the afflicted house, and business was at once suspended as an appropriate show of public mourning.

"But the obligation to obey the divine injunction demanded poor Psyche for her appointed punishment. Therefore, the ceremonial preparations for this funeral marriage were completed in utmost [249] grief, the living corpse was led from the house accompanied by the entire populace, and a tearful Psyche marched along, not in her wedding procession but in her own funeral cortège. Her parents, dejected and overwrought by this great misfortune, hesitated to perform the heinous deed, but their daughter herself urged them on.

"'Why,' she asked, 'are you torturing your unhappy old age with prolonged weeping? Why are you exhausting your life's breath – really my own – with constant wailing? Why are you marring with useless tears those features that I revere? Why do you wound my eyes in wounding your own? Why are you tearing your grey hair? Why are you beating your bosoms and the breasts that fed me? Are these sufferings to be your glorious reward for my outstanding beauty? Too late you realise that the blow which destroys you is dealt by wicked

---

[2] I.e. Apuleius.

Envy. When countries and peoples were giving me divine honours, when with a single voice they were all calling me a new Venus, that is when you should have grieved, that is when you should have wept, that is when you should have mourned me as if I were already dead. Now I understand. Now I see that it is Venus' name alone that has destroyed me. Take me and put me on the cliff appointed by the oracle. I hasten to enter into this happy marriage, I hasten to see this high-born husband of mine. Why should I postpone and shun the coming of him who was born for the whole world's ruin?'

[251] "After this pronouncement the maiden fell silent, and with firm step joined the procession of escorting citizens. They came to the appointed crag of the steep mountain and placed the girl, as decreed, on its very summit, where they abandoned her one and all. The bridal torches, with which they had lighted the way, now extinguished by their tears, they left behind; and with heads bent low they began their homeward journey. Her unhappy parents, shattered by this great catastrophe, shut themselves up in the darkness of their house, resigning themselves to perpetual night.

"Psyche, meanwhile, frightened, trembling and weeping at the very top of the cliff, was slowly lifted by a gentle breeze from the softly-blowing Zephyr, which stirred her raiment on this side and on that, and caused her dress to billow. With its tranquil breath it gradually carried her down the slopes of the high cliff, and in the valley deep below laid her tenderly on the lap of the flowery turf.

BOOK V

[253] "As Psyche lay pleasantly reclining in the soft lawn on her bed of dew-covered grass, her great mental distress was relieved and she fell peacefully asleep. When she had been restored by enough slumber, she arose feeling calm. She saw a grove planted with huge, tall trees; she saw a glistening spring of crystal water.

"At the midmost center of the grove beside the gliding stream is a royal palace, constructed not with human hands but by divine skills. You will know from the moment you enter that you are looking at the resplendent and charming residence of some god. High coffered ceilings, exquisitely carved from citron-wood and ivory, are supported on golden columns. All the walls are covered with silver reliefs, with wild beasts and herds of that kind meeting your gaze as you enter. It was indeed a miraculous man, or rather a demigod or even a god, who used the refinement of great art to make animals out of so much silver. Even the floors are zoned into different sorts of pictures made from precious stones cut in tiny pieces. Truly blessed – twice so and even more – are those who tread upon [255] gems and jewellery! All the other quarters of the house throughout its length and breadth are likewise precious beyond price, and all the walls are constructed of solid gold masonry and sparkle with their own brilliance, so that the house creates its own daylight even though the sun deny his rays. The rooms, the colonnades, even the doors flash lightning. Every other luxury too is equally matched with the house's magnificence, so that you may quite correctly think it a heavenly palace constructed for great Jupiter's use in his human visitations.

"Psyche, attracted by the allurement of this beautiful place, came closer, and as she gained a little more confidence, crossed the threshold. Soon her eagerness to look at such beautiful things drew her on to examine every object, and on the other side of the palace she spotted storerooms built with lofty craftsmanship and heaped high with vast treasures. Nothing exists which is not there. But beyond her wonderment at the enormous quantity of wealth, she found it especially amazing that there was not a single chain or lock or guard protecting this treasure-house of all the world. As she was gazing at all this with rapturous pleasure, a voice without a body came to her. 'Mistress,' it said, 'why are you so astounded at this great wealth? All this belongs to you. So retire to your room and soothe your weariness upon a bed, and when you wish, take a bath. We whose voices you hear are your servants who [257] will wait on you diligently, and when your body is refreshed you shall straightway have a royal feast.'

"Psyche felt the blessing of divine Providence, and she obeyed the suggestions of the disembodied voice, washing away her weariness first with sleep and then with a bath. And suddenly she saw near her a raised semicircular platform, and judging from the dinner setting that it was meant for her own refreshment, she promptly reclined there. Instantly trays loaded with nectarous wine and various foods appeared, with no one serving; it was only some breath of air[1] that wafted them and placed them before her. She could see no one, but merely heard words emanating from somewhere; her servants were only voices. After her sumptuous dinner someone unseen came in and sang, and someone else played a lyre, which was invisible too. Then the compact sound of a large melodious group came to her ears; although no human being appeared, it was obviously a choir.

"When the pleasures were over, at the evening star's urging Psyche retired to bed. Then, when night was well advanced, a dulcet sound impinged upon her ears. Now being all alone she feared for her virginity.

---

[1] The Latin *spiritu* might possibly be translated "spirit."

She trembles and shudders, and fears worse than anything the thing she is ignorant of. Now her unknown husband had arrived, had mounted the bed, had made Psyche his wife, and [259] had quickly departed before the rising of daylight. At once voices-in-waiting in the bedchamber cared for the new bride whose virginity was ended. This happened thus for a long time, and, as nature provides, her new condition through constant habituation won her over to its pleasure, and the sound of a mysterious voice gave comfort to her loneliness.

"In the meantime her parents were growing old in their tireless mourning and grief. The story had spread widely, and when her older sisters learned all that had happened, in sorrow and mourning they hastily deserted their own homes and vied with each other in their rush to see and console their parents.

"That very night Psyche's husband spoke to her: though she could not see him, he was none the less sensible both to her hands and to her ears.

"'My dearest Psyche,' he said, 'my darling wife, cruel Fortune is threatening you with a deadly danger, which I advise you to guard against with the utmost caution. Your sisters are now upset by the belief that you are dead, and in searching for some trace of you they will very soon come to that cliff. If you should happen to hear any of their laments, do not answer; no, do not even look in their direction. Otherwise you will cause me the most bitter pain, and yourself utter destruction.'

"She nodded assent and promised to behave as her husband wished. But when he and the night had both slipped away, she spent the whole day miserably weeping and lamenting, saying repeatedly [261] that now she really was utterly dead: fenced in by the confinement of her luxurious prison, and bereft of human company and conversation, she could not even help to save her own sisters in their mourning for her; and worse, she could not even see them at all. With neither bath nor food nor any other refreshment to restore her, she retired to sleep weeping profusely. In no time her husband came to bed, a little earlier than usual, and finding her still crying as he took her in his arms, he scolded her.

"'Is this what you promised me, my Psyche?' he asked. 'What am I, your husband, to expect of you now? What am I to hope from you? All day and all night you never stop torturing yourself, even in the midst of love-making. Very well, do as you like and obey your heart's ruinous demands. Only remember my earnest warning, when you begin to repent too late.'

"Then she pleaded with him and threatened to die until she wrenched from her husband his consent to her wishes: to see her sisters, to soothe their grief, and to converse with them. Thus he gave in to his new bride's entreaties, and in addition he permitted her to present them with whatever gold or jewellery she might wish. But he warned her time and again, often with threats, never to yield to her sisters' pernicious advice to investigate her husband's appearance. Otherwise, through her sacrilegious curiosity, she would cast herself down from the exalted height of her fortunes and never afterwards [263] enjoy his embrace.

"She thanked her husband and, feeling happier now, said, 'I would rather die a hundred times than be robbed of your sweet caresses. For I love and adore you passionately, whoever you are, as much as my own life's breath, and I would not even compare Cupid[1] himself with you. But please grant me this favour also, I beg you: instruct your servant Zephyr to bring my sisters here to me the same way he carried me.' And she began to press persuasive kisses upon him and pile on caressing words and entwine him with her irresistible limbs, adding to her charms expressions like 'My honey-sweet,' 'My husband,' 'Sweet soul of your Psyche.' Her husband reluctantly succumbed to the force and power of her alluring whispers and promised he would do everything. Then as daylight drew near he vanished from his wife's embrace.

"Meanwhile her sisters, having ascertained the location of the cliff where Psyche had been abandoned, hurried there and began to weep their eyes out and beat their breasts until the rocks and crags reverberated with the echo of their repeated howls. Then they started summoning their poor sister by her own name until, as the penetrating sound of their wailing voices slipped down over the slopes, Psyche came running out of her house, distraught and trembling.

[265] "'Why needlessly destroy yourselves,' she cried, 'with pitiful lamentation? I, whom you are mourning, am here. Stop those mournful sounds and at last dry your cheeks soaked so long in tears, for you can now embrace the girl for whom you were grieving.'

"Then she called Zephyr and reminded him of her husband's instructions. Instantly he obeyed the command and immediately, with a harmless ride on the gentlest of breezes, they were carried down to their destination. First the sisters took their delight in mutual embraces and eager kisses, and the tears that had been allayed came back again at joy's urging.

"'But come under our roof,' Psyche said, 'enter our home in happiness, and refresh your troubled souls together with your Psyche.'

---

[1] The first mention of his name in the story.

"After this welcome she pointed out the supreme riches of the golden house[1] and showed their ears the large staff of voices-in-waiting. She refreshed them luxuriously with a beautiful bath and the delicacies of her unearthly table; with the result that, glutted with the abundant plenty of this truly heavenly wealth, they began to nourish envy deep in their hearts. One of them then began to interrogate her minutely and inquisitively without stopping. Who was the owner of these heavenly [267] objects? Who was her husband? What sort of man was he? But Psyche did not in the least violate her husband's command nor banish it from her heart's secret keeping; but extemporising she pretended that he was a young and handsome man, just beginning the shadow of a downy beard on his cheeks, and that he spent much of his time hunting in the fields and on the mountains. But afraid that, if the conversation continued, with some slip she might betray her counsel of silence, she loaded them with wrought gold and jewelled necklaces, quickly summoned Zephyr, and handed them over to his charge for transport back.

"This was accomplished right away. Now returning home those worthy sisters were consumed with the gall of swelling Envy and complained loud and long to each other.

"'O blind, cruel, unjust fortune!' began the one. 'Was that your pleasure, then, for us daughters of the same parents to suffer such a different lot? Indeed, are we, the older, surrendered as slaves to foreign husbands and banished from home and country too, to live like exiles far from our parents; while she, the youngest, the last product of our mother's weary womb, has acquired all that wealth and a god for a husband? Why, she does not even know how to use all those possessions properly. Did you see, sister, how much jewellery was lying around in her house, and how fine it was? Did you see those shining clothes and sparkling gems, and [269] all that gold under foot everywhere? And if she has and holds such a handsome husband, as she says, there is not a luckier woman now alive in the whole world. But maybe, as their familiarity continues and their affection increases, her divine husband will make her a goddess too. That's it, by Hercules! That is the way she was acting and behaving. The woman is already looking skywards and aspiring to godhead, the way she has voices for maids and gives orders even to the winds. But look at poor me! In the first place I drew a husband older than my father, and besides he is balder than a pumpkin and punier than any child, and he keeps the whole house locked up with bolts and chains.'

---

[1] Nero's luxurious palace in Rome had also been called the "Golden House" (Suetonius, *Nero* 31).

"The other sister took over. 'As for me, I have to put up with a husband who is even doubled over and bent with arthritis, and therefore hardly ever pays homage to my Venus. I am forever rubbing his twisted and petrified fingers and burning these delicate hands of mine with smelly fomentations and dirty bandages and stinking poultices. Instead of playing the dutiful part of a wife, I have to endure the laborious role of a doctor. You, sister, may decide for yourself with what attitude of patience and servility – I shall say frankly what I feel – you may tolerate this situation. But as for me, I can no longer endure the fact that so blessed a fortune befell an undeserving girl. Just remember how haughtily, how arrogantly she dealt with us; and how she revealed her swollen pride by the very [271] boastfulness of her immoderate display; and how she reluctantly tossed us a few little things from all that treasure; and then, burdened by our presence, she hastily ordered us to be driven out, blown off, and whistled away. I am no woman, I have no breath in me at all, if I do not cast her down from that pile of wealth. And if you too, as you ought, have felt the sting of this insult to us, let us devise some effective plan of action together. Let us not show our parents or anyone else these things that we are bringing back – no, let us not even be aware that she is alive. It is enough that we ourselves saw things that we regretted seeing, let alone that we should proclaim such glorious tidings of her to her parents and to all the world. They are not glorious whose riches nobody knows. She will discover that she does not have maids, but older sisters. And so now let us go back to our husbands and return to our poor but respectable hearths. Then, after we have fortified ourselves with deep deliberation, let us return in greater strength to punish her pride.'

"This wicked plan seemed a good idea to the two wicked women. They hid all their costly gifts; then, tearing their hear and scratching their cheeks – precisely as they deserved – began renewing their mock lamentations. Thus they quickly frightened their parents by reopening the wound of their grief too. Then, swollen with madness, they hastened to their own homes to plot some heinous crime – even murder – against their innocent sister.

[273] "Meanwhile Psyche was again being warned by her unknown husband in his nightly talks with her. 'Do you see how much danger you are in?' he asked. 'Fortune is now firing at long range, and unless you take very strong precautionary measures, she will soon attack at close quarters. Those deceitful bitches are making great efforts to execute a villainous plot against you, the gist of which is to persuade you to examine my face. As I have often told you before, if you see it, you

will never see it again. Therefore, if those horrible harpies armed with their pernicious thoughts come again – and they will come, I know – you must not talk to them at all. And if you cannot bear that because of your simple innocence and tenderheartedness, then at least, if they talk about your husband, neither listen nor answer. You see, we are now about to increase our family, and your womb, still a child's, bears another child for us, who will be a god if you guard our secret in silence, but a mortal if you profane it.'

"Psyche blossomed with happiness at the news, hailed the comfort of a divine child, exulted in the glory of the baby to be born and rejoiced in the honour of the name of mother. She anxiously counted the growing days and the departing months, and, being a new recruit who knew naught of the pack she bore, she was amazed at such a pretty swelling of her fertile womb from just a tiny pinprick.

"But already those pests and foulest of Furies [275] had set sail, breathing viperous poison and hastening with impious speed. Then for a second time her transient husband warned his Psyche. 'The critical day,' he said, 'the ultimate peril, the malice of your sex, and your blood in hatred have now taken arms against you: they have struck camp, are arrayed for battle, and have sounded the charge. Now your wicked sisters have drawn the sword and are attacking your throat. O my sweetest Psyche, what disasters are upon us! Have mercy on yourself and me. By resolute self-restraint free your home, your husband, yourself, and our little one from the catastrophe of ruin which threatens. Those vile women – you cannot call them sisters after their murderous hatred and their trampling on the ties of blood – do not look at them or listen to them when they lean out over the cliff like Sirens[1] and make the rocks resound with their fatal songs.'

"Psyche answered, making her words indistinct through her tearful sobbing. 'Some time ago, I think, you assayed proofs of my loyalty and discretion; now too you will no less approve the resolution of my mind. Just give your servant Zephyr his orders again. Let him perform his duty. To compensate for forbidding me a sight of your holy face, at least grant me a look at my sisters. I beg you, by [277] those cinnamon-scented curls hanging around your head, by those soft round cheeks so like my own, by your breast so wonderfully aflame with heat: please, as I hope to know your looks at least in my unborn babe's, be conquered by the loving prayers of an anxious suppliant and grant me the enjoyment of a sisterly embrace. Revive with joy the

[1] Half women, half birds, who lured sailors to their death with enchanting songs (cf. Homer, *Odyssey* XII 165–200).

soul of your devout and dedicated Psyche. I shall ask no further about your appearance. Not even the night's darkness hurts me now, because I have you in my arms, my light.'

"Bewitched by her words and soft caresses, her husband dried her tears with his hair and promised assent; and then instantly departed ahead of the light of the newborn day.

"Yoked in a conspiratorial faction, the two sisters never stopped to visit their parents but headed straight from the ships to the cliff at breakneck speed. Nor did they await the arrival of a carrying wind, but with unbridled recklessness leapt out into the chasm. Zephyr, mindful of the royal edict, caught them, albeit with reluctance, in the bosom of his airy breeze and deposited them on the ground. With no hesitation they instantly penetrated the house side by side and embraced their prey, falsely calling themselves sisters. Masking the storehouse of their deeply hidden treachery behind cheerful faces, they began to flatter her.

"'O Psyche,' they said, 'you are not the tiny little Psyche you used to be, but you are now yourself a [279] mother! Think what a good thing for us you are carrying in your purse! With what pleasure you will gladden our whole house! O how lucky we are! How much joy we will have bringing up that golden baby! If he resembles his parents – as he ought to – in beauty, he will be born an absolute Cupid!'

"Thus with their pretended affection they gradually invaded their sister's heart. As soon as they had been relieved of their travel-weariness by resting and refreshed by the steamy waters of the baths, she feasted them most beautifully in her dining room with those marvellous rich foods and sausages. She commanded a lyre to speak and there was strumming; flutes to perform and there was piping; choirs to sing and there was singing. All those sounds with no one present caressed the listeners' spirits with the most delightful melodies. But the wickedness of the accursed women was not mollified even by the mellifluous sweetness of the music. They turned the conversation to the deceitful trap they had plotted, and casually began to enquire about her husband: what sort of man he was, what his origins were, what sort of background he came from. In her excessive simplicity Psyche forgot her earlier story and invented a different fiction. She said that her husband came from the next province, was a merchant dealing in large sums, and was now middle-aged with a sprinkling of grey in his hair. Without lingering a moment longer in the conversation, she loaded them down once [281] more with lavish gifts and sent them back by their aerial conveyance.

"While they were returning home, raised aloft on Zephyr's gentle breath, they angrily discussed the situation. 'Well, sister, what do we say about that silly girl's monstrous lie? First he was a young man just growing a beard of soft down; next he is middle-aged, distinguished by silvery white hair. Who can he be who is suddenly transformed by such a short space of time into an old man? The only answer, my sister, is that the wicked woman is either telling us a string of lies or she does not know what her husband looks like. Whichever is the case, she must be dislodged as quickly as possible from her riches. If she is ignorant of her husband's appearance, then surely she must have married a god, and is carrying a god for us in that pregnancy of hers. Well, if – god forbid – she becomes known as the mother of a divine child, I shall immediately knot a noose and hang myself. In the meantime, then, let us go back to our parents and weave a woof of guile to match the colour of our discussion's warp.'

"Enflamed as they were, they greeted their parents haughtily and spent a disturbed and wakeful night. Early in the morning those damned women flew to the cliff, and thence with the wind's customary help swooped violently downward. Having pressed their eyelids to force tears, they greeted the girl with their display of guile: 'Here you sit, happy and fortunate in your very ignorance of [283] your great misfortune. You are not even curious about the danger you are in, while we have been awake all night in sleepless concern over your situation, pitifully tortured by your calamities. We now know the truth, you see, and since of course we share your pain and plight, we cannot conceal it from you. It is a monstrous snake gliding with many-knotted coils, its bloody neck oozing noxious poison and its deep maw gaping wide, that sleeps beside you hidden in the night. Remember now Apollo's[1] oracle, which proclaimed that you were destined to marry a savage beast. Moreover, several farmers and people who hunt hereabouts and many residents of the neighbourhood have seen him coming home from feeding in the evening, and swimming in the shallows of the river nearby. They all say that he will not long continue to fatten you with the charming indulgences of nourishment, but as soon as a full womb brings your pregnancy to completion and endowed you with more luscious fruit, he will eat you up. Given these facts, it is now your decision. Are you willing to listen to your sisters in their concern for your dear safety and avoid death and live with us free from peril? Or do you prefer to be buried in the bowels of a ferocious beast? If you really enjoy the voiceful loneliness of this country place, or the stinking and perilous copulations of [285] furtive love

---

[1] The Latin says "Pythian," i.e. "Delphic," but in fact (cf. IV 32) the oracle was given at Miletus, not Delphi.

and the embraces of a poisonous snake – at least we will have done our duty as loving sisters.'

"Then poor little Psyche, artless and tenderhearted as she was, was seized with terror at their grim words. Driven beyond the limits of her own mind, she completely shed the memory of all her husband's warnings and her own promises, and hurled herself headlong into an abyss of disaster. Trembling, pallid, the blood drained from her face, barely able to stammer her words through half-open lips, she answered them as follows.

"'You, my dearest sisters, as was only right, are being true and firm in your family loyalty. And I do not think that the people who told you these stories are telling a lie. In fact I have never seen my husband's face, and I have no knowledge at all where he comes from. I only barely hear his talking at night, and I must endure a husband of unknown standing who totally shuns the light. You must be right when you say he is some beast, I agree. He is always intimidating me from looking at him, and threatening some great punishment for any curiosity about his features. If now you can bring some salvation to your sister in her danger, help me right now. Otherwise, your subsequent neglect will undo all the benefits of your concern thus far.'

"The gates were open now, and those vicious women, having reached their sister's defenceless mind, quit the concealment of their covered artillery, [287] unsheathed the swords of their deception, and assaulted the timorous thoughts of the guileless girl.

"One of them said, 'Since the bond of our common origin compels us to disregard all possible danger when your life is at stake, we shall show you the only way which promises a path to salvation, which we have been planning for a long, long time. Take a very sharp razor, whet it with the application of your soft stroking palm, and secretly conceal it on that side of the bed where you usually lie. Then get a lamp, trimmed and filled with oil and burning with a clear light, and hide it beneath the cover of a little pot. Dissemble all this preparation very carefully; and then, after he has drawn along his furrowing gait and mounted the bed as usual, when he is stretched out entangled in the first threads of oppressing sleep and begins to breathe deep slumber, slip off the couch, and, with bare feet lessening little by little your airy tread, free the lamp from the prison of its blind darkness. From the light's good counsel borrow the occasion for a glorious deed of your own: boldly grasping your double-edged weapon, first raise your right hand high; then, with as strong a stroke as you can, sever the knot that joins the poisonous serpent's neck and head. We shall not fail to support you, but as soon as you have won safety by his death we will hasten anxiously to your side; and after bringing back along with you all this treasure, we will make a [289] desirable marriage for you, human to human.'

"With this blaze of words they inflamed their sister's burning heart, for in truth it was already on fire, and then straightway left her, for they were greatly afraid even to be in the neighbourhood of such an evil deed. As usual they were carried to the top of the cliff by the wafting of the winged breeze and rushed away at once in rapid retreat; they boarded their ships at once and were gone.

"Psyche was left alone, except that a woman driven by hostile furies is not alone. In her grief she ebbed and flowed like the billows of the sea. Although she had determined her plan and her mind was made up, nevertheless, as she turned her hands toward the act itself, she still wavered irresolutely, torn apart by the many emotions raised by her dilemma. She felt haste and procrastination, daring and fear, despair and anger; and worst of all, in the same body she loathed the beast but loved the husband. But as evening began to bring on the night, she prepared the apparatus for her abominable crime with frantic haste. Night came, and her husband came, and after skirmishing in love's warfare he dropped into a deep sleep.

"Then Psyche, though naturally weak in both body and spirit, was fed with strength by the cruelty of Fate. She brought out the lamp, seized the razor, and in her boldness changed her sex. But as soon as the bed's mysteries were illumined as the lamp was brought near, she beheld that wild creature who is [291] the gentlest and sweetest beast of all, Cupid himself, the beautiful god beautifully sleeping. At the sight of him even the light of the lamp quickened in joy, and the razor repented its sacrilegious sharpness. But Psyche was terrified at this marvellous sight and put out of her mind; overcome with the pallor of exhaustion she sank faint and trembling to her knees. She tried to hide the weapon – in her own heart. And she would certainly have done so, had not the blade slipped out and flown away from her reckless hands in its horror of so atrocious a deed. She was now weary and overcome by the sense of being safe, but as she gazed repeatedly at the beauty of that divine countenance her spirit began to revive.

"On his golden head she saw the glorious hair drenched with ambrosia: wandering over his milky neck and rosy cheeks were the neatly shackled ringlets of his locks, some prettily hanging in front, others behind; the lightning of their great brilliance made even the lamp's light flicker. Along the shoulders of the winged god white feathers glistened like flowers in the morning dew; and although his wings were at rest, soft and delicate little plumes along their edges quivered restlessly in wanton play. The rest of his body was hairless and resplendent, such as to cause Venus no regrets for having borne this child. By the feet of the bed lay a bow and quiver and arrows, gracious weapons of the mighty god.

[293] "Insatiably, and with some curiosity, Psyche scrutinised and handled and marvelled at her husband's arms. She drew one of the arrows from the quiver and tested the point against the tip of her thumb; but her hand was still trembling and she pushed a little too hard and pricked too deep, so that tiny drops of rose-red blood moistened the surface of her skin. Thus without knowing it Psyche of her own accord fell in love with Love. Then more and more enflamed with desire for Cupid[1] she leaned over him, panting desperately for him. She eagerly covered him with impassioned and impetuous kisses till she feared about the depth of his slumber. But while her wounded heart was swirling under the excitement of so much bliss, the lamp – either from wicked treachery or malicious jealousy or simply because it too longed to touch and, in its way, kiss such a beautiful body – sputtered forth from the top of its flame a drop of boiling oil on to the god's right shoulder. O bold and reckless lamp, worthless servant of Love, to scorch the very god of all fire, when it must have been some lover who first invented you that even by night he might the longer enjoy the object of his desire! Thus burnt the god jumped up, and seeing the ruin of betrayed trust, straightway flew up from the kisses and embraces of his poor unhappy wife without a word.

[295] "But as he rose Psyche quickly grasped his right leg with both hands, forming a pitiable appendage to his soaring flight and a trailing attachment in dangling companionship through the cloudy regions. At last, exhausted, she fell to the ground. Her divine lover did not desert her as she lay on the ground, but flew to a cypress nearby, from whose high summit he spoke to her in deep distress.

"'My poor naive Psyche!' he said. 'I in fact disobeyed the orders of my mother Venus, who had commanded me to chain you with passion for some wretched and worthless man and sentence you to the lowest sort of marriage. Instead I flew to you myself as your lover. But that was a frivolous thing to do, I know. Illustrious archer that I am, I shot myself with my own weapon and made you my wife, for the pleasure, it seems, of having you think me a wild beast and cut off my head with a sword, the head that holds these eyes which are your lovers! I told you time and time again that you must always be on your guard against this, and I kept warning you about it for your own good. As for those excellent advisers of yours, I shall soon be revenged on them for their disastrous instructions. But I shall punish you merely by leaving.'

---

[1] The Latin for "desire" is *cupido*. For his names, see note 3, p. 182.

"And as his words ended he took wing and soared into the sky.

"Psyche lay flat upon the ground and watched her husband's flight as far as her sight enabled her, tormenting her soul with the most piteous lamentations. [297] But after her husband, speeding on his oarage of wings, had been removed from her view by vastness of distance she threw herself over the edge of a nearby river. The gentle stream, however, no doubt respecting the god who can kindle even water but also apprehensive for himself, quickly caught her in his harmless current and deposited her on a bank deep in grass. At that moment the rustic god Pan happened to be sitting beside the stream's brow, embracing the mountain goddess Echo and teaching her to sing back to him all kinds of tunes. Near the bank wandering she-goats grazed and frolicked as they cropped the river's hair. The goat-like god saw Psyche sad and weary, and being not unaware of her misfortune, he called her gently over to him and calmed her with soothing words.

"'Pretty maiden,' said he, 'although I am a country fellow and a herdsman, by benefit of an advanced old age I have been schooled by much experience. Now if I guess rightly – though wise men call it not guessing but divination – from your weak and oft tottering footsteps, your extremely pale complexion, your constant sighing, and still more by your sad eyes, you are suffering from an overdose of love. Listen to me, therefore, and do not try to kill yourself again by a fatal leap or any other sort of suicide. Stop your mourning and put away your grief. Instead pray to Cupid, the greatest of the gods, and worship him and earn his favour with flattering deference, since he is a pleasure-loving [299] and soft-hearted youth.'

"When the shepherd god had finished speaking, Psyche did not reply, but merely gestured reverently to the beneficent deity and went her way. After she had wandered a rather long way in her weary walking, she took an unfamiliar road, and as daylight was fading she came to a city where the husband of one of her sisters was king. When she discovered this, Psyche asked that her presence be announced to her sister. She was soon invited in, and when they had had their fill of embracing and greeting each other, her sister enquired into the reasons for her coming. Psyche began:

"'You remember that advice of yours: I mean when the two of you persuaded me to take a double-edged razor and kill the beast who was sleeping with me under the false name of husband, before my wretched body was swallowed in his greedy maw. Well, as soon as I had taken the light as my accomplice – in which I concurred with your advice – and looked at his face, I saw an amazing and utterly divine spectacle: the goddess Venus' son in person, I mean Cupid himself, lying peacefully asleep. Excited by the spectacle of so much bliss and confused by an overabundance of delight, I was feeling distress at my inability to enjoy it fully when, obviously through some terrible misfortune, a drop of burning oil spurted on to his shoulder. Immediately the pain jolted him from sleep, and when he saw me armed with fire and sword he declared: "On [301] account of your dreadful crime, you are forthwith to depart from my couch and take what is yours with you. I shall now wed your sister in holy matrimony"[1] – and he spoke your full name. Then at once he commanded Zephyr to waft me beyond the boundaries of his house.'

"Psyche had not even finished talking before her sister, goaded by the spurs of insane passion and poisonous jealousy, contrived on the spot a lie to deceive her husband, pretending that she had just heard the news of her parents' death, then instantly boarded a ship and went straight to the cliff. Although a different wind was blowing, in the blind hope of her desire she cried out, 'Take me, Cupid, a wife worthy of you! And you, Zephyr, catch your mistress!' and made a great leap. She plunged downward, but even in death she could not reach that destination: her body was tossed and torn apart by the crag's jutting rocks, and, just as she deserved, with entrails ripped open her corpse provided a ready meal for bird and beast.

"Nor was the infliction of the second punishment slow in coming, for resuming her wandering steps Psyche arrived at another city, in which that other sister was living in similar style. She too, likewise led on by her sister's false story, and an eager claimant for the wicked possession of her sister's [303] marriage, hastened to the cliff and fell to the self-same deadly doom.

"Psyche meanwhile, intent on her search for Cupid, was travelling about the country, while he lay groaning in pain from the lamp's wound, in his mother's own bedchamber. At this point a bird, the white seagull who swims on wings above the waves, dived hurriedly down deep into Ocean's bosom, where she at once found Venus as she bathed and swam. The bird stood beside her and informed her that her son had been burned, that he was in grievous pain from the wound, that he had taken to his bed, and that his recovery was uncertain. 'Furthermore,' she said, 'because of various rumours and reproaches circulating by word of mouth throughout the whole world, Venus' entire household is getting a bad reputation. They are saying that the two of you have gone off on vacation, he to his mountainside whoring, you to swimming in the sea; and so there is no joy any more, no grace, no charm. Everything is unkempt and boorish and harsh. Weddings and social intercourse and the love of children are gone, leaving only a

---

[1] *Tibi res tuas habeto* was the customary formula for divorce, and *confarreatio* the most ancient and solemn form of marriage among Romans.

monstrous mess and an unpleasant disregard for anything as squalid as the bonds of marriage.' Thus did that talkative and altogether interfering bird cackle into Venus' ear, tearing her son's reputation to shreds.

"Venus was furious and burst out: 'So now that virtuous son of mine has a girlfriend, has he? Come on, then, my only loyal servant, and tell me the [305] name of the creature who seduced that simple and innocent boy. Is she of the tribe of Nymphs, or the band of Hours, or the choir of Muses, or my own company of Graces?

"The loquacious bird did not hold her tongue. 'I do not know, mistress. But I think that he is desperately in love with a girl, who is known, if I remember correctly, by the name of Psyche.'

"Then Venus indignantly screamed at the top of her voice: 'Psyche! Is it really Psyche he loves, that whorish rival of my beauty, that pretender to my name? The young imp must have thought I was a madam who was showing him the girl so that he could get to know her.'

"With these loud plaints she speedily surfaced from the sea and headed immediately for her golden bedroom, where she found her ailing boy, just as she had heard. From the doorway she bellowed at him for all she was worth. 'What fine behaviour! And how appropriate to your parentage and your virtuous character! First you trample underfoot your mother's commands – your queen's I should say – and fail to torture my enemy with some low-class passion. And furthermore at your age, a mere boy, you couple with her in your unrestrained, immature lovemaking, evidently supposing that I would tolerate as a daughter-in-law a woman I hate. You must presume, you good-for-nothing, unlovable seducer, that you alone are the prince and that I am too old to conceive. Well, I want you to know that I [307] will produce another son much better than you. Indeed, in order to make you feel the insult all the more I will adopt one of my young slaves and make over to him those wings of yours and torches, your bow and arrows, and the rest of my equipment, which I did not give you to use that way. Remember, there was no allowance granted from your father's property for outfitting you. But you were badly trained as a baby, and you have sharp hands, and you disrespectfully strike your elders all the time, and you expose me your mother to shame every day, you monstrous son! You have beaten me several times and you scorn me as if I were a widow and you have no respect for your stepfather, who is the world's strongest and greatest warrior.[1] Why should you, when you are always supplying him with girls to torment

---

[1] Mars. Venus here legitimises their relationship, which is usually not presented as marriage; similarly at the end of chapter 29 she represents herself as divorced from Cupid's father Vulcan.

me with his adultery? But now I will make you sorry for mocking me, and that marriage of yours will taste sour and bitter.

"'But now that I have been made a laughing-stock, what am I to do? Where can I turn? How am I going to repress this reptile? Should I ask for help from my enemy Temperance, whom I have so often offended precisely because of my son's extravagance? But I shudder at the thought of talking to that crude and dirty woman. Still the consolation of [309] revenge is not to be rejected, whatever the source. I really must employ her and her alone to give the harshest possible punishment to that good-for-nothing, dismantle his quiver and disarm his arrows, unknot his bow, defuse his torch, yes and even curb his body with harsher medicines. I shall not consider my humiliation atoned for until she has shaved off his hair, which I with my own hands have often brushed to a golden sheen, and clipped his wings, which I have dyed in my bosom's fount of nectar.'

"So saying, she rushed out of doors, furious and angry with passion's own bitterness. Ceres and Juno came up to her at that very moment, and when they saw her wrathful countenance asked why she spoiled the charm of her flashing eyes with such a sullen frown. 'How opportune!' she replied. 'My heart is quite on fire, and I suppose you have come to coerce me to desist. But please use all your powers to help me hunt out Psyche, my elusive runaway. I assume that the notorious tale about my family and the exploits of my unspeakable son have not escaped your notice.'

"Not unaware what had happened they tried to soothe Venus' savage anger. 'My lady,' they asked, 'what fault did your son commit so grave as to make you attack his pleasures so determinedly and also be so keen to destroy the girl he loves? What crime is that, we ask you, if he likes smiling at a pretty girl? Or are you not aware that he is male, and a [311] young man at that? Or perhaps you have forgotten how old he is now? Just because he carries his years prettily, do you think of him as being for ever a child? Now, you are a mother, and a sensible woman besides. Will you never stop spying inquisitively into your son's pastimes, blaming self-indulgence in him, scolding him for his love-affairs, and, in short, finding fault with your own talents and your own delights in the case of your handsome son? What god, what human will tolerate your scattering the seeds of desire all over the world while in your own house you bitterly restrict love-affairs and close down the factory in which the natural faults of women are made?'

"Thus, in fear of his arrows they flattered Cupid with an obliging defence, although he was not in the courtroom. But Venus, offended that her wrongs were being treated with ridicule, swept past them on the other side and set out quickly toward the sea.

BOOK VI

[313] "Meanwhile Psyche wandered this way and that, restlessly track-
ing her husband day and night, so eager was she, even if she could
not soften his anger with a wife's allurements, at least to try to appease
him with a slave's prayers. When she spotted a temple at the top of a
high mountain, she said, 'How do I know if perhaps that is not where
my master lives?' At once she began to walk rapidly toward it; although
she was very weary from continuous effort, hope and desire quickened
her pace. When she had valiantly climbed the lofty ridge, she went in
and stood near the holy couch. There she saw ears of grain in a heap
and others woven into wreaths, and ears of barley. There were sickles
too, and all the implements of harvest work, but everything was lying
scattered about and in careless disorder, as if tossed from the labourers'
hands in the summer heat. Psyche carefully separated all these objects
one by one and arranged them properly in distinct piles, evidently
believing that she ought not to neglect any god's shrines and rituals,
but appeal to the benevolence and pity of them all.

[315] "When bountiful Ceres discovered her attentively and diligently taking care of her shrine, she instantly exclaimed from afar:
'What's this, pitiable Psyche? All over the world Venus is making an
intense investigation to track you down, raging in her heart. She seeks
to inflict condign punishment upon you and demands vengeance with
all the power of her godhead. But here you are, acting as caretaker of
my property. How can you be thinking about anything except your
own safety?'

"Then Psyche fell before her, drenching the goddess's feet with a
flood of tears and sweeping the ground with her hair. She uttered
manifold entreaties as she sought to win her favour. 'I beseech you by
your fertile right hand, by the fructifying rites of the harvest, by the
silent mysteries of the sacred baskets; and by the winged course of
your dragon-servants, the furrows of the Sicilian soil, the ravisher's
chariot and the grasping ground, Proserpina's descent to a lightless
wedding and your daughter's lamplit discovery and ascent; and by all
other secrets which the sanctuary of Attic Eleusis cloaks in silence[1]:

---

[1] Ceres (the Greek Demeter) was a goddess of agriculture. Her daughter Proserpina was
abducted in Sicily by Pluto and removed to the underworld, and her mother's grief
brought infertility upon the world: a compromise was reached whereby the daughter
would spend part of the year above ground and part below. Her most famous cult-centre
was at Eleusis, near Athens, where mysteries were celebrated involving death and resurrection. Sacred objects in her cult were concealed in a basket (*cista*), and Ceres is
sometimes represented as travelling in a dragon-drawn chariot. See Ovid, *Metamorphoses* v 341–661.

succour the pitiable soul of Psyche, your suppliant. Let me hide here for a few days at least, among your stores of grain, until the [317] powerful goddess's raging anger is softened by the passing of time, or at least until my strength, which is exhausted from my long toil, is soothed by an interval of rest.'

"Ceres replied, 'Your tearful prayers move me deeply and I long to come to your aid, but Venus is my relative and we have old ties of friendship. Besides she is a good woman, and I cannot risk causing bad feelings between us. So depart from this house at once, and count yourself lucky that I did not detain you as my prisoner.'

"Driven out, disappointed in her hopes, and doubly afflicted with grief, Psyche retraced her steps. In a valley below, in the middle of a faintly lighted grove, she caught sight of an artfully constructed shrine. Unwilling to omit any possible path, however doubtful, toward improved hopes, and willing to seek favour from any divinity, she approached the consecrated doors. She saw costly offerings and ribbons lettered in gold attached to the tree-branches and doorposts, which bore witness to the name of the goddess to whom they had been dedicated, along with thanks for her deed. Psyche knelt and embraced in her arms the altar still warm with sacrifice, dried her tears, and then prayed.

"'O sister and consort of great Jupiter — whether you dwell in the ancient sanctuary of Samos, which alone glories in your birth and infant wails and nursing; or whether you frequent the blessed site of lofty Carthage, which worships you as a virgin who [319] travels through the sky on the back of a lion; or whether you protect the renowned walls of the Argives beside the banks of Inachus, who proclaims you now the Thunderer's bride and queen of goddesses — you whom all the East adores as "Yoker" and all the West calls "Bringer into Light" — be you Juno Saviouress to me in my uttermost misfortunes.[1] I am so weary from enduring great toils. Free me from fear of the danger threatening me, for I know you are wont to come freely to the aid of pregnant women in peril.'

"While she was making this supplication Juno suddenly appeared to her in all the august majesty of her godhead. 'In faith, how I wish,'

---

[1] Juno (the Greek Hera) is here learnedly and accurately invoked by Psyche with a syncretistic mixture of references to Greek, Roman, and Punic cult-centres, titles and functions. Samos is an island in the Eastern Aegean. At Carthage, the Romans assimilated the Punic goddess Tanit, calling her Juno Caelestis. Argos was a city-state in the Peloponnese; its personified river Inachus was the father of Io, whom Jupiter raped and Juno mercilessly persecuted. The titles Zygia (Greek) and Lucina (Latin) refer to Juno's primary function in the Greco-Roman world, that of woman's protector in marriage and childbirth.

she said at once, 'that I could accommodate my will to your petitions. But I would be ashamed to set myself against the will of my daughter-in-law Venus,[2] whom I have always loved as a daughter. And besides I am prevented by laws forbidding anyone to harbour the fugitive slaves of others without their masters' consent.'[3]

[321] "Terrified by this second shipwreck of her fortunes, and now unable to reach her winged husband, Psyche gave up all hope of being saved and took counsel with her own thoughts.

"'What more can I try now? What other aids can be applied to my tribulations, since even the votes of the goddesses, favourable as they are, could not help me? Where else can I turn my steps, caught as I am in such a powerful noose? What roof or darkness can I hide beneath to evade the inescapable eyes of mighty Venus? So why not finally take courage like a man and bravely abandon your vain hopes? Hand yourself over voluntarily to your mistress and soften her furious attacks by submission, late though it be. Besides, who knows but what you will actually find the one you have long been searching for, there in his mother's house?'

"In this way, prepared to risk the uncertain consequences of compliance – or rather sure destruction – she pondered how she should begin her coming appeal.

"Venus, meanwhile, had abandoned her attempts to track her down on earth and was making for heaven. She ordered her chariot fitted out, the one that Vulcan the goldsmith had carefully embellished with refined craftsmanship and offered her as a wedding gift before their first experience of marriage. It shone more brightly for what had been rubbed away by the refining file, and had become more valuable from the very loss of gold. From the [323] flock stabled round their mistress's bedroom, four white doves step forward and with joyful gait twist their painted necks and walk beneath the jewelled yoke, then lift their mistress and happily take flight. Sparrows follow in the train of the goddess's chariot, frisking about with merry chirping; and all the other kinds of songbird too proclaim the goddess's approach by delightfully sounding their sweet melodies. The clouds make way and Heaven opens up to its daughter[1] and the topmost ether receives the

---

[2] Vulcan was Juno's son.

[3] E.g. *Codex Iustinianus* VI i 4: "Whoever shall harbour a runaway slave in his house or on his land without the owner's knowledge shall return him, together with another slave of equal value or twenty solidi."

[1] See note on p. 181.

goddess in gladness. Nor is great Venus' song-filled retinue afraid of swooping eagles or preying hawks along their path.

"Then she went straight to the royal citadel of Jupiter and declared in a haughty petition that she urgently required to borrow the services of Mercury, the herald god.[2] Nor did Jupiter's cerulean brow nod nay. At once Venus triumphantly descended from heaven, with Mercury too in her train, to whom she spoke the following earnest words:

"'Arcadian brother, you know full well that your sister Venus has never accomplished anything without Mercury's presence, and it has surely not escaped your notice that I have long been vainly trying to find my runaway slave-girl. Nothing else is left then but for you to proclaim publicly a reward for whoever finds her. So see to it that you execute my commission quickly, and clearly describe the features by which she can be recognised. I do not want anyone who may be faced with the charge of [325] illegal concealment to be able to defend himself with a plea of ignorance.' With these words she handed him a handbill containing Psyche's name and all other particulars, and immediately departed home.

"Mercury did not fail to comply, but ran from person to person everywhere, fulfilling his assigned responsibility with the following proclamation: 'If anyone can arrest the flight or reveal the whereabouts of a runaway princess, a slave-girl of Venus, known as Psyche, he should meet this announcer, Mercury, behind the Murcian turning-post.[1] There as a reward for his information he will receive from Venus herself seven delicious kisses plus one more, deeply sweetened by the touch of her caressing tongue.'

"At this proclamation from Mercury, the lust for so splendid a reward aroused the competitive zeal of every mortal man. This circumstance more than all else put an end to Psyche's hesitation. As she was approaching her mistress's door, one of Venus' domestic staff, named Habit, ran towards her and instantly began shouting at the top of her voice. 'So you have finally come to recognise that you have a mistress, you worthless hussy! This would be just like your usual thoughtless behaviour, pretending not to know how much trouble we have had to suffer in our search for you. But it's a good job that I'm the [327] one into whose hands you have fallen, for now you are caught in the very

---

[2] In epic, Mercury functions as messenger between gods and men.

[1] A spot in the Circus Maximus at Rome, where there was a shrine of Venus Murcia. The passage suggests that Apuleius was writing at Rome for a Roman audience.

clutches of Death[1] and you will certainly pay the penalty without delay for your gross insubordination.'

"With that she boldly seized her by the hair and dragged her inside. Psyche offered no resistance, and was brought in and presented to Venus. The instant the goddess caught sight of her, she burst out in wild laughter, as men are wont to do in rage. Then shaking her head and scratching at her right ear, she exclaimed: 'So, you have finally deigned to call on your mother-in-law, have you? Or have you come rather to visit your husband, who is in critical condition from that wound you gave him? But don't you worry: I shall receive you now in the proper way for a good daughter-in-law.' And she called out, 'Where are my servants Trouble and Sadness?'

"When they had been summoned in, she handed Psyche over to them for torture. Following their mistress's orders they scourged poor Psyche with whips and tortured her with every other sort of device, and brought her back to Venus' presence. Then Venus burst out laughing again. 'Look at her!' she said. 'She is moving us to pity with that alluring swollen belly of hers. With that illustrious progeny she no doubt means to make me a happy grandmother. Lucky me! In the very flower of my youth I shall be called grandmother; and the son of a cheap slave-girl will be known as Venus' grandson. But how foolish I am to misuse the word "son," since the [329] marriage was between unequals[1]; besides, it took place in a country house without witnesses and without the father's consent. Hence it cannot be regarded as legal and therefore your child will be born illegitimate – if indeed we allow you to go through with the birth at all.'

"Having delivered this tirade Venus flew at her, ripped her dress into several pieces, tore her hair, and beat her head, hurting her sorely. Next she took some wheat and barley and millet and poppyseed and chickpeas and lentils and beans, jumbled them up by the heapful and poured them together in a single mound. Then she turned to Psyche. 'You are such a hideous slave,' she said, 'that I do not think you can attract lovers by anything except hard work. Therefore I shall now test your worth myself. Sort out that motley mass of seeds and put each grain properly in its own separate pile. Finish the job before this evening and show it to me for my approval.'

---

[1] Literally "the crabs of Orcus": the expression is puzzling, for we expect *fauces*, "jaws," as at VII 7 *mediis Orci faucibus*.

[1] Under Roman law marriage could not take place between parties of widely different social position (e.g. free and servile).

"After assigning her this mountain of seeds, she herself went off to a wedding dinner. Psyche, instead of applying her hands to that disordered and unresolvable mass, sat silently dumbfounded and dismayed by the enormity of the task. Then an ant – the little country ant – recognising the great difficulty and toil involved, pitied the bride of the [331] great god and abominated the cruelty of her mother-in-law. Running strenuously this way and that, it convoked and assembled an entire squadron of neighbourhood ants, shouting, 'Have pity, ye nimble nurselings of Earth, the mother of all, have pity, and be prompt and quick to aid Love's wife, a pretty girl in peril.' Wave after wave of the six-footed folk came rushing up. With indefatigable industry they individually took the entire heap apart, grain by grain, distributed and sorted the different kinds in separate piles, and then speedily disappeared from sight.

"At nightfall Venus returned from her wedding banquet, soaked in wine and smelling of balsam, her whole body wreathed in glistening roses. When she saw the wonderful industry with which the task had been performed, she exclaimed: 'This is not your work, vile creature, nor the accomplishment of those hands of yours, but rather his, the boy who fell in love with you, to your misfortune, and his too.' Then she tossed her a piece of bread for her supper and went off to bed.

"In the meantime Cupid was being kept under close guard, locked up in solitary confinement in one room in the inner part of the house, partly for fear that he would aggravate his wound by wanton self-indulgence, and partly to keep him from meeting his beloved. Thus, sundered and separated under one roof, the lovers dragged out an anguished night.

"Just as Dawn came riding in, Venus summoned [333] Psyche and addressed her. 'Do you see those woods that fringe the long banks of the river flowing past, where dense thickets look down upon a nearby spring? Sheep whose fleeces shine with the pure hue of gold wander there and graze unguarded. Procure a hank of their fleece of precious wool in any way you please, and bring it to me at once. That is my decree.'

"Psyche set out with a will, not indeed to fulfil the assignment but to find rest from her ills by throwing herself off the cliff into the river. But, there from the stream, a green reed, nurse of melodious music, divinely inspired by the gentle stirring of a sweet breeze, prophesied as follows. 'Poor Psyche, you are assailed by so many sorrows. Do not pollute my sacred waters with your pitiful suicide. And do not approach those fearsome wild sheep at this time of day, when they borrow heat from the burning sun and often break out in fierce madness, venting their fury in the destruction of men with their sharp horns and rock-like foreheads, and sometimes even with poisonous bites. But until the afternoon allays the sun's heat and the flock settles down under the calming influence of the river breeze, you can hide in concealment under this tall plane-tree which drinks from the same current as I. And then as soon as the flock's madness is assuaged and their spirit relaxed, if you shake the foliage in the adjacent woods, you will find some of the woolly gold clinging here and there to the bent branches.'

[335] "Thus a kind and simple reed taught suffering Psyche how to save herself. Once she had been carefully instructed she never faltered or had reason to regret obeying. She heeded all the advice, and with facile thievery filled the folds of her dress with the softness of yellow gold and brought it back to Venus. But, in her mistress's eyes at least, the danger of her second labour earned her no favourable commendation. Venus knitted her eyebrows and said with a bitter smile, 'I am well aware of the illicit prompter of this accomplishment too! But I shall now seriously put you to the test to find out if you really are endowed with courageous spirit and singular intelligence. Do you see that steep mountain-peak standing above the towering cliff? Dark waves flow down from a black spring on that peak and are enclosed by the reservoir formed by the valley nearby, to water the swamps of Styx and feed the rasping currents of Cocytus. Draw me some of the freezing liquid from there, from the innermost bubbling at the top of the spring, and bring it to me quickly in this phial.' With that she handed her a small vessel hewn out of crystal, and added some harsher threats for good measure.

"Psyche eagerly and speedily began walking toward the top of that mountain-peak, determined there at least to end her wretched life. But when she reached the area adjacent to the aforementioned ridge, she saw at once the deadly difficulty of her enormous task. A towering rock of monstrous size, [337] precariously jagged and inaccessible, belched from its stony jaws hideous streams, which issuing immediately from the chinks of a vertical opening flowed down over the slopes. Then, concealed in the path of a narrow channel that it had furrowed out for itself, the water slipped unseen down into the neighbouring valley. To right and left fierce snakes crawled out of the pitted crags, snakes which stretched out long necks, their eyes pledged to unblinking wakefulness and their pupils keeping nightwatch in ceaseless vision. And now even the water was defending itself, for it could talk, and it repeatedly cried out: 'Go away!' 'What are you doing? Look out!' 'What are you up to? Be careful!' 'Run!' 'You will die!' In her utter helplessness Psyche was transformed into stone. Although present in the body, she had taken leave of her senses, and, completely overwhelmed by the magnitude of her inescapable danger, she lacked even the last solace of tears.

"But the serious eyes of good Providence did not miss the tribulation of an innocent soul. Almighty Jupiter's royal bird, both wings outstretched, was there to help her: the rapacious eagle recalled that old service he had performed, when under Cupid's command he carried the Phrygian cupbearer[1] up to Jupiter; now he was bringing timely assistance and honouring the god's claim on him during his wife's ordeal. He abandoned the bright paths of heaven's [339] high summit and swooped down in front of the girl's face.

"'Do you,' he began, 'naive and inexperienced as you are in such matters, really expect to be able to steal, or even touch, a single drop from that holiest – and cruelest – of springs? Even the gods and Jupiter himself are frightened by these Stygian waters. You must know that, at least by hearsay, and that, as you swear by the powers of the gods, so the gods always swear by the majesty of the Styx. But here, give me that phial!'

"He snatched it out of her hands and hurried off to fill it with the water. Balancing his massive waving pinions he flew between the serpents' jaws, with their savage teeth and three-furrowed flickering tongues, plying his oars both right and left. The water resisted and threatened to harm him if he did not depart, but he took some, alleging that he was making his petition at Venus' orders and acting as her agent, on which account he was granted somewhat easier access.

"So Psyche joyfully took the full pitcher and speedily brought it back to Venus. But even then she still could not appease the cruel goddess's will. Menacing her with stronger and more terrible threats, Venus said to her with a baleful smile: 'I am convinced now that you must be some sort of great and mighty sorceress, seeing how thoroughly you have carried out these difficult tasks of mine. But there is still one more service you must perform, my [341] pet. Take this jar and go straight down from the daylight to the underworld and Orcus' own dismal abode. Then hand the jar to Proserpina and say: "Venus requests that you send her a little of your beauty, just enough to last her one brief day, because she has used up and exhausted all she had while caring for her sick son." But do not be too late coming back, because I have to rub some of it on before I go to attend the congress of the gods.'

"Then Psyche felt more than ever that her fortunes had reached the end: the veil had been drawn aside, and she realised clearly that she was being driven to immediate destruction – obviously, since she was

---

[1] Ganymede.

being compelled to take a voluntary trip on her own two feet to Tartarus[1] and the shades of the dead. Without further delay she headed towards a very high tower, with the intention of jumping off it, since she thought this was the most direct and decorous route by which she could descend to the underworld.[2] But the tower suddenly broke into speech: 'Why, unhappy girl, do you want to destroy yourself in a suicide-leap? And why rashly succumb now to this task, which is the last of your labours? Once your breath is separated from your body, you will indeed go straight down to the bottom of Tartarus, but in no way will you be able to return from there. Listen to my advice. The famous Achaean [343] city Lacedaemon is not far from here. Ask for Taenarus, hidden in a remote area bordering Lacedaemon.[1] There is Dis's breathing-vent,[2] and through wide-gaping doors one is shown a dead-end road. Once you cross the threshold and commit yourself to this road, you will continue by a direct track to Orcus' palace. But you must not go forward into that shadowy region empty-handed. In each hand you must carry a barley-cake soaked in mead, and hold two coins in your mouth.[3] Now, when you have completed a good part of your deathly journey you will meet a lame ass carrying wood, with a driver lame as well, who will ask you to hand him some twigs that have fallen off his load. But you must not utter a single word and must pass by him in silence. Very soon you will come to the river of the dead,[4] where the administrator Charon immediately demands the toll and then ferries travellers to the farther bank in his patched skiff. We see that greed is alive even among the dead; and Charon, Dis's tax-gatherer, great god that he is, does nothing unpaid. A poor man who is dying must find his passage-money, and unless a copper happens to be [345] on hand no one will let him breathe his last breath. For your fare you will give that filthy old man one of the coins you are carrying; but make him take it out of your mouth with his own hand. Likewise, while you are crossing that sluggish steam a dead old man, floating on the surface, will lift up his rotting hands and beg you to pull him into the boat. But be not swayed

---

[1] The underworld.
[2] Cf. Aristophanes, *Frogs* 117–33, where this is the jesting advice of Heracles to Dionysus.

[1] The Roman province Achaea included Lacedaemon (Sparta) and Cape Taenarus, where there was a temple and cave traditionally considered an entrance to the underworld.
[2] The expression comes from Vergil, *Aeneid* VII 568, and in this and the following chapter there are several other echoes of the poet.
[3] The dead were often buried with a small coin in the mouth to pay the ferryman Charon.
[4] Or "the dead river," if *mortuum* is read as neuter accusative singular instead of genitive plural.

by unlawful pity. After you have crossed the river and gone on a little farther, some old women weaving at a loom will ask you to lend a hand for a moment. But you must not touch this either. All this and much more will arise from traps for you laid by Venus, to make you let at least one cake out of your hands. Do not suppose that this paltry loss of a barley-cake is of no consequence: if you lose either cake you will never see the daylight again. For there is a huge dog with a triple head of vast size, a monstrous, fearsome creature who barks with thundering jaws, trying in vain to frighten the dead, to whom he can do no harm now. He lies in constant watch in front of the threshold outside Proserpina's black halls, guarding the insubstantial house of Dis. If you restrain him with one cake for prey, you will easily get by him and pass directly into Proserpina's presence. She will receive you courteously and kindly and try to persuade you to sit down comfortably beside her and eat a sumptuous supper.[1] But you must sit on the floor and ask [347] for common bread and eat that. Then announce why you have come, take what is put before you, and return, buying off the dog's cruelty with the remaining cake. Then give the greedy sailor the coin you have kept in reserve, cross his river, and by retracing your earlier steps you will return to this choir of heavenly stars. But above all else, I advise you to be especially careful not to open or look into the jar that you will be carrying, and in fact do not even think too inquisitively about the hidden treasure of divine beauty.'

"Thus that far-seeing tower performed its service of revelation. Without delay Psyche went to Taenarus, and when she had duly acquired the coins and cakes, she raced down the path to the underworld. She passed by the crippled ass-driver in silence, gave river-toll to the ferry-man, ignored the pleas of the floating corpse, spurned the cunning requests of the weaver-women, drugged the dog's terrifying madness by feeding him a cake, and penetrated the house of Proserpina. She embraced neither the luxurious seat nor the rich food which her hostess offered, but sitting on the ground at her feet and contenting herself with ordinary bread, she carried out Venus' commission. Quickly the jar was filled and closed in secret, and Psyche took it. She silenced the dog's barking with the trick of the second cake, paid her remaining coin to the sailor, and ran even more nimbly back from the underworld. When she had returned to the bright [349] daylight and worshipfully saluted it, despite her haste to be finished with her term of service, her mind was overcome by rash curiosity. 'Look,' she said

---

[1] An allusion to the trick practised on Theseus, by which he was compelled to sit there for ever (see *Aeneid* VI 617–618).

to herself, 'I am a fool to be a porter of divine beauty and not take out a tiny drop of it for myself. It might even enable me to please my beautiful lover.'

"No sooner said than done. She opened the jar, but there was nothing there, not a drop of beauty, just sleep – deathlike and truly Stygian sleep. Revealed when the cover was removed, it attacked her instantly, enveloping her entire body in a dense cloud of slumber. She collapsed on the path where she stood and the sleep took possession of her. She lay there motionless, no better than a sleeping corpse.

"But Cupid, recovering now that his scar had healed, could no longer endure the long absence of his beloved Psyche, and slipped out of the high window in the bedroom where he was confined. Since his wings had been restored by a period of rest, he flew much more rapidly; he rushed to his Psyche's side, carefully wiped off the sleep, and returned it to its original place in the jar. Then he roused her with a harmless prick of his arrow. 'See,' he said, 'you almost destroyed yourself again, poor girl, by your incurable curiosity. But now be quick and complete the commission assigned you by my mother's orders. I will take care of everything else.' With these words her lover lightly took to his wings. For her [351] part, Psyche speedily carried Proserpina's gift back to Venus.

"Cupid, meanwhile, consumed with uncontrollable love and pale of face, was apprehensive of his mother's sudden austerity and so turned back to his old tricks.[1] On rapid wings he penetrated heaven's summit, where he knelt before great Jupiter and tried to win support for his case. Jupiter, pinching Cupid's cheek and raised his hand to his lips, kissed it, and then replied. 'My lord son,' he said, 'despite the fact that you have never preserved the respect decreed to me by the gods' permission, but have wounded my heart with repeated blows and shamed it with frequent failings of terrestrial passion, who ordain the laws of the elements and the orbits of the stars; and despite the fact that, in defiance of the laws – including the Julian decree itself[2] – and of public order, you have injured my good name and reputation through scandalous adulteries by vile transformations of my serene countenance into snakes, flames, beasts, birds, and herd-cattle[3]; nevertheless, mindful of my moderate disposition and the fact that you grew up in my

---

[1] Literally "went back to the wine-jug," a proverbial phrase.

[2] The Lex Julia *de adulteriis*, of about 18 B.C., in which Augustus prescribed the penalties for adultery.

[3] In his seductions Jupiter employed many disguises: e.g. snake (Proserpina), flame (Aegina), swan (Leda), bull (Europa). See Ovid, *Metamorphoses* VI 103–114.

own arms, I shall do everything you ask; but only on the condition that you know how to take precautions against your competitors, and also, if there is now on the earth a girl of outstanding beauty, you must give me [353] her as repayment for my present favour.'

"So saying he ordered Mercury to summon an immediate assembly of all the gods, announcing that anyone who absented himself from the meeting of the celestial citizens would be fined ten thousand sesterces. At this threat the celestial assembly-theatre was filled at once. Tall Jupiter, seated in his throne on high, made the following pronouncement:

"'O gods enrolled in the Muses' register, you all surely know that I raised this boy with my own hands. I have decided that the hot-blooded impulses of his early youth must be restrained by some bridle. There has been enough scandal from the daily tales of his adulteries and all sorts of immoralities. We must remove every opportunity, and chain his boyish self-indulgence with the shackles of matrimony. He has selected a girl and robbed her of her maidenhood: let him keep her to have and to hold, and in Psyche's arms let him indulge his passion forever.'

"Then he added, turning to Venus, 'Now, my daughter, do not be so gloomy and do not be afraid for your excellent pedigree and your status because of a mortal marriage. I will make the wedding no longer uneven, but legitimate and in accordance with civil law.'

"He immediately ordered Mercury to take hold of Psyche and bring her to heaven. Then he handed her a cup of ambrosia, saying, 'Drink this, Psyche, and you will be immortal. Cupid will never leave your embrace, and your marriage will last for ever.'

[355] "Instantly there appeared a rich wedding-banquet. The bride-groom reclined on the couch of honour, clasping Psyche in his arms. Jupiter with his wife Juno were similarly placed, and then all the gods in order of rank. Jupiter was served a cup of nectar – the wine of the gods – by his shepherd cupbearer[1]; and the others were served by Liber.[2] Vulcan was cooking the dinner,[3] the Hours were colouring everything with roses and all the other flowers, the Graces were sprinkling balsam, and the Muses too were there, singing melodiously. Apollo chanted to the accompaniment of his lyre,[4] and Venus danced gorgeously, stepping to the tune of the lovely music. She had arranged

---

[1] Ganymede (cf. VI 15).
[2] Bacchus (the Greek Dionysus), god of the vintage.
[3] In his capacity as god of fire.
[4] He was associated with music and poetry, and is often portrayed holding a lyre.

the stage so that the Muses were singing in chorus, a Satyr blew the flute, and a Paniscus[5] played on the reed-pipes.

"Thus in proper form Psyche was given in marriage to Cupid. And when her time was come, a daughter was born to them, whom we call by the name Pleasure."

---

[5] A type of woodland creature who were associated with Pan and shared some of his goat-like qualities.

Notes

1 The areas of research that seek to address women's absence from specific areas of social and intellectual life include philosophy and political thought, as in Susan Moller Okin's *Women in Western Political Thought*, Sheila Rowbotham's *Women's Consciousness, Man's World*, and Mary O'Brien's *The Politics of Reproduction*; culture, religion, and art, as in Michelle Zimbalist Rosaldo and Louise Lamphere's (eds.) *Woman, Culture, and Society*, Mary Daly's *Beyond God the Father*, Merlin Stone's *When God Was a Woman*, Elaine Pagels's *The Gnostic Gospels*, Estella Lauter's *Women as Mythmakers*, and Lucy Lippard's *Overlay*; and literature, as in Sandra M. Gilbert and Susan Gubar's *The Madwoman in the Attic*, Elaine Showalter's *A Literature of Their Own*, and Tillie Olson's *Silences*. Other texts, such as Susan Brownmiller's *Against Our Will,* deal with the physical violence used against women that accompanies such erasures. Ann Jones's *Next Time She'll Be Dead* exposes the ways in which our cultural attitudes continue to allow and re-enforce men's violence and physical abuse against women.

2 See, for example, Charlotte Bunch and Sandra Pollack's (eds.) *Learning Our Way*, Margot Culley and Catherine Portuges's (eds.) *Gendered Subjects*, Arlene Fausto-Sterling's *Myths of Gender: Biological Theories about Women and Men*, and Angela Miles and Geraldine Finn's (eds.) *Feminism in Canada*.

3 See Sherry B. Ortner's "Is Female to Male as Nature Is to Culture?" and Susan Griffin's *Woman and Nature: The Roaring inside Her*.

4 Perhaps the clearest example of the way in which men's ideas and attitudes, men's power and learning, have controlled how women perceive themselves and their lives is in the role male physicians have played in

the traditionally female responsibilities of childbirth and child rearing. Women's experience of the male control of childbirth is variously documented by Marilyn French, Germaine Greer in *Sex and Destiny,* and Emily Martin in *The Woman in the Body.* The movement towards reclaiming a measure of control over the birthing experience was illustrated by the natural childbirth movement beginning in the sixties and by the LaLeche League. Women's own descriptions of the birthing experience were important components of publications such as Sheila Kitzinger's *Giving Birth, How It Really Feels.*

5 For an account of the ramifications this has for all women, see Dale Spender's *Women of Ideas.* In the texts examining the issues in women's learning, scholars such as Judith Thompson, Sybil Shack, Anne Dagg, and Patricia J. Thompson articulate women's experience in education as variously as Shack's reference to women teachers as a "two-thirds minority" and Spender's description of women in education as "invisible." A similar displacement from language of an authentic voice for female experience is discussed by M.M. Jenkins and Cheris Kramarae and by Robin Lakoff. My own 1987 article in *Art Education* dealt with the ways in which even progressive curriculum changes could actually handicap girls in their searches for self-expressive ways of working and for women artists as role models.

6 Paulo Friere's *Pedagogy of the Oppressed* introduces a concept for education in the Third World that distinguishes a teaching/learning metaphor of banking from one of midwifery. This implies that this more woman-centred metaphor could manifest a more egalitarian, family, and human-centred approach.

7 The title of the myth is usually presented in the reverse order, as, for example, it is in Erich Neumann's reference to *Amor and Psyche.* Because I construe Psyche's importance as central in the myth, I order the names to reflect this importance.

8 Unless otherwise indicated, all definitions are taken from *The Compact Edition of the Oxford English Dictionary* (1986, 1971).

CHAPTER ONE

1 For a critical examination of the quilt in American women's experience and literature, please see *Alice Walker: "Everyday Use,"* edited by Barbara T. Christian. Of the different ways of constructing quilts, the pieced quilt image that I employ is closely associated with the practice on the North American frontier (and that of my paternal grandmother) and is, therefore, more personal as an analogy for my own interdisciplinary research.

2 For confirmation of the importance of paying attention to the way power structures influence educational practice and change, thereby controlling

change in the learning experience, see Joan S. Walters's *Three Case Studies.*

3 These distinctions of Signature and Archetype, cultic practice and myth underscore the work of revisioning myth that is a central project of feminism. Works as various as Barbara G. Walker's *The Woman's Dictionary of Symbols and Sacred Objects* and *The Woman's Encyclopedia of Myths and Secrets* and M. Esther Harding's *Woman's Mysteries* reclaim and revalue the roles of the goddesses, women and the feminine, within the history of Western myth. Jack Zipes brings together a collection of feminist fairy tales that includes literary criticism in *Don't Bet on the Prince.* More recently, *Women Who Run with the Wolves* by Clarissa Pinkola Estes and *Cassandra* by Christa Wolf incorporate interdisciplinary research with retelling stories to reclaim women's lived experience underlying the patriarchal signatures of these ancient traditional stories.

4 In the listing of dichotomies or contradicting categories, I place the positively valued terms (in the Western tradition), like male, active, culture, masculine, and science, always on the "right" side; and I place the less positively valued, like female, passive, nature, feminine, and arts, on the *(sinister)* left. This visually clarifies the unequal value "balance" or weighting bestowed in such categorizations. The left side readily slips below the right, becomes "lower" to the "upper" and more "important," and thereby further clarifies the teleological import of dualistic classifications.

CHAPTER TWO

1 My own investigation of the myth of Narcissus is necessarily limited. For a more comprehensive analysis and investigation of the complex of issues surrounding the myth of Narcissus, narcissism, psychoanalysis, subjectivity and literature, see Gray Kochlar-Lindgren's *Narcissus Transformed.* I especially endorse his observation that "myth is a story that renews itself through interpretation" (3).

2 I use D.E. Hill's translation of Ovid's *Metamorphoses I–IV*, within which the myth of Narcissus appears on pages 107–15. I do not provide parenthetical page numbers because the passage in question is brief. A recent translation, Hill's edition supplies valuable linguistic and historical information. Whereas Hill translates from the Latin and uses the Latin names for gods and goddesses, I include the Greek names to suggest their more ancient associations.

3 In *Sowing the Body*, Page DuBois refers to "the male narcissism of traditional scholarship" (7) and warns: "Our paradoxical enterprise is to be both within and outside the sex gender system, to see the ways in which it enables our being, but to call to the foreground its bias, its historicity"

(9). My own enterprise is to bring to light what I see as the other and very real system that is represented by the "outside" and Echo's place.

4 Feminist art practice and criticism present both a reclamation and redefinition of those practices named craft. See Germaine Greer's *The Obstacle Race*, Estella Lauter's *Women as Mythmakers: Poetry and Visual Art by Twentieth Century Women*, Lucy Lippard's *Overlay*, and Rozsika Parker and Griselda Pollack's *Old Mistresses: Women, Art and Ideology*.

5 In Virginia Woolf's *A Room of One's Own*, a similar quality of wonderment and the wonderful is evoked. She describes the patriarchal need for creating woman as a mirror "possessing the magic and delicious power of reflecting the figure of man at twice its natural size" (53).

6 This is a splintering and fragmentation that Naomi Wolf, too, emphasizes as detrimental to women's psychological health and development. In *The Beauty Myth*, she describes how this male vision of women is culturally mirrored to constrict women's sense of authentic being.

7 In *Herself Beheld*, Jenijoy La Belle uses mirror scenes in literature as a way of examining feminine consciousness. She writes about the relationship between the woman and the mirror as a reciprocal one that is certainly conflicted, and yet, she notes, in many ways women are searching for a truth about "what they really are" (9). This corroborates my own interpretation of Aphrodite's mirror, which appears at the end of chapter 3.

CHAPTER THREE

1 Translations of Apuleius's *Metamorphoses* are offered by William Adlington, H.E. Butler, Robert Graves, and J. Arthur Hanson. Robert Graves provides a second later and separate edition of the Psyche myth with an introduction by Marian Woodman. The story of Cupid and Psyche also appears within Walter Pater's *Marius the Epicurean*. In *Till We Have Faces*, C.S. Lewis retells the myth from the point of view of the eldest sister.

2 I use Hanson's translation throughout this study because it is, I believe, the most recent. The fact that it is not to my knowledge associated with any previous interpretations is also a factor in my decision. In most instances, my parenthetical references are to the page numbers of the material supplied in the Appendix. Hanson's translation exists in two volumes whose pages are not sequentially numbered, but only in the rare instances where I need to reference the second volume will I include the original volume and page number, as in (2:299).

3 For an investigation into these sources and their motifs, see Jan-Ojvind Swahn's *The Tale of Cupid and Psyche* and Ben Edwin Perry's *The Ancient Romances: A Literary-Historical Account of Their Origins*. For

an analysis of the sources of motif and literary techniques involved in the conversion story as metamorphosis, see Judith K. Krabbe's *The Metamorphoses of Apuleius*. In *The Novel before the Novel: Essays and Discussions about the Beginnings of Prose Fiction in the West*, Arthur Heisman suggests an Egyptian influence in the way the episodes are linked by a storyteller "who is in some sort of predicament" (152). Elizabeth Hazelton Haight in *Apuleius and His Influence* gives a history of the ideas of love and soul and includes information on their earliest representations.

4 Apuleius, of course, uses the Latin names for the goddesses and gods. I prefer and have inserted the older Greek variants, for I rely on the reclamations and reinterpretations of these more ancient representations. Obviously I mean to suggest the fullest possible interpretation of Aphrodite's capacities.

5 Because of her associations with maidens and childbirth, Artemis might arguably be the most appropriate goddess for Psyche to seek. As the myth has been recorded by Apuleius and as my own interpretations suggest, for many and far-reaching reasons, I believe that Aphrodite is the most appropriate goddess to foster personal growth in Psyche.

6 See Naomi Goldenberg's *The Changing of the Gods* and Elaine Pagels's *The Gnostic Gospels* for discussions of the ways in which the female divine has been appropriated in patriarchal culture.

CHAPTER FOUR

1 Here again, while Artemis is the goddess of the wild or of the wilderness and wild animals, the integration of palace, cultural artifacts, and sensuousness makes the presence of Aphrodite more prominent. The "wild beasts and herds" are in silver reliefs and not living presence (253).

2 The problems in the designation "Mistress" are explored in Parker and Pollack's *Old Mistresses: Women, Art and Ideology*. Alluding to the honorific title "old masters," they point out how patriarchal attitudes have undermined the female ownership of what might be roughly equivalent titles of respect. By acknowledging Psyche's ownership of the title, I intend that the authority it represents is at least equivalent to what we automatically grant "master."

3 Explaining early methods of birth control, Sarah B. Pomeroy supplies information that suggests a knowledge of reproductive responsibility that joins together Psyche's first two tasks: "Mixed with ineffective techniques [of birth control] were effective methods including the use of occlusive agents which blocked the os of the uterus. Oils, honey, and soft wool were employed" (167).

4 The mother's absence from literature is presented in Di Brandt's *Wild Mother Dancing*. In her discussion of Canadian women writers, she

examines aspects of the mother's silencing as each writer attempts to deal with it and the ways in which each reclaims the mother as subject of her own story.

CHAPTER FIVE

1 This attitude recalls the kind of feminist scientific practice Evelyn Fox Keller describes in the work of Barbara McClintock. Of equal interest is the paper on Native observational attitudes and practice given by scientist Pamela Colorado.

2 In Kent and Morreau's *Women's Images of Men*, Sarah Kent describes how the male body is objectified in homoerotic art. Male bodies are rendered as passive for the visual consumption of a male audience, but not for women's appreciation; the male viewer continues powerful. See "The Erotic Male Nude" (75–82).

3 Kristeva terms this time sense "monumental" temporality in its association with the maternal (192). This link with myth and motherhood, she cautions, brings with it the possibility of a "fantasy of totality," of "narcissistic completeness," yet she sees also the possibility of an "apprenticeship in attentiveness" within child care (206). As can be seen, my own definition of this third sense of time differs markedly from Kristeva's.

4 This pattern of heredity, "call" and wisdom/foreknowledge as women's shamanic pattern, also exists in the story of Cassandra: her knowledge also was lost; her society refused to hear her warnings. See Christa Wolf's *Cassandra: A Novel and Four Essays*.

5 Though McClelland does distinguish between a male and female attitude towards power and sex-role differentiation, his emphasis on power as a power-over is like the attitudes that I have questioned in my discussion of power in chapter 3. To indicate the attitude appropriate to Psyche's story, I will call this kind of quest an empowerment vision. The pattern, however, remains the same.

CHAPTER SIX

1 One episode of the *Travels* television series, entitled *Madagascar: Isle of the Ancestors*, provides a comparison by way of a similar ritual of spiritual significance. Travel writer Helena Drysdale describes the journey of a family group to disinter the bodies of dead ancestors in order to replace their shrouds. While she describes her own anxiety at what she believed would be a macabre ritual, she is surprised that it is so joyous an occasion, that the bodies had decomposed to a rich loamy earth, and that the ritual celebrated the continuity of life rather than the individual deaths.

What is equally interesting is her observation that the removed and "earth stained" shrouds were prized as blankets on which to conceive new life and so linked death to conception and birth, to regeneration. Ancestors and the yet unborn are linked together in a profoundly metaphoric way (PPTV, ch. 3, 5/4/93, 7 p.m.).

2 This "Stygian sleep" further supports an interpretation of Psyche as shaman. In *Sanctuary of the Goddess: The Sacred Landscape and Objects*, Peg Streep describes the association of foul smell and oracular prophecy. According to her, one of the sources of prophetic trance was "the frenzied ecstasy of a priestess who inhaled the mystic but foul smelling vapours of the earth itself that came up through the cleft (the *chiasma*) in the floor." Streep notes that the name of Apollo's priestess, Pythia, is derived "from *pythein*, or 'rotting,' a reference to the rotting corpse of the snake which makes the sanctuary Apollo's" (180).

3 Earlier, I noted how the crone-mother-daughter triad of female relationship has been dualized. (Not for nothing is "trivialize" pejorative.) Awareness of the significance and importance of post-menopausal female life experience is variously documented (and valued) by Gail Sheehy in *Menopause: The Silent Passage*, Germaine Greer in *The Change*, and Janine O'Leary Cobb in *Understanding Menopause*. This "Hecate" aspect may be translated into a larger social responsibility – for example, in the political activism of "The Raging Grannies" and in the anti-nuclear demonstrations of the women at Greenham Common. Other cultures include this wisdom into a female life pattern. In *Grandmothers of the Light: A Medicine Woman's Sourcebook*, Paula Gunn Allen describes the seven steps to becoming a medicine woman. The last two stages, of teacher and wise woman, occur in the post-menopausal years when the woman becomes "a transmitter of spiritual and social wisdom" (14).

CHAPTER SEVEN

1 In keeping with my decision to use the more ancient Greek names, I substitute *Voluptas* for the Latin *Voluptatem*. Rachel Blau DuPlessis translates *Voluptatem* into English as "Joy" (90).

2 It will have become obvious that I am avoiding "trinity" and using "triplicity" instead. As the means of registering transformational movement, individuality, and family relationship, "triplicity" circumvents the connotative meanings of "trinity" in the way it is used. In patriarchal religions, its usefulness for me has been weakened by the absence of the female principle and by the implication of unitary oneness.

3 Nor Hall reduces this to one hour: "The hour of the wolf is the time between night and dawn. It is the hour when most people die, when sleep is deepest, when nightmares are most palpable, when ghosts and demons

hold sway. The hour of the wolf is also the hour when most children are born" (117).

4 The direct references to these paradoxes in Josselson's text are as follows: holding and attachment (53), passion (77–8, 80), eye-to-eye (106, 108), idealization and identification (128), mutuality (156), embeddedness (178), and tending (203).

5 This placentally based metaphor also recalls Kegan's *The Evolving Self* and provides a way of bringing together the theories of the separate and symbiotic self. For an analysis of the self described as "twice" born into a later psychological separateness, see Margaret Mahler's *The Psychological Birth of the Human Infant.*

6 In *The Language of the Goddess*, archeologist Marija Gimbutus describes the presence throughout Europe of ancient symbolic representations that combine the omphalos as navel with goddess representations. For example, she documents an ancient frog goddess with a navel represented by concentric circles; she links the depiction with regeneration (252).

7 Brian McHale, in his analysis of postmodernist fiction, describes narrative circularity as one "possible structure of textual non-ending" (110). The spiral is a means of ascending to a higher level and "metalepsis" is the way to leap the gap which the spiral passes through (119). This leaping of the gap, however, bypasses the continuity that the spiral implies and substitutes instead a series of presumably concentric circles or centres such as Eliade discusses.

8 For popular examples and discussions of boys' initiation ceremonies and the hero journey, see Robert Bly's *Iron John* and Joseph Campbell's *Myths to Live By.*

9 O'Brien notes that the stages of male initiation are remarkably like couvade. As husbands in some societies take to their beds in the appearance of giving birth like their wives do, so, likewise, do men appropriate the forms of menstruation, pregnancy, and birth as a means of signifying magic and power (149–56).

10 Kurt Weitzmann states that, in ancient sculptural representations of Cupid and Psyche, both are winged creatures. Such a representation serves to mark each as devotees of the winged Bird Goddess but perhaps not necessarily as transcendent beings. Most birds fly, but they remain creatures of earth.

CHAPTER EIGHT

1 I use Psychean as an adjective to characterize a view of women's life journeys that emphasizes possibility and opportunity, that sees work, growth, relationship, and spiritual connection as integral within embodied experi-

ence, and that suggests the complexity of the learning that is possible beyond dichotomies.

2 The issues surrounding the definition of the self and individuality are recurrent in the analyses of women's autobiographies. Obviously my own view is necessarily limited in its ability to address these larger questions directly. For the moment, and in the light of the way I have revisioned birth, I am arguing the real and centred presence of a self in text and a self concept that is not "split" but transformative, able to act with a "response-ability." For an examination of the "discontinuities" of women's narratives see *The Female Autograph: Theory and Practice of Autobiography from the Tenth to the Twentieth Century*, edited by Domna C. Stanton.

3 For a discussion of the ways in which this mirror representation and the dichotomized image of self both affect and fail to explain women's autobiographical practice, see *The Private Self: Theory and Practice of Women's Autobiographical Writings*, edited by Shari Benstock. See especially the article by Kathleen Woodward for the discussion of mourning and loss in the context of Simone de Beauvoir's autobiography. As an example of a search for a metaphor for articulating identity in a context that includes geography, Helen M. Buss suggests mapping as a way to understand the relationships among reader, text, and writer. See her *Mapping Ourselves: Canadian Women's Autobiography in English*.

4 For comparison, an examination of the titles of twentieth-century men's autobiographies reveals motifs more in keeping with those characteristics I have discussed with respect to the Icarus complex and which appear in Eros's story. Roald Dahl's *Going Solo* emphasizes separation and recalls his first flight as a qualifying pilot. Arthur Miller's *Timebends: A Life* plays with the ideas of time and life changes but in a way that implies force, confrontation, resistance, and the laws of physics. While *Treasure in Clay: The Autobiography of Fulton J. Sheen* combines paradoxical notions of value (in the work, he describes himself as the clay and the treasure as gift, given from outside, "desire flourishing in clay" [29]), it is his being called by God to be a priest that is the treasure, not his existence as an embodied being. The title of James A. Michener's memoir, *The World Is My Home*, suggests a place in the world of man, in culture and society, and ease therein. Conrad Black's title, *A Life in Progress*, clearly states the sense of life as means and ends rather than process or continuity. Finally, George Burns's saucy *Living It Up: Or They Still Love Me in Altoona* combines the world and the flesh in an attitude that Eros surely would approve and enjoy.

5 *Outercourse* is an intense and complex expression of a formidable intellect trained in two of the most patriarchal of disciplines: Christian

theology and philosophy. In spite of her exodus from that religion, Daly would be the first to acknowledge her debt to that tradition for enabling her to critique it on its own terms (74–6). What this tradition brings with it is the focus on "gaps" and the necessity for the "leap," which recalls the dichotomy inherent in Narcissus's gaze and sexual union. While I see the Psychean pattern in her writing, I am fully aware and cannot stress enough that she sees something different. The most obvious is in the three-ness of my interpretation of Psyche's journey and Daly's preference for four and the quaternity in her spiral galaxies. As I see it, however, her Fourth Galaxy is the new being, another beginning in continuing process, and she herself notices that four may be seen as three-plus-one (373). Rather than the stasis of quaternity, it becomes process.

Works Cited

Abrams, M.H. *A Glossary of Literary Terms*. 5th ed. Fort Worth, TX: Holt, Rinehart & Winston, 1988.

Allen, Charlotte Vale. *Daddy's Girl*. New York: Berkley, 1980.

Allen, Paula Gunn. *Grandmothers of the Light: A Medicine Woman's Sourcebook*. Boston: Beacon Press, 1991.

Angelou, Maya. *I Know Why the Caged Bird Sings*. New York: Random, 1970.

Apuleius, Lucius. *The Golden Ass: Being the Metamorphoses of Lucius Apuleius*. Trans. W. Adlington. London: Heinemann, 1919.

– *Metamorphoses*. Ed. and trans. J. Arthur Hanson. 2 vols. Cambridge, MA: Harvard University Press, 1989.

– *The Tale of Cupid and Psyche*. Trans. Robert Graves. Intro. Marian Woodman. Boston: Shambhala, 1993.

– *The Transformations of Lucius: Otherwise Known as The Golden Ass*. Trans. Robert Graves. Harmondsworth, UK: Penguin Books, c.1950.

Baird, James. *Ishmael: A Study of the Symbolic Mode in Primitivism*. Baltimore: Johns Hopkins University Press, 1958.

Barber, Elizabeth Wayland. *Women's Work: The First 20,000 Years, Women, Cloth, and Society in Early Times*. New York: Norton, 1994.

Bardige, Betty. "Things so Finely Human: Moral Sensibilities at Risk in Adolescence." In *Mapping the Moral Domain: A Contribution of Women's Thinking to Psychological Theory and Education*. Ed. Carol Gilligan, Janie Victoria Ward, and Jill McLean Taylor. Cambridge, MA: Harvard University Press, 1988.

Barry, Judith, and Sandy Flitterman-Lewis. "Textual Strategies: The Politics of Art-Making." In *Feminist Art Criticism: An Anthology*. Ed. Arlene Raven, Cassandra L. Langer, and Joanna Frueh, 87–131. New York: Icon Books, 1988.

Baruch, Grace, Rosalind Barnett, and Caryl Rivers. *Lifeprints: New Patterns of Love and Work for Today's Women*. New York: McGraw, 1983.

Bassin, Donna, Margaret Honey, and Meryl Mahrer Kaplan, eds. *Representations of Motherhood*. New Haven, CT: Yale University Press, 1994.

Battersby, Christine. *Gender and Genius: Towards a Feminist Aesthetics*. London: Women's Press, 1989.

Belenky, Mary Field, Blythe McVicker Clinchy, Nancy Rule Goldberger, and Jill Mattuck Tarule. *Women's Ways of Knowing: The Development of Self, Voice, and Mind*. New York: Basic, 1986.

Bell, Linda A. *Rethinking Ethics in the Midst of Violence: A Feminist Approach to Freedom*. Lanham, MD: Roman & Littlefield, 1993.

Benjamin, Jessica. *The Bonds of Love: Psychoanalysis, Feminism, and the Problem of Domination*. New York: Pantheon, 1988.

Benstock, Shari, ed. *The Private Self: Theory and Practice of Women's Autobiographical Writings*. Chapel Hill: University of North Carolina Press, 1988.

Berger, John. *Ways of Seeing*. London: Penguin Books, 1972.

Berman, Jeffrey. *Narcissism and the Novel*. New York: New York University Press, 1990.

Bettelheim, Bruno. *The Uses of Enchantment: The Meaning and Importance of Fairy Tales*. New York: Knopf, 1976.

Betterton, Rosemary. *Looking On: Images of Femininity in the Visual Arts and Media*. New York: Pandora Press, 1987.

Blackburn, Regina. "In Search of the Black Female Self: African American Women's Autobiographies and Ethnicity." In *Women's Autobiography: Essays in Criticism*. Ed. Estelle C. Jelinek, 133–48. Bloomington: Indiana University Press, 1980.

Bly, Robert. *Iron John: A Book about Men*. Reading, MA: Addison-Wesley, 1990.

Boothby, Richard. *Death and Desire: Psychoanalytic Theory in Lacan's Return to Freud*. New York: Routledge, 1991.

Bourne, Gordon. *Pregnancy*. London: Pan Books, 1972.

Brandt, Di. *Wild Mother Dancing: Maternal Narrative in Canadian Literature*. Winnipeg: University of Manitoba Press, 1993.

Breslin, James E. "Gertrude Stein and the Problems of Autobiography." In *Women's Autobiography: Essays in Criticism*. Ed. Estelle C. Jelinek, 149–62. Bloomington: Indiana University Press, 1980.

Brooks, Peter. "Freud's Masterplot." In *The Critical Tradition: Classical Texts and Contemporary Trends*. Ed. David H. Richter, 710–20. New York: St Martin's Press, 1989.

Brown, Lyn Mikel, and Carol Gilligan. *Meeting at the Crossroads: Women's Psychology and Girls' Development*. Cambridge, MA: Harvard University Press, 1992.

Brownmiller, Susan. *Against Our Will*. New York: Simon & Schuster, 1975.

Bunch, Charlotte, and Sandra Pollack, eds. *Learning Our Way: Essays in Feminist Education*. New York: Crossing Press, 1983.

Buss, Helen M. *Mapping Ourselves: Canadian Women's Autobiography in English*. Montreal and Kingston: McGill-Queen's University Press, 1993.

Caccavo, Penny W. "The Forbidden Room: A Pair of Fairy Tales as Developmental Metaphor." In *Psychoanalytic Perspectives on Women*. Ed. Elaine V. Siegel, 130–49. New York: Brunner/Mazel, 1992.

Campbell, Joseph. *Myths to Live By*. New York: Bantam, 1972.

Campbell, Maria. *Half-breed*. Halifax, NS: Goodread, 1983.

Carr, Emily. *Growing Pains: An Autobiography*. Toronto: Irwin, 1946.

Carroll, Noel. *Mystifying Movies: Fads and Fallacies in Contemporary Film Theory*. New York: Columbia University Press, 1988.

Carson, Anne. *Eros the Bittersweet*. Princeton, NJ: Princeton University Press, 1986.

– "Putting Her in Her Place: Woman, Dirt, and Desire." In *Before Sexuality: The Construction of Erotic Experience in the Ancient Greek World*. Ed. David M. Halperin, John J. Winkler, and Froma I. Zeitlin, 135–69. Princeton, NJ: Princeton University Press, 1990.

Cell, Edward. *Learning to Learn from Experience*. Albany: State University of New York Press, 1984.

Chase, Karen. *Eros and Psyche: The Representation of Personality in Charlotte Bronte, Charles Dickens, George Eliot*. New York: Methuen, 1984.

Chodorow, Nancy J. *Feminism and Psychoanalytic Theory*. New Haven, CT: Yale University Press, 1989.

Christ, Carol P. *Diving Deep and Surfacing: Women Writers on Spiritual Quest*. Boston: Beacon Press, 1980.

Christian, Barbara T., ed. *Alice Walker: "Everyday Use."* New Brunswick, NJ: Rutgers University Press, 1994.

Cobb, Janine O'Leary. *Understanding Menopause*. Toronto, Key Porter, 1988.

Colorado, Pamela. *American Indian Science*. Unpublished paper, 1988.

Culley, Margot, and Catherine Portuges, eds. *Gendered Subjects*. London: Routledge, 1985.

Dagg, Anne Innis, and Patricia J. Thompson. *MisEducation: Women & Canadian Universities*. Toronto: OISE Press, 1988.

Daloz, Laurent A. *Effective Teaching and Mentoring: Realizing the Transformational Power of Adult Learning Experiences*. San Francisco: Jossey-Bass, 1986.

Daly, Mary. *Beyond God the Father*. Boston: Beacon Press, 1978.

– *Outercourse: The Be-Dazzling Voyage*. San Francisco: Harper San Francisco, 1992.

Danica, Elly. *Don't: A Woman's Word*. Toronto: McClelland and Stewart, 1990.

Davis-Floyd, Robbie E. *Birth as an American Rite of Passage*. Berkeley: University of California Press, 1992.

de Lauretis, Teresa. *Alice Doesn't: Feminism, Semiotics, Cinema*. Bloomington: Indiana University Press, 1984.

Dexter, Miriam Robbins. *Whence the Goddesses: A Sourcebook*. New York: Bantam, 1990.

Donaldson-Evans, Lance K. *Love's Fatal Glance: A Study of Eye Imagery in the Poets of the Ecole Lyonnaise*. No. 39. University, MS: Romance Monographs, 1980.

Dowden, Ken. "Approaching Women through Myth: Vital Tool or Self-Delusion?" In *Women in Antiquity: New Assessments*. Ed. Richard Hawley and Barbara Levick, 44–57. London and New York: Routledge, 1995.

– *Death and the Maiden: Girls' Initiation Rites in Greek Mythology*. London and New York: Routledge, 1989.

Downing, Christine. *The Goddess: Mythological Images of the Divine Feminine*. New York: Crossroad, 1988.

– *Psyche's Sisters: ReImagining the Meaning of Sisterhood*. San Francisco: Harper San Francisco, 1988.

DuBois, Page. *Sowing the Body: Psychoanalysis and Ancient Representations of Women*. Chicago: Chicago University Press, 1988.

DuPlessis, Rachel Blau. "Psyche or Wholeness." *Massachusetts Review* 20, no. 1 (1979): 77–96.

– *Writing beyond the Ending: Narrative Strategies of Twentieth Century Women Writers*. Bloomington: Indiana University Press, 1985.

Edwards, Betty. *Drawing on the Right Side of the Brain: A Course in Enhancing Creativity and Artistic Confidence*. Los Angeles: J.P. Tarcher, 1979.

Edwards, Lee R. *Psyche as Hero: Female Heroism and Fictional Form*. Middletown, CN: Wesleyan University Press, 1984.

Eliade, Mircea. *The Myth of the Eternal Return: Or, Cosmos and History*. Princeton, NJ: Princeton University Press, 1954.

– *Rites and Symbols of Initiation: The Mysteries of Birth and Rebirth*. Trans. Willard R. Trask. New York: Harper & Row, 1958.

– *Shamanism: Archaic Techniques of Ecstasy*. Bollingen series no. 76. Trans. Willard R. Trask. New York: Pantheon, 1964.

Estes, Clarissa Pinkola. *Women Who Run with the Wolves: Myths and Stories of the Wild Woman Archetype*. New York: Ballantine, 1992.

Fausto-Sterling, Anne. *Myths of Gender: Biological Theories about Women and Men*. New York: Basic, 1985.

Ferguson, Mary Anne. "The Female Novel of Development and the Myth of Psyche." *Denver Quarterly* 17, no. 4 (1983): 58–74.

Fiedler, Leslie A. *No! in Thunder*. Boston: Beacon Press, 1960.

Franz, Marie-Louise von. *An Interpretation of Apuleius' Golden Ass with the Tale of Eros and Psyche*. Irving, TX: Spring, 1980.

French, Marilyn. *Beyond Power: On Women, Men, and Morals*. New York: Simon & Schuster, 1985.

Freud, Sigmund. "On Narcissism." In *Freud on Women: A Reader.* Ed. Elizabeth Young-Bruel. New York: Norton, 1990.

- *Totem and Taboo.* Trans. James Strachey. New York: Norton, 1952.

Friedrich, Paul. *The Meaning of Aphrodite.* Chicago: University of Chicago Press, 1978.

Friere, Paulo. *Pedagogy of the Oppressed.* Trans. Myra Bergman Ramos. New York: Seabury, 1970.

Frueh, Joanna. "Towards a Feminist Theory of Art Criticism." *Feminist Art Criticism: An Anthology.* Ed. Arlene Raven, Cassandra L. Langer, and Joanna Frueh, 153–65. New York: Icon Books, 1988.

Frye, Marilyn. *The Politics of Reality: Essays in Feminist Theory.* Freedom, CA: Crossing Press, 1992.

- *Willful Virgin: Essays in Feminism.* Freedom, CA: Crossing Press, 1992.

Fulton, Keith Louise. "Journalling Women: The Authentic Voice and Intellectual Cross-Dressing." In *A Reader in Feminist Ethics.* Ed. Debra Shogan, 425–37. Toronto: Canadian Scholars' Press, 1993.

Gallop, Jane. *Reading Lacan.* Ithaca and London: Cornell University Press, 1985.

Gardiner, Howard. "Multiple Intelligences: Implications for Art." In *Artistic Intelligences: Implications for Education.* Ed. William J. Moody, 11–27. New York: Teachers College Press, 1990.

Garnett, Angelica. *Deceived with Kindness: A Bloomsbury Childhood.* London: Hogarth Press, 1984.

Gilbert, Sandra M., and Susan Gubar. *The Madwoman in the Attic: The Woman Writer and the Nineteenth Century Imagination.* New Haven, CT: Yale University Press, 1979.

Gilligan, Carol. *In a Different Voice: Psychological Theory and Women's Development.* Cambridge, MA: Harvard University Press, 1982.

Gilligan, Carol, Janie Victoria Ward, and Jill McLean Taylor with Wendy Bardige, eds. *Mapping the Moral Domain: A Contribution of Women's Thinking to Psychological Theory and Education.* Cambridge, MA: Harvard University Press, 1988.

Gimbutus, Marija. *The Language of the Goddess.* San Francisco: Harper San Francisco, 1989.

Goldenberg, Naomi. *The Changing of the Gods: Feminism and the End of Traditional Religions.* Boston: Beacon Press, 1979.

Gollnick, James. *Love and the Soul: Psychological Interpretations of the Eros and Psyche Myth.* Waterloo, ON: Wilfrid Laurier University Press, 1992.

Greer, Germaine. *The Change: Women, Aging and the Menopause.* London: Hamilton, 1991.

- *The Obstacle Race.* London: Martin, Secker and Warburg, 1979.

- *Sex and Destiny.* Toronto: Stoddart, 1984.

Griffin, Susan. *Woman and Nature: The Roaring inside Her.* New York: Harper & Row, 1980.

Grigson, Geoffrey. *The Goddess of Love: The Birth, Triumph, Death and Return of Aphrodite.* London: Constable, 1976.

Grim, John A. *The Shaman: Patterns of Siberian and Ojibway Healing.* Norman: Oklahoma University Press, 1983.

Grosz, Elizabeth. *Jacques Lacan: A Feminist Introduction.* London: Routledge, 1990.

Grunberger, Bela. *New Essays on Narcissism.* Trans. and ed. David Macey. London: Free Association Books, 1989.

Haight, Elizabeth Hazelton. *Apuleius and His Influence.* New York: Longmans, 1927.

Halifax, Joan. *Shamanic Voices: A Survey of Visionary Narratives.* New York: Dutton, 1979.

Hall, Nor. *The Moon and the Virgin: Reflections on the Archetypal Feminine.* New York: Harper & Row, 1980.

Harding, M. Esther. *Woman's Mysteries: Ancient and Modern.* Boston: Shambhala, 1971.

Harner, Michael. *The Way of the Shaman.* Toronto: Bantam, 1982.

Harrison, Jane Ellen. *Prolegomena to the Study of Greek Religion.* London: Merlin, 1962, 1980.

Hayes, Elizabeth T., ed. *Images of Persephone.* Gainsville: University of Florida Press, 1994.

Heisman, Arthur. *The Novel before the Novel: Essays and Discussions about the Beginnings of Prose Fiction in the West.* Chicago: University of Chicago Press, 1977.

Hillman, James. *The Myth of Analysis: Three Essays in Archetypal Psychology.* Evanston, IL: Northwestern University Press, 1972.

Hinz, Evelyn J. "Hierogamy vs Wedlock: Types of Marriage Plots and Their Relationship to Genres of Prose Fiction." *Periodical of Modern Language Association* 91, no. 5 (1976): 900–13.

Houle, Cyril O. *The Inquiring Mind (A Study of the Adult Who Continues to Learn).* Madison: University of Wisconsin Press, 1963.

Huber, Barbara Weir. *Feminism, Manitoba Artists for Women's Art and Art Education: A Woman-Centred Examination of the Learning Experience in the Mentor Program of MAWA.* Unpublished master's thesis, 1989.

– "What Does Feminism Have to Offer DBAE? Or, So What If Little Red Riding Hood Puts aside Her Crayons to Deliver Groceries for Her Mother?" *Art Education* 40, no. 3 (1987): 36–41.

Hurston, Zora Neale. *Dust Tracks on a Road.* New York: HarperCollins, 1991.

Jelinek, Estelle C. "Introduction: Women's Autobiography and the Male Tradition." In *Women's Autobiography: Essays in Criticism.* Ed. Estelle C. Jelinek, 1–10. Bloomington: Indiana University Press, 1980.

Jenkins, M.M., and Cheris Kramarae. "A Thief in the House: Women and Language." In *Men's Studies Modified*. Ed. Dale Spender, 11–22. Oxford: Pergamon, 1981.

Johnson, Buffie. *Lady of the Beasts: Ancient Images of the Goddess and Her Sacred Animals*. San Francisco: Harper & Row, 1980.

Johnson, Robert A. *She: Understanding Feminine Psychology*. New York: Harper & Row, 1989.

Jones, Ann. *Next Time She'll Be Dead: Battering and How to Stop It*. New York: Beacon Press, 1993.

Joseph, R. *The Right Brain and the Unconscious: Discovering the Stranger Within*. New York: Plenum, 1992.

Josselson, Ruthellen. *The Space between Us: Exploring the Dimensions of Human Relationships*. San Francisco: Jossey-Bass, 1992.

Jung, Carl G. *Psyche and Symbol: A Selection from the Writing of C.G. Jung*. New York: Doubleday, 1958.

Jung, Carl G., and C. Kerenyi. *Introduction to a Science of Mythology: The Myth of the Divine Child and the Mysteries of Eleusis*. Trans. R.F.C. Hull. London: Routledge, 1951.

Kegan, Robert. *The Evolving Self: Problem and Process in Human Development*. Cambridge, MA: Harvard University Press, 1982.

Keller, Evelyn Fox. *A Feeling for the Organism: The Life and Work of Barbara McClintock*. New York: Freeman, 1983.

– *Reflections on Gender and Science*. New Haven: Yale University Press, 1985.

Kent, Sarah, and Jacqueline Morreau, eds. *Women's Images of Men*. London: Writers and Readers, 1985.

Kingston, Maxine Hong. *The Woman Warrior: Memoirs of a Girlhood among Ghosts*. New York: Knopf, 1977.

Kinsley, David. *The Goddesses' Mirror: Visions of the Divine from East to West*. Albany, NY: State University Press, 1989.

Kitzinger, Sheila. *Giving Birth, How It Really Feels*. London: Victor Gollancz, 1983.

Knowles, Malcolm S. *Self-Directed Learning: A Guide for Learners and Teachers*. New York: Association Press, 1975.

Kochlar-Lindgren, Gray. *Narcissus Transformed: The Textual Subject in Psychoanalysis and Literature*. University Park, PA: Pennsylvania State University Press, 1993.

Krabbe, Judith K. *The Metamorphoses of Apuleius*. New York: Peter Lang, 1989.

Kristeva, Julia. *The Kristeva Reader*. Ed. Toril Moi. New York: Columbia University Press, 1986.

Kubler-Ross, Elizabeth. *Death: The Final Stage of Growth*. Englewood Cliffs, NJ: Prentice Hall, 1975.

La Belle, Jenijoy. *Herself Beheld: The Literature of the Looking Glass*. Ithaca, NY: Cornell University Press, 1988.

Labouvie-Vief, Gisela. *Psyche and Eros: Mind and Gender in the Life Course*. Cambridge: Cambridge University Press, 1994.

Lacan, Jacques. *Ecrits: A Selection*. London: Tavistock, 1977.

Lakoff, George, and Mark Johnson. *Metaphors We Live By*. Chicago: University of Chicago Press, 1980.

Lakoff, Robin. *Language and Woman's Place*. New York: Harper & Row, 1975.

Langer, Cassandra. "Against the Grain: A Working Gynergenic Art Criticism." In *Feminist Art Criticism: An Anthology*. Ed. Arlene Raven, Cassandra Langer, and Joanna Freuh, 111–32. New York: Icon, 1988.

Laurence, Margaret. *Dance on the Earth: A Memoir*. Toronto, Coach House Press, 1989.

Lauter, Estella. *Women as Mythmakers: Poetry and Visual Art by Twentieth Century Women*. Bloomington: Indiana University Press, 1984.

Lawrence, Amy. *Echo and Narcissus: Women's Voices in Classical Hollywood Cinema*. Berkeley: University of California Press, 1991.

Levinson, Daniel J. *The Seasons of a Man's Life*. New York: Knopf, 1978.

Lewis, C.S. *Till We Have Faces: A Myth Retold*. San Diego: Harvest, 1957.

Lippard, Lucy. *Overlay*. New York: Pantheon, 1983.

Lowell, Amy. *Selected Poems*. Ed. John Livingston Lowes. Boston: Houghton Mifflin, 1928.

McClelland, David C. *Power: The Inner Experience*. New York: Irvington, 1975.

McHale, Brian. *Constructing Postmodernism*. New York: Routledge, 1992.

McLeish, John A.B. *The Ulyssean Adult: Creativity in the Middle and Later Years*. Toronto: McGraw-Hill, 1976.

Mahler, Margaret. *The Psychological Birth of the Human Infant: Symbiosis and Individuation*. New York: Basic, 1975.

Martin, Emily. *The Woman in the Body: A Cultural Analysis of Reproduction*. Boston: Beacon Press, 1989.

Maynard, Fredelle Bruser. *Raisins and Almonds*. Toronto: Doubleday, 1972.

Miles, Angela, and Geraldine Finn, eds. *Feminism in Canada*. Montreal: Black Rose Books, 1982.

Minnich, Elizabeth Kamarck. *Transforming Knowledge*. Philadelphia: Temple University Press, 1990.

Montgomery, L.M. *The Alpine Path: The Story of My Career*. Toronto: Fitzhenry & Whiteside, 1990.

Neumann, Erich. *Amor and Psyche: The Psychic Development of the Feminine, A Commentary on the Tale by Apuleius*. Trans. Ralph Manheim. New York: Bollingen, 1956.

O'Brien, Mary. *The Politics of Reproduction*. London: Routledge, 1981.

Okin, Susan Moller. *Women in Western Political Thought.* Princeton, NJ: Princeton University Press, 1979.

Olney, James. *Metaphors of Self: The Meaning of Autobiography.* Princeton, NJ: Princeton University Press, 1972.

Olson, Tillie. *Silences.* New York: Delta/Seymore Lawrence, 1978.

Ortner, Sherry B. "Is Female to Male as Nature Is to Culture?" In *Women and Values: Readings in Recent Feminist Philosophy.* Ed. M. Pearsall, 62–75. Belmont, CT: Wadsworth, 1986.

Otto, Rudolf. *The Idea of the Holy.* London: Oxford University Press, 1923.

Ovid. *Metamorphoses I–IV.* Ed. and trans. D.E. Hill. Warminster, UK: Aris & Phillips, 1985.

Pagels, Elaine. *The Gnostic Gospels.* New York: Random, 1979.

Parker, Rozsika. *Mother Love/Mother Hate: The Power of Maternal Ambivalence.* New York: Basic, 1995.

Parker, Rozsika, and Griselda Pollock. *Old Mistresses: Women, Art and Ideology.* New York: Pantheon, 1981.

Pater, Walter. *Marius the Epicurean: His Sensations and Ideas.* 2 vols. London: Macmillan, 1910.

Pearson, Carol, and Katherine Pope. *The Female Hero in American and British Literature.* New York: Bowker, 1981.

Perera, Sylvia Brinton. "The Descent of Inanna: Myth and Therapy." In *Feminist Archetypal Theory: Interdisciplinary Re-Visions of Jungian Thought.* Ed. Estella Lauter and C.S. Rupprecht, 137–86. Knoxville: University of Tennessee Press, 1985.

Perry, Ben Edwin. *The Ancient Romances: A Literary-Historical Account of Their Origins.* Berkeley: University of California Press, 1967.

Perry, William G. Jr. *Forms of Intellectual and Ethical Development in the College Years: A Scheme.* New York: Holt, Rinehart & Winston, 1968.

Pollock, Griselda. *Vision and Difference: Femininity, Feminism and the Histories of Art.* London: Routledge, 1988.

Pomeroy, Sarah B. *Goddesses, Whores, Wives, and Slaves: Women in Classical Antiquity.* New York: Schocken, 1975.

Pratt, Annis. *Archetypal Patterns in Women's Fiction.* Bloomington: Indiana University Press, 1981.

Rabuzzi, Kathryn Allen. *Motherself: A Mythic Analysis of Motherhood.* Bloomington: Indiana University Press, 1988.

– *The Sacred and the Feminine: Toward a Theology of Housework.* New York: Seabury, 1982.

Raven, Arlene. "The Last Essay on Feminist Criticism." In *Feminist Art Criticism: An Anthology.* Ed. Arlene Raven, Cassandra L. Langer, and Joanna Frueh, 227–38. New York: Icon Books, 1988.

Rich, Adrienne. *Diving into the Wreck: Poems 1971–1972.* New York: Norton, 1973.

– *Of Woman Born: Motherhood as Experience and Institution*. New York: Norton, 1986.

Rivers, Caryl, Rosalind Barnett, and Grace Baruch. *Beyond Sugar and Spice: How Women Grow, Learn and Thrive*. New York: Putnam's, 1979.

Rosaldo, Michelle Zimbalist, and Louise Lamphere, eds. *Woman, Culture, and Society*. Stanford, CA: Stanford University Press, 1974.

Rosenblatt, Sidney M. "Thumbelina and the Development of Female Sexuality." In *Psychoanalytic Perspectives on Women*. Ed. Elaine V. Siegel, 121–9. New York: Brunner/Mazel, 1992.

Rowbotham, Sheila. *Woman's Consciousness, Man's World*. Harmondsworth, UK: Penguin Books, 1973.

Roy, Gabrielle. *Enchantment and Sorrow*. Trans. Patricia Claxton. Toronto: Lester & Orpin Dennys, 1987.

Rubin, Lillian B. *Women of a Certain Age: The Midlife Search for Self*. New York: Harper & Row, 1979.

Ruddick, Sara. "Maternal Thinking." *Feminist Studies* 6 (1980): 70–96.

Salverson, Laura Goodman. *Confessions of an Immigrant's Daughter*. Toronto: University of Toronto Press, 1981.

Shack, Sybil. *The Two-Thirds Minority*. Toronto: University of Toronto Press, 1973.

Sheehy, Gail. *Menopause: The Silent Passage*. New York: Simon & Schuster, 1991.

Showalter, Elaine. *A Literature of Their Own: British Women Novelists from Bronte to Lessing*. Princeton, NJ: Princeton University Press, 1977.

Shuttle, Penelope, and Peter Redgrove. *The Wise Wound*. New York: Bantam, 1978.

Silverman, Kaja. *The Acoustic Mirror: The Female Voice in Psychoanalysis and Cinema*. Bloomington: Indiana University Press, 1988.

Smith, Sidonie. *Subjectivity, Identity, and the Body: Women's Autobiographical Practice in the Twentieth Century*. Bloomington: Indiana University Press, 1993.

Spender, Dale. *For the Record: The Making and Meaning of Feminist Knowledge*. London: Women's Press, 1985.

– *Invisible Women, the Schooling Scandal*. London: Writers & Readers, 1982.

– *Women of Ideas – and What Men Have Done to Them*. London: Routledge, 1982.

–, ed. *Men's Studies Modified*. Oxford: Pergamon, 1981.

Spretnak, Charlene. *Lost Goddesses of Early Greece*. Boston: Beacon Press, 1978.

Stanton, Domna C., ed. *The Female Autograph: Theory and Practice of Autobiography from the Tenth to the Twentieth Century*. Chicago: Chicago University Press, 1987.

Stein, Gertrude. *The Autobiography of Alice B. Toklas*. New York: Random, 1933.

Steinem, Gloria. *Revolution from Within: A Book of Self-Esteem*. Boston: Little, 1992.

Steiner, Wendy. *Pictures of Romance: Form against Context in Painting and Literature*. Chicago: University of Chicago Press, 1988.

Stern, Daniel L. *The Interpersonal World of the Infant*. New York: Basic, 1985.

Stone, Merlin. *When God Was a Woman*. San Diego: Harvest, 1976.

Streep, Peg. *Sanctuary of the Goddess: The Sacred Landscapes and Objects*. Boston: Bulfinch Press, 1994.

Swahn, Jan-Ojvind. *The Tale of Cupid and Psyche*. Lund: C.W.K. Gleerup, 1955.

Tavris, Carol. *Anger: The Misunderstood Emotion*. New York: Simon & Schuster, 1989.

Thompson, Judith. *Learning Liberation: Women's Response to Men's Education*. London: Croom Helm, 1983.

Tomm, Winnie. *Bodied Mindfulness: Women's Spirits, Bodies and Places*. Waterloo, ON: Wilfrid Laurier University Press, 1995.

Trevathan, Wenda R. *Human Birth: An Evolutionary Perspective*. New York: De Gruyter, 1987.

Turner, Victor. *The Ritual Process*. Chicago: Aldine, 1989.

– "Variations on a Theme of Liminality." In *Secular Ritual*. Ed. Sally F. Moore and Barbara G. Myerhoff, 36–52. Assen/Amsterdam: Van Gorcum, 1977.

Ulanov, Ann Bedford. *The Feminine in Jungian Psychology and Christian Theology*. Evanston, IL: Northwestern University Press, 1971.

Walker, Barbara G. *The Woman's Dictionary of Symbols and Sacred Objects*. San Francisco: Harper & Row, 1988.

– *The Woman's Encyclopedia of Myths and Secrets*. San Francisco: Harper & Row, 1983.

Walsh, P.G. *The Roman Novel: The 'Satiricon' of Petronius and the 'Metamorphoses' of Apuleius*. Cambridge: Cambridge University Press, 1970.

Walters, Joan S. *Three Case Studies to Examine Factors Which Influence Effective Implementation of an Elementary Art Curriculum in Manitoba Schools*. Ann Arbor: UMI Research Press, 1987.

Warner, Marina. *From the Beast to the Blonde: On Fairy Tales and Their Tellers*. London: Vintage, 1994.

Weitzmann, Kurt. *Ancient Book Illumination*. Cambridge, MA: Harvard University Press, 1959.

Williams, Linda Verlee. *Teaching for the Two-Sided Mind*. Englewood Cliffs, NJ: Prentice Hall, 1983.

Wolf, Christa. *Cassandra: A Novel and Four Essays*. Trans. Jan Van Heurck. New York: Farrar Straus & Giroux, 1984.

Wolf, Naomi. *The Beauty Myth*. Toronto: Vintage, 1990.

Woodward, Kathleen. "Simone de Beauvoir: Aging and Its Discontents." In *The Private Self: Theory and Practice of Women's Autobiography*. Ed. Shari Benstock, 90–113. Chapel Hill: University of North Carolina Press, 1988.

Woolf, Virginia. *Moments of Being*. Ed. and intro. Jeanne Schulkind. San Diego: Harvest, 1985.

– *A Room of One's Own*. London: Hogarth Press, 1929.

Young-Bruel, Elizabeth, ed. *Freud on Women: A Reader*. New York: Norton, 1990.

Zeitlin, Froma I. *Playing the Other: Gender and Society in Classical Greek Literature*. Chicago: University of Chicago Press, 1996.

Zipes, Jack. *Don't Bet on the Prince: Contemporary Feminist Fairy Tales in North America and England*. New York: Routledge, 1986.

Index

Abrams, M.H., 27, 104
Adlington, W., 122, 218n1
adolescence: girls loss of self-esteem in, 49
adult: gendered definition of, 22
aesthetics: and repetition, 29, 33–4
allegory, 57
Allen, Charlotte Vale: autobiography by, 145, 155–6
Allen, Paula Gunn, 221n3
alma mater, 117
Amor, 216n7. *See also* Eros
androcentrism, 56, 122, 135. *See also* patriarchy
Angelou, Maya, 145, 154–5
anger: and envy, 66–70, 73; and Eros, 71; and the sisters, 68–70
anima, 59, 105–6
ants: as Psyche's helpers, 91; symbolism of, 91–2
Aphrodite: anger of, 51–2; attributes of, 52–5, 71, 96; in conflict with Psyche, 6, 46, 48; and Demeter, 52, 55, 61; and Eros, 62, 109, 113; and "green world," 60–2; as liminal figure, 134–5; and motherliness, 55, 131; origins of, 9, 93; and Persephone, 78, 81, 112–4; powers of, 54–9, 80, 85, 93; and Psyche, 48, 75, 83–4, 90, 117; and Psyche's tasks, 76–7, 83–4, 113; representations of, 153; and sexual desire, 47, 62–4, 71; and sister goddesses, 70–1, 81; and Zeus, 55, 96, 100

Apollo, 48, 57–8
Apuleius, Lucius: on Aphrodite, 57, 58, 75, 77; as author, 21, 51; critical interpretations of his *Metamorphoses*, 45, 218n3; general references to, 57, 101, 102, 156; on Isis, 45, 77, 112; on Oracle, 57; on Psyche's experience, 61, 74; on Psyche's sisters, 66, 69–71, 74; on sister goddesses, 70–1; translations of his *Metamorphoses*, 45, 218n1, n2
archetype: Jungian, 6; and signature, 21, 217n3
arrows: of Eros, 63, 86; as eye beams, 35, 86
art: feminist analyses of, 218n4; depiction of women in, 43–4; and male nudes, 43; repetition and, 33–4; women's, 34
Artemis: and childbirth, 118, 219n5; as huntress, 48, 52, 57; and wild animals, 71, 118, 219n1
Astarte, 53
Athena, 52, 93
authority: failed male, 91, 111
autobiography: titles of men's, 223n4; by women writers, 10, 139–60

Baird, James, 58, 66
Barber, Elizabeth Wayland: on spinning, 93
Bardige, Betty, 16
Barry, Judith, and Sandy Flitterman-Lewis, 33–4